Unwilling to Bend

Unwilling to Bend

True Stories of Courageous and Determined Women

Priya Somaiya

BLOOMSBURY
NEW DELHI • LONDON • OXFORD • NEW YORK • SYDNEY

BLOOMSBURY INDIA
Bloomsbury Publishing India Pvt. Ltd
Second Floor, LSC Building No. 4, DDA Complex, Pocket C – 6 & 7,
Vasant Kunj New Delhi 110070

BLOOMSBURY, BLOOMSBURY INDIA and the Diana logo are trademarks of
Bloomsbury Publishing Plc

First published in India 2019
This edition published 2019

ISBN: TPB: 978-93-88414-78-4; eBook: 978-93-88414-80-7

2 4 6 8 10 9 7 5 3 1

Typeset in Charter by Manipal Digital Systems
Printed and bound in India by Replika Press Pvt Ltd

Contents

Introduction

The myth that change and transformation are only possible through physical, political or economic powers needs to be challenged. While these powers do exert influence and control, the strength to transform lives, societies and nation-states resides more in determination, courage, empathy, unconditional love, a sense of purpose and a value-based service orientation. The change and growth thus facilitated are positive for everyone involved and are long-lasting.

These qualities have prompted many living in abject poverty and unimaginable adversity to take charge of their lives and destiny. With stoic silence and a sense of responsibility, hundreds have looked after their growing children and supported their education and career progression. Many have found a credible sense of purpose after a personal tragedy and mentored or coached those going through troubled times. There are many illiterate individuals who have resolved to educate themselves and make something of their lives. At the same time, many have learnt to survive in penury while some others have made efforts to become financially stable and successful.

This book, based on true stories, celebrates the lives of women who have demonstrated these qualities and achieved not only an astonishing personal metamorphosis but transformed the social status and the culture of their families and communities. Their stories teach us lessons in self-management and leadership and how the power of positive values can transform personal and collective experiences.

Even today, a number of women face discrimination, domestic violence, emotional and physical harm and trauma. In many remote and backward rural areas of our country, there is a lack of awareness and education resulting in prejudice, superstition and gender stereotypes. Women are perceived to be the weaker section of society and hence are deprived in many ways. This thinking is also prevalent in tradition-bound communities even in the urban areas. There are hundreds of girls dropping out of school because of the financial condition of the family even when the family manages to send their brothers to school. Young girls are still forced to get married and girls, as young as 14 years old, are giving birth. There are dowry deaths, hundreds of rape cases, the girl child succumbing to malnutrition and adult women dying during childbirth. Lack of family planning and other medical aid is also becoming rampant in many parts of India.

Even though there is a positive perceptible shift brought about by the government and civil society initiatives in women's education, financial and social emancipation and empowerment, we still have a long way to go.

Many women, as also in these stories, have made huge strides towards the betterment of their lot through personal commitment, hard work, positivity and fortitude. There have been many stories of such women in the past and throughout our history who have demonstrated enormous spiritual and emotional strength. Such women have made us proud and continue to do so.

1

Scarred at Eighteen

Living in a bungalow has its own charm, thought Sunita Sharma as she arranged the roses, plucked from her own garden, in the ornate vase placed at the centre of the meticulously laid-out table. Late breakfast on a Sunday was such a welcome change for Sunita who preferred to call it an 'exciting brunch' because she felt that egg *bhurji*, and not scrambled eggs, made a world of difference to the menu, especially when accompanied with large, brown and crisp *parathas*. Sunita looked forward to having the entire family on the breakfast table and receive everyone's appreciation for her cooking as well as for the way she laid the table and arranged the flowers in the dining or the living areas of their rather large bungalow. The upper middle class have a number of status symbols, the size of the bungalow being one. The Sharmas' bungalow boasted of large, beautifully manicured green lawns on three sides of the house; the front one, exquisitely landscaped. Sunita was very proud of her garden and always made sure to convey the smallest of its details—the variety of flowers, the marble fountain that was lit in the evenings, the porch—to her kitty party friends. Her husband Sahil had spent a fortune on the upkeep of the garden because it seemed to make Sunita happy.

The Sharmas resided in Maharani Bagh. It was a posh locality with old and new bungalows. It was a known fact that only the very well-to-do stayed in Maharani Bagh. The families living in this neighbourhood were highly status-conscious and interacted only with people from their own class, social status and financial background. Most families ran their own businesses—some were first-generation business families and many were families who were running established businesses for three or four generations. There was a perceptible difference in the culture and the habits of these two categories. The more established and older families were members of the India International Centre, a very well-known cultural centre with exclusive membership which included senior bureaucrats, ministers, doctors, authors and poets as well as owners, managing directors and presidents of companies. Sahil and his family were members of the Delhi Gymkhana Club, another elite association. He had managed to get the club's membership through his contacts about five years ago. The new members were families who had recently acquired wealth and believed in more ostentatious display of their material acquisitions. Most of them were loud and boisterous who preferred to dress flashily which betrayed the subtlety and the quiet charm of the older gentry. The Sharmas belonged to this category, but only to a certain extent.

The wealth from Sahil's successful business was clearly evident in the décor of their home. The drawing room was oval-shaped with light pink Italian marble flooring. Like all families with newly acquired wealth, Sunita's family was also happy to include more and more artefacts in their home, even better if they came from countries like Italy and France which were famous for their sculptures and art.

However, the similarities with the 'new-money' families ended there. The rooms were tastefully done-up and added beauty to their home; they also made a stylish statement about the residents. Beige sofas with sap green and gold cushions complemented the blue, green and beige Bukhara carpet and looked very elegant. The teak furniture was crafted very delicately with little carved edges and light brown marble tops. The coffee table with its silver legs looked slightly incongruous but Sunita had insisted on buying it. Maybe the silver attracted her with its opulence and when people complimented her taste and asked her how much it cost, she always felt important. She had to have these expensive things in her home because, after all, her husband was not a small businessman. His name had been mentioned in the list of the hundred most important businessmen of the country in a leading trade journal.

Sahil came to the breakfast table in a chirpy mood and said, 'Rather appetising breakfast Sunita. Your egg *bhurji* is really colourful, the coriander and the tomato look so nice together. Where is Janvi? I have not seen her since morning. Have you?'

'Oh yes, she was with me in the kitchen a while ago. She is such a big help! After all, my girl is just like me. I am glad to see her taking so much interest in the kitchen; she's turning into an excellent cook, Sahu. You'll love the chicken which she has cooked for lunch. Can you believe it, lunch is already done and ready. She doesn't let me feel Mahinder's absence at all!'

While Sunita was giving this long explanation, Sahil anxiously glanced towards Janvi's room and called out to her twice. She had turned 17 a week ago and was a tall, slim girl with long and lustrous black hair and large black eyes that looked deep and affectionate. Janvi was growing up well, though a bit reticent, but displayed all the traits of a well-brought-up girl from a good family. Apart from cooking, she was passionate about music of all types—from jazz to north Indian classical—and sang songs from old Hindi films rather well. She had completed her 12th board examinations and was awaiting the results which were to be announced in the month of May. She was a student of the arts, history being her favourite subject. She was expecting decent results and if all went well, she hoped to be admitted to one of the better colleges in Delhi.

'Papa, would you like some fresh sweet lime juice? I am going to make some for Ma and myself.'

'Yes, please. Thanks, Janu. That'll be great. I haven't had fruit juice all week; instead I ended up drinking a lot of tea and coffee in office. I think tomorrow onwards I will carry some juice in that new crystal flask your mom bought from Prague last year.'

'No, not at all!' Sunita said with complete disbelief. How could Sahil even think of doing such a thing? That flask came out of the cabinet only during parties to store hot water for after-dinner coffee. A number of people had admired her crystal crockery from Czechoslovakia and she used it very sparingly, only for parties which Sahil threw for top government officials or for some of the richest business families of Delhi.

Janvi did not like her mother's rather abrupt response and immediately retorted, 'Come on, Ma, you have other jugs in that cabinet. We also deserve to use some of the good things; they are not here only to be showed off to people during parties.' As she spoke, she went to the cabinet and took out the crystal flask. Then, she walked into the kitchen and came out carrying the juice in her hand. Sahil smiled and thanked her. Sunita also had a faint smile on her rather pale face and mentioned quietly that she can always get more stuff through her embassy friends in Prague.

Life for the Sharmas was going smoothly. Sahil was as hard-working as any other businessman; he worked long hours and travelled a lot which kept him away from home for 10–15 days a month. Even though Sunita kept telling her friends, giggling quite peculiarly, how much she missed him and longed for his company—especially in the evenings and after dinner—she knew, in her heart, that this was not true. She was quite relieved when she bade goodbye to Sahil whenever he left home for his tours. She felt less tense and had a little more time in hand which she spent on herself. She would visit the salon to get a facial and a massage and had enough time to catch up on her reading. She often borrowed magazines from her friends when they met on weekends or holidays, since she thought buying magazines was a real waste of money. And, she never did have the patience to visit libraries.

Sahil seemed to create a lot of work for her and the servants when he was around. Like all Indian men, he was spoilt to the hilt; he was his mother's darling little boy and Sunita hated his mother pampering him when she visited them during winters. Her mother-in-law was growing old and every year Sunita hoped that she would avoid the bitter cold of Delhi. Hyderabad, where she had been staying for more than two decades now, was much better for her with its mild winters. But, people like Sahil's mother never understood the huge amount of trouble they caused others in the family, with their demands and their fussing over things like a little spot over the dining table cloth. Sunita couldn't stand her pointing out these small things. After all, she was a guest and should behave like one. Sahil couldn't say a word to his mother and readily agreed to her demands and tolerated all her tantrums.

Presently though, Sunita was a little worried about Janvi and her lifestyle. She waited for the right time to share her worries with Sahil but didn't ever seem to find him alone. Of late, whenever he was back home from office, he had the tendency to sit with Janvi for hours, discussing current affairs and her career plans. Sunita didn't grudge the father-daughter bonding sessions but lately, she had started feeling a little neglected and isolated.

Sunita understood that their marriage was complicated and there were a lot of conflicts, but which marriage was perfect? Agreed, their relationship was under a lot strain and Sunita disliked many of Sahil's habits and even, sometimes, the way he treated her, but she, like all wives, still aspired for her husband's attention. Sahil had to understand that she too needed some time with him, and it was his responsibility to take care of his wife's needs and aspirations.

'Ma, will you be home today? Why don't you go out with Chandni aunty and your gang to the flower show? I saw your invitation cards. What a waste if you don't go! You should have told me about this, I would have called up Anjali and dragged her to the show. But, now she has gone shopping with her mom.'

'I haven't seen Anju in so long. What's wrong with her? She has stopped coming over. Is everything alright?'

'Yes Ma, I spoke with her this morning and she sounded perfectly fine. In fact, she mentioned that she has not seen you for almost three months and would like to drop in soon.'

'That'll be nice, ask her to come for dinner tomorrow.'

'Oh, she can't because she's off to Leh tomorrow in the morning. We can invite her when she comes back.'

'How nice, she'll probably be on the same flight with Sahu. Tomorrow he is flying off to Leh as well, for some board meeting. You can tell Anju, that if need be, she can travel to the airport with your father.'

'Not a bad idea, I'll do that.'

Janvi picked up her mobile phone and called Anjali to give her the information. Then, she told her mother that she would like to wear her mauve dress in the evening for her trip to the party, and quietly moved towards Sunita's bedroom.

The lines on Sunita's forehead had begun to show; she was 49 but looked much older. Her hair had greyed a lot in the last two years and she appeared to be losing interest in herself. Unlike her younger self, she did not care much about what she wore at home. Her wardrobe was quite disorganised and anyone looking at it would say that this woman was really not interested in dressing well. She had a number of clothes that needed mending, and quite a few were just thrown in a bundle and stuffed in one of the drawers.

That evening, when she had some time, she decided to arrange her clothes and throw away some of the clutter. Lazily and with thoughts of the impending dinner preparation occupying her mind, she went into her bedroom and saw the wardrobe door wide open. She remembered that Janvi had wanted to borrow her mauve dress and, as usual, she had left the wardrobe open.

She started taking her clothes out of the wardrobe absentmindedly, when her eyes fell on the small drawer which was not properly closed. She opened it and noticed that the bundle of cash inside looked thinner than what she had seen about two days ago. Sahil would not have touched it and she didn't remember giving any money to Mahinder, their servant. He had not been home for a week now and had settled all accounts with her before he left for his leave. Mahinder, who had managed her kitchen for 16 years now, hardly ever entered her bedroom and was an honest person. She thought that maybe the cleaning lady might have...? But, how was that possible? Whenever she came in to sweep and mop the rooms, Sunita would never leave her alone. She sat on her bed, took out the bundle of notes and counted the money. To her shock, she found almost a lakh missing. This was a huge amount and she wondered whether Janvi could have taken it? She didn't want to call Sahil because she knew that he would be worried. Sunita decided to wait for Janvi to return.

Janvi returned home 40 minutes past midnight and the first thing that Sunita noticed was that she was not wearing the mauve dress. So, she didn't even think it necessary to inform me that she is not taking the dress, thought Sunita. She realised that Janvi had started taking advantage of being an only child and was getting more arrogant and callous with every passing day. And, she also knew, to a large extent, Sahil was responsible for the same.

Janvi went straight to her bedroom and Sunita decided to not reprimand her for coming back late. Recently, whenever she went out, she would come back around midnight and always avoided telling Sunita where she was and the reason for her delay. Sunita also noticed that she looked rather strange; her lipstick was smudged and her hair was strewn loosely all over her face. Her dress was unbuttoned at the back and she had a glazed expression in her eyes.

Sunita slumped on the sofa with her eyes shut as her mind raced with hundreds of negative thoughts. She sipped water from a glass that she held tightly in her left hand lest, out of sheer worry, it slipped. She couldn't fathom what was going on with Janvi, but she knew that there was something seriously amiss. She was tempted to go into her room and talk to her but it was too late, almost one in the morning, and Janvi didn't seem to be in a state to talk about serious issues. Sunita kept sitting on the sofa with her eyes closed. Five minutes later, her mobile phone rang and with a startle, she opened her eyes bringing the phone close to her face as she didn't have her spectacles on. She could barely decipher the number and to her total disbelief, it was Sahil!

He never called so late when he was travelling. In fact, he barely even called her. Sunita panicked seeing Sahil's number and, for a second, didn't have the courage to take his call. What if something bad had happened? Some accident or worse...? Then, controlling her fear, she answered the phone. Sahil sounded a little drunk and asked, in a rather indifferent tone, 'How's Janu? Hope she's OK. Is she asleep or, like you, she is still up and about? You sound pretty wide awake.'

'How do you know? And, what an unearthly hour to call! What's the matter with you?'

'Nothing really; I just felt like saying hi to Janu.'

'In that case, why don't you call on her number?'

Sunita snapped and hung up. She slumped on the sofa, feeling exhausted and wondered about Sahil and Janvi's behaviour. It was beyond her comprehension. Her mind wandered and she thought about the months before Janvi's birth. Her pregnancy had been extremely difficult and there was no one to support her in those nine months. She had developed hyperemesis gravidarum which caused incessant vomiting, extreme weakness and weight loss. Sahil had just started his business and as they were badly off, financially, she couldn't afford maids and cooks and thus, she had to cook and clean the house herself. Sahil's mother was no help at all. Instead, she was a source of tension most of the time and didn't have one good word to say to her.

Sahil's family was orthodox and patriarchal. It was only after Sunita came into their family that their standard of living and their social circle improved. Sahil's father belonged to a village called Sagarkunj near Hapur which is a small town in western Uttar Pradesh. Sagarkunj had this rather pompous name because it had a huge rainwater lake and a hilly terrain. The Sharmas owned some land there but they were not big landlords. However, being educated Brahmins, the Sharmas were respected by all in Sagarkunj and its neighbouring villages.

Sunita clearly remembered all the times when she had to sleep on the floor because they would have to move out of their bedroom whenever an elderly relative came to visit and stayed on for weeks. How embarrassed she would feel coming out of the tiny washroom adjacent to the dining area where the whole family and guests congregated! She had even noticed the servants using this washroom stealthily whenever they thought that no one was keeping an eye on them. Every day was more miserable than the last but, she had weathered all storms and spent so many years supporting Sahil, his immediate as well as extended family and, of course, looking after the house and their pampered daughter. Sunita had no qualms in admitting that Sahil had spoilt their daughter. Even now, he gave in to all her whims and fancies while overlooking her misbehaviour. 'What a life… he'll pay for it heavily one of these days…' she muttered these words as she moved quietly into her bedroom.

Janvi woke up very late the next day. It was almost lunch time when she entered the kitchen. Knowing that Mahinder was not around, she started to fix a cup of coffee on her own. She looked for the instant coffee bottle and found her favourite mug. She had had the same mug for the last five years with not one chip on it. Mahinder handled the entire kitchen so well! She opened the fridge and picked up a muffin along with a slice of bread, which she topped with two slices of salami and a bit of mayonnaise. Then, she walked out of the kitchen towards the dining area. Sunita was in the living room settling the cushions and cleaning the centre tables. The maid was mopping the floor and sharing some neighbourhood gossip with Sunita who looked completely disinterested.

Hearing Janvi approach, Sunita glanced at her daughter with extreme indifference. Janvi also didn't offer any greeting or any explanation for her coming in late the previous night. Sunita wondered whether to broach the subject but decided to avoid mentioning this to Janvi in front of the maid. She didn't want Janvi to become the latest topic of gossip. Also, she didn't want to get into a pointless argument with her in the morning, rather afternoon. After about 15 minutes, Janvi walked up to her and asked if she wanted a cup of coffee. Sunita said that she had finished her lunch and kept cleaning the sides of the coffee table. Janvi started giving her a long description of the party that she had attended at the Hyatt the previous night and was just getting into the details of the menu when Sunita stopped her and asked about her coming back home late. Sunita's tone was cold, cutting and sharp.

Janvi looked at her angrily and said, 'Why do you need to know everything about me? Papa doesn't ask me such questions. He leaves me alone. Why are you prying all the time? I can look after myself. This house is becoming impossible to live in! Why do you want to control everyone's life? Even *Dadi* feels so.'

Sunita heard her daughter yelling at her and stood still. The Janvi who was standing in front of her, defiant and rebellious, was not the Janvi she knew—well-behaved, well-brought-up, disciplined and an overall happy child. This was some other Janvi. For quite some time, she had been noticing subtle changes in Janvi's behaviour but the extent of her transformation was a shock to her. Sunita couldn't believe what she had just heard. Without responding to Janvi, Sunita went out on the lawn and walked silently, her mind in turmoil, towards the huge neem tree in the centre. She sat on a chair kept under the tree, numb, and looked blankly towards the house. After a while, she saw Janvi walking out into the garden. It took her five minutes to walk up and in those few moments, Sunita had made up her mind to not bring up her misbehaviour. She didn't want to rake up the issue and create a scene or cause another tantrum. But, she was very certain that things were not normal with Janvi as she was noticing a complete metamorphosis of her daughter's personality. What has happened to her, she wondered. She couldn't lay her finger on anything for certain. Sahil, as usual, was very lenient when it came to Janvi, so, she had become strict in the matters of her mobility, her staying out of the house and returning late at night. However, she soon fell back on her methods because, after all, Janvi was the only one in her life. What if she also got angry and stopped talking to me? She shuddered at that thought.

Janvi did well academically, so there was no major concern in that area. She didn't have any relationship with a boy, at least nothing that Sunita knew of. She was sure that Janvi, being brought up within the social circle they frequented, would not hide her relationship from her parents. Would she? She was perplexed and completely at a loss. Being a mother, she was very worried.

'Hi, Ma. I finished dusting the living room for you. Sorry, I couldn't join you for lunch. Got late last night and then woke up late. I just had a sandwich with some tomato and salami. Quite yum! Do you want some coffee? I can make some for you,' Janvi said, nonchalantly, as if the earlier outburst hadn't happened.

'No, thanks. I won't be able to sleep if I have coffee now,' Sunita replied, matching her daughter's easygoing tone.

After a pause, Janvi added, 'Sorry, I reacted like that before. I am under a little pressure because of the results. Everything hinges on these examinations. Last night, I met a few friends who told me that college admissions will be tougher this year as the cut-off percentages in all the colleges will be higher.'

'Why is that?'

'The colleges want only the highest scoring students as these students can help them maintain their reputation.'

'Things are so different these days. We didn't know anything about cut-off percentages in our time. However, seats were reserved then also, and preference was given to first division students before others. Anyway, it's OK. I understand you are under pressure. I'll go now and get some sleep,' Sunita said, walking back inside.

Sahil returned from Leh after four days looking relaxed and happy. He was all praises for the food that his hotel served and how well appointed the rooms were. Sunita asked him about the conference and for a moment he looked quite lost before replying hurriedly that it went off well but nothing much was achieved in the meetings. Three of his team members had dropped out at the last minute so quite a few important issues couldn't be discussed. Nevertheless, it was a good break from the usual work routine.

Of late, Sunita had been noticing a change in Sahil's attitude towards his business. He didn't seem to be concentrating as much on his work and his focus had shifted from the targets he had set for himself. He spoke more about vacations and recreation, health and personal grooming. He also became more careful with his diet and was worried about his paunch and receding hairline. Sunita found these changes a little odd. She remembered reading about mid-life crisis in some magazine and wondered whether Sahil, being 50 now, was going through one as well.

They all sat down for a rather lacklustre dinner. Normally on Sahil's return, Sunita would prepare his favourite chicken curry and *raita* with cucumbers, onions, tomatoes and coriander leaves. However, tonight, she was not in the mood to do anything. The atmosphere in the house was a bit strained and tense. Everyone was pretending to be normal with each other but she knew that something was definitely amiss. Janvi had emerged from her bedroom after a good three hours and didn't make any attempts to enter the kitchen, even though she knew that Sunita would be cooking alone in the absence of Mahinder. All through dinner, she was completely quiet, but for a cursory nod or two when Sahil asked her about her results or college admissions.

'What's the matter Janu? You look quite preoccupied. You haven't even spoken a word to me, are you feeling alright?' Sahil asked, concerned.

'Nothing, Papa. I am just a little tense about my results and my admissions. I want to get in to the right college.'

'Your results will be great and you will get admission into the college of your choice. You leave that to me. You know, these days, everything can be done with right contacts and a little bit of money. Your father is a competent fellow. Don't forget that you belong to a well-to-do family. People know us in this city and we can get things done. So, relax and enjoy your holidays. If I am right, you have another fortnight left before the college admissions start?'

'Yes, Pa. Thanks for reassuring me, you always managc to boost my morale.'

Janvi got up, went over to Sahil's side of the table and gave him a peck on his cheek. Holding his hand for a fleeting second and after wishing him goodnight, she went into her bedroom. Sunita looked at her daughter's retreating back with a mixture of sadness and disappointment.

She felt ignored and left out and then suddenly realised that her relationship with Sahil was weakening and Janvi was merely filling the gap in their lives created by their limited interactions. She wondered whether every relationship outgrows its attraction and freshness, and there comes a time when the signs of fatigue start setting in.

Janvi's results were declared on a Monday morning. She was fast asleep after finishing a thriller which she had borrowed from the library sometime back. James Hadley Chase wrote gripping and hair-raising stories and Janvi found herself getting addicted to his books. It was past 10 in the morning when Sunita knocked on Janvi's bedroom door.

'Baby get up, I have to tell you something…' She whispered urgently.

'Not again, Ma. You have a habit of waking me up at the wrong time. I slept very late, I was reading a book,' Janvi mumbled.

'Alright, open the door for only two minutes and then you can go back to sleep.'

Janvi reluctantly opened the door and found her mother holding a white sheet of paper in her right hand and her favourite Parker pen in her left. She, with a wide smile on her face and a sense of noticeable happiness, told Janvi that she had secured the highest marks in her batch in school. She added, with a note of pride, that Janvi had cleared the board examinations with an aggregate score of 94 per cent. Sunita had also spoken with the school's principal who had requested Janvi to be in school in another hour for some celebration. Janvi held her mother's hand and, very softly and gently, thanked her for her support, 'It would not have been possible without you, Ma. Thank you for all the early morning revision sessions and those endless cups of coffee in the night'

Sunita hugged her and both of them stood together in an affectionate embrace, forgetting all their altercations of the recent past. . Both mother and daughter looked happy and it was clear that despite bickering now and then, they shared a very close bond.

Janvi reached school to find all her classmates there, except Anjali. On inquiring, she was told that Anjali was not well and was at home. Sujata, another close friend of theirs, mentioned that Anjali had just about managed to pass the examinations and had the lowest percentage among all their classmates. Her results had surprised the whole school as she was a good student and the principal and teachers were expecting a lot from her.

Janvi called Anjali on her mobile phone but the automated voice recording continuously said that it was out of network range. She wondered where Anjali could be; maybe with her friend Amjad, who was a close friend of her brother's. Amjad's family and Anjali's family were also very close and Amjad was a kind of guide and mentor for her. Whenever Anjali needed advice, she would ask Amjad.

Sahil called and Janvi answered with subdued excitement. She waited for Sahil to congratulate her about her excellent result.

'Where are you, Janvi? I assumed you would be with Anjali and called her but, her phone was out of network range. I thought of speaking to both of you together but, never mind. How was the overall result of the school? What is your percentage?'

Janvi found this conversation very odd. He should have called her instead of Anjali. However, without thinking further, she quietly said that she had scored 94 per cent, the highest in her school.

'Oh, that's very good. It certainly deserves a celebration. What about Anjali's result? Have you spoken to her?'

'No, I haven't,' she replied curtly, hurt at her father's lack of enthusiasm.

'OK, that's alright. I will try her phone later.'

Janvi was a little surprised. In fact, she was speechless and couldn't comprehend what was happening. On returning home, she found Sunita in the kitchen busy preparing Janvi's favourite dish. She spontaneously hugged her mother and planted a big kiss on her cheek. Sunita, smiling ear to ear, patted her on the cheek and told her that she was very proud of her and her achievements.

Janvi told Sunita about Anjali's unexpected result and the conversation she had had with her father a few minutes ago. Sunita stopped stirring the pot and sat down on a beautifully carved teak chair placed in the corner of the kitchen. She looked at Janvi with confusion, itching to ask her a number of questions. For almost a minute, she was unable to speak. After taking a few sips of water, she asked Janvi, 'Why do you think Anjali did so poorly?'

Janvi, without thinking too much but with a lot of certainty, responded, 'Ma, I think Anjali was not at all serious about the examinations. For the last few months, she had been saying that she wanted to try modelling and get a job as an air hostess. She said that she wanted to travel and start earning straight away. I think she is no longer interested in higher education. Throughout last year, she was meeting designers and models. She has changed a lot, Ma. Sometimes, I feel that I do not know this new Anjali at all; she has become aloof and as you also noticed, she has practically stopped visiting us.'

'Yes, I did notice that.' Sunita did not mention but she had noticed other things too.

That evening, they decided to head out for dinner, in celebration of Janvi's excellent result. Janvi looked beautiful.

She wore a long pink and orange flowing dress; pink and burnt orange is a rare combination but, somehow, it suited Janvi a lot. Youth has a freshness that cannot be replaced by any beauty product. The tightness of the skin, the colour of health and vigour and the tautness of the muscles, all combine to produce the magical aura of youth. Her lustrous hair and its black sheen added to her charm. With a gentle smile playing around the corners of her lips, she held Sunita's hand and climbed the steps of the restaurant. Sahil had called, at the last moment, to say that he had an urgent meeting and won't be able to join them for dinner but that he would be planning an evening out with them the following day. Janvi, though a little disappointed, thanked him and told him about her mother's plan of taking her to her favourite Chinese restaurant, Ming Room.

However, when they were leaving the house, Sunita suggested that they go to the lovely *kebab* and *biryani* restaurant instead which had opened recently and, in no time, had become the talk of the town for its superb North-West Frontier cuisine. Janvi, always up for new experiences, had readily agreed. Mother and daughter sat on a table near the inner window which was secluded but provided a great view of the garden outside. The lanterns, the brightly-lit fountain with its silvery water and the large green and blue pool looked beautiful, almost like a painting. The chef walked up to them and greeted them warmly. He suggested they begin with some delicious *malai kebabs,* which were his specialty.

They placed their order and sat together in companionable silence. Janvi looked at her mother. She had a certain dignity about her and Janvi thought that despite the early struggles in her married life and with her grandmother, Sunita had courageously stood her ground and made something of their lives. She had indeed been an asset to her father—looking after him as well as the house and bringing up Janvi with diligence and great responsibility. Janvi knew that Sunita, during the days of their family's immense financial difficulties, had even sold off her jewellery to contribute to Sahil's business. She had never complained about this fact and was very proud of Sahil's achievements. Without her, it would not have been possible for Sahil to come so far and gain the social standing he enjoyed in Delhi. However, of late, Janvi had noticed that Sunita was snappy and irritable with Sahil and they both appeared to be drifting apart. They hardly spent any time together, except for one or two calls they made during the day. But, even those were mostly about household chores or their many social engagements. Their going out together for parties and other social events had also decreased considerably. Working late was taking up most of Sahil's time, and Sunita had become more disciplined with her exercises, early dinners and sleeping before 10 pm.

Janvi reminded herself to get rid of these negative thoughts as this was her big day. She also had a week of celebrations planned with her friends. While sipping the cold and tangy mixed fruit juice, she looked around and was astonished to see Anjali and her own father walking, hand in hand, towards a table 12 to 15 feet away from where she was sitting. She shook her head and blinked a couple of times; she couldn't believe what was happening. Wasn't her father busy with some important meeting? At that precise moment, Anjali turned and their eyes met. Janvi saw Anjali's smile freeze on her face and her eyes widen in shock. Before Janvi could even move or utter a single word, Anjali rushed out of the restaurant. Sahil too, without looking right or left, darted out with his head bent low, following Anjali.

Janvi could feel tears welling up in her eyes and a lump form in her throat. She concentrated on the glass in her hand, furiously blinking back tears. Sunita inquired, concerned, 'Why are you staring into the glass, Janu? Is there something wrong with the fruit juice?' Sunita patiently waited for her answer but, when Janvi didn't reply, she extended her hand and touched Janvi's arm. Shaking her gently, Sunita asked Janvi if she was alright. Janvi got up, adjusted her dress and wiped her lips with an embroidered napkin. She requested Sunita to take her home as she was not feeling well. Without saying anything more, she walked out, her mother hurrying after her. Janvi was quiet in the car, staring out of the window. On reaching home, she quickly went to her room and shut the door leaving behind a confused mother trying to understand her daughter's mood swings. Sahil came home late that night and Sunita informed him how Janvi had suddenly taken ill at the restaurant. Neither Sahil nor Janvi mentioned a word about that chance encounter to Sunita.

A fortnight passed since their evening at the restaurant but Janvi remained unwell, eating poorly and saying little. 'Emotional shock can cause many symptoms, some of which can be severe,' the doctor conveyed to Sunita over the telephone. Sahil was perturbed as he was sure that Janvi had seen him with Anjali. He had been receiving very short and cryptic responses from Janvi whenever he attempted a conversation with her. Janvi was laid up in bed for weeks and the doctors again said that her menstruation bleeding, which wouldn't stop even after 15 days, was on account of immense emotional shock. Whenever Sunita made an attempt to speak to Janvi about that evening to understand what had actually happened that led to her troubled state of mind, Janvi's bleeding worsened. Finally, when her condition seemed to deteriorate, the doctors forbade Sunita to initiate any conversation of that nature.

Mahinder's return was a big relief for Sunita. She had toiled for over two months in the kitchen since Sahil was no help in the running of the house. She had long stopped expecting any assistance from him and this realisation had made her life easier with less conflicts and complaints.

With Mahinder's arrival, the colour in Janvi's cheeks also started returning slowly. Mahinder's presence always made her happy as he had seen her grow up and spoilt her a lot. Sunita had even called him in his village and given him the good news about Janvi's result. She knew that Mahinder was a sensitive man and he would never forgive her if she forgot to inform him. After all, Janvi was like his own daughter.

Mahinder had bought a gift for Janvi—it was a brass and copper swan beautifully engraved and studded with stones. He had purchased the gift from a neighbouring village which was famous for its handicrafts; he had paid a handsome amount for it. When Janvi inquired about the price, Mahinder simply said that nothing in this world was more precious than his beautiful Janu. They hugged each other and Sunita, seeing their affection, smiled and quietly left them to catch up.

Almost six weeks had passed since the day of Janvi's breakdown. There had hardly been any communication between father and daughter, which left Sunita perplexed. She didn't have the courage to broach the topic with Sahil who continued to avoid any discussion about Janvi's health or her visits to the doctor. Janvi was being treated for anxiety and what the doctors called a panic disorder.

With time, her condition improved and she also got admission in her preferred college. Three months passed smoothly for Janvi in her new alma mater studying sociology. The faculty in the department was excellent and she particularly enjoyed attending the classes of Prof. Pooja Sharma who had been a brilliant student and was now an equally erudite, well informed and articulate teacher. Janvi would always be on time for her classes, prepared and attentive. She had struck a chord with the professor from day one and whenever Prof. Sharma had some time between classes, she would ask Janvi to meet her in the staff room and recommend interesting books and articles to her.

It was a Friday morning when Janvi, on entering the college premises, saw Prof. Sharma drive past in a shimmering white Honda City. The professor also noticed her, stopped the car and asked Janvi to meet her in the staff room. Janvi, excited to read more interesting books, ran towards the staff room but as she took a turn, she saw Amjad. He looked at her angrily and asked about her father.

'He is fine, just very busy with work,' she replied.

'I bet he is,' he mumbled.

Janvi decided to ignore Amjad's tone and asked about Anjali, 'Have you spoken with Anjali? Is she alright?'

'Why don't you ask your father!' Amjad almost spat the last word out before walking away.

Janvi wondered what the matter with Amjad was because from their past interactions, she knew that he was an affable person, very down to earth and courteous. She hoped that his anger was not directed at her but, at someone else. She decided to call him once she was done meeting her professor.

On entering the staff room, Janvi found Prof. Sharma filling up some forms. The professor informed her that she was invited for a conference in Bangalore, scheduled towards the end of the month, where she would present a paper and chair a couple of panel discussions. She also said that she wanted Janvi to accompany her and attend the seminar and, if she felt confident, also participate in a few panel discussions. Janvi knew that travelling and interacting with faculty and other students is an enriching experience. She told the professor that she would ask her parents but added that she did not foresee any problem. In fact, it would be her pleasure to accompany her to Bangalore. As she came out of the staff room, Janvi saw Amjad again. He had his back towards her. For a moment, she thought that she would stop and say hello to him, but then her instinct told her not to and she walked towards her class. However, she still could not forget that expression of anger and disgust on Amjad's face.

'Janu, what will be the date of your Bangalore departure? Has it been decided?' asked Sunita.

'No, Ma. Not yet, but it should be around the 14th or the 15th of this month. Why do you ask?'

'I was just thinking about visiting your Sulakshana Masi in Kolkata. She has been asking me to come and spend some time with her. It isn't a bad idea. I will anyway not have much to do when you are not here.'

'Seems good, Ma. Why don't you do that? Call up Sulak Masi today and get your tickets booked.'

'I will do that Janu. I think it's great that you have met someone like Pooja. I would like to meet her some time too, she seems great. You don't find teachers like her these days, universities and colleges pay their staff so poorly that most talented young people move on to running businesses or to universities and colleges abroad.'

'Ma, sometimes you surprise me with your knowledge and understanding of what is happening in India and the world today. I wish you had got a job or something, you have such a sharp mind and so many interests.'

'Well, I don't have any regrets Janu. I brought you up and raising you has been my biggest joy. Half my life is gone anyway. Now, I just want to see you happy and settled, that's it. Then, I would have performed all my duties and have nothing left to do. I want to die while I am still young and active.'

'Ma, come on! You still have lots to do... you need to get Mahinder's kids married off! I am sure you'll love doing that, his daughter will be 20 this year! Mahinder and his wife must be extremely worried. Seriously, why don't you start planning for that?'

'Not a bad idea at all!' Sunita said, grinning.

Both mother and daughter started planning for the impending wedding, discussing themes and venues before realizing the lack of a groom. Laughing at their folly, they went into their bedrooms to catch up on their personal chores.

Sahil called to say that he won't be home for dinner as there was an inspection at the factory and he would be required to sign the final reports as well as spend time with the team of government inspectors. Sunita called out to Janvi from her room and asked, 'Janu, would you like to try the Ming Room today? Papa is coming home late, he is dining with some factory inspectors. Let's go and try the food there. Mahinder will also get some respite; he's been cleaning up the kitchen all day.'

Even though Janvi felt a little trepidation with the thought of going to a restaurant considering what happened last time, she agreed and went in to her room to change. Mangal, their trusted driver, took out the black Mercedes. Mother and daughter sat at the back and looked chic in their similar white and salmon-pink dresses. They smiled indulgently and complimented, rather teased, each other on their exquisite taste. Both looked forward to spending an evening out of the house, relishing the delicious Ming Room food. Sunita, especially, felt less claustrophobic when she stepped out of the house. Lately, her own room had started to depress her and make her feel tired and irritable.

Ming Room was a little far away from their house so Janvi asked Mangal to put on the songs from her favourite Hindi film, which Sunita also enjoyed. Sunita smiled and settled in against some cushions. Mangal always made sure that the plush cushions were available in the car as they prevented jerks which aggravated Sunita's back pain. At 49, almost every woman suffered from either knee or back pain. While the poor didn't speak about it and went ahead with their jobs of mopping and sweeping the floors of the rich women who lived in bungalows, the affluent women had the luxury to complain.

Sunita was enjoying the songs when Mangal, with a sudden brake, stopped the car at a red light crossing. Sunita opened her eyes and looked outside. She thought she saw Anjali in the car which had stopped a couple of lanes next to theirs. Somehow, the car also looked a little familiar. Then, to her amazement, she realised that it was Sahil's black BMW! Craning her neck a little, she saw Sahil at the steering wheel. Janvi had her eyes closed. Sunita shut her eyes too and understood everything in a flash. The signal turned green and Sahil drove away. Sunita wondered whether Sahil had seen them. That did not matter, in any case.

She enjoyed the Ming Room dinner, the five glasses of red wine which she had had after years might have contributed to her enjoyment. She had drunk so much wine only one time, six years ago, when her maid had complained about Sahil's misbehaviour with her teenage daughter. Sunita had not believed a word of what the maid had said and had fired her immediately. Today, the pieces of that puzzle finally clicked into place. Later that night, Mangal and Janvi escorted her back to her room. Janvi tucked her safely in bed, before switching off the lights. She was happy that her mother had let her hair down and enjoyed dinner after a really long time.

*****

'Ma'am, your presentation was very good,' Janvi told Pooja after the Bangalore conference as they sat together in the flight. She had also successfully participated in a panel discussion as a student representative. They talked about the various discussions that happened at the conference and the professor was happy to see Janvi's confidence in putting across her points of view. For a beginner, Janvi showed good understanding of the sociological concepts and research methodologies for family structures in South-East Asian social systems.

'Janvi, I must appreciate your reading in sociology. I am happy to see that you are putting serious effort into academics. If you carry on like this, you could consider being an academic after your graduation. You stand a good chance at getting through a great university for your post-graduation and later working in research and teaching,' Pooja said as they waited for their baggage.

'Thank you, Ma'am. It's so nice of you to say that and also thanks a lot for bringing me to the conference. It has been great exposure.'

'You are welcome, Janvi. I am sure that this is just the beginning. See you in college.'

Janvi bade goodbye to her professor at the airport and got into her car. She was surprised to find that Sunita was not there. Usually, Sunita always picked her up from stations and airports. Mangal responded to Janvi's questions about Sunita, in an off-hand manner, 'Kindly ask your mother when you meet her at home, Baby. I won't be able to tell you.'

The air around the bungalow was heavy and didn't feel natural at all. Normally, Sunita turned on all the living room lamps along with the lights in the garden and around the fountain. But today, there was only one light on in the porch and the rest of the house was in pitch darkness. Janvi got off the car and looked around, perplexed. She was worried to see the house all dark and gloomy. For a moment, she thought that there could have been a major electricity breakdown. But then, how could the porch light be on? She tentatively tiptoed inside the house and walked towards Sunita's bedroom. There was no one there and the house staff couldn't be seen either. She called out to Mahinder and after about five minutes, he rushed into the living room—panting and looking forlorn.

'Where is Ma, Mahinder?' Janvi asked, almost in a whisper.

'Oh! Sahib has taken her to the hospital. She fainted in her room and was lying on the floor when Sir came back from the factory, about an hour back.'

'Is there any news from the hospital?' Janvi said, walking back towards the entrance.

'Yes, they have admitted her for a day. The doctors say, as Sahib told me, that she has low blood pressure. In fact Baby, she has not been eating at all since you left for Bangalore... no breakfast, no lunch and very little dinner. I told her that she would get very weak.'

Janvi heard the noise of a car in the porch. She looked through the living room window and saw Sahil closing the car door.

'Hello, Papa. What happened to Ma?' she asked as soon as Sahil stepped inside.

'Oh, this behavior is so typical of your mother! She is hell-bent on losing weight and was apparently starving for four or five days. This had to happen! Anyway, there is nothing to worry about; she just has low blood pressure and blood sugar. They have kept her in the hospital for the night to monitor her BP and will release her tomorrow,' he said and continued in a matter-of-fact tone, 'By the way, I have an important meeting in Chandigarh tomorrow...the opening of a government tender. I would have fetched her back from the hospital but, it seems now that you'll have to do it tomorrow morning.'

Then, looking at Janvi's incredulous expression, he mumbled, 'I can stay back, if you want me to.'

'That's all right, I'll manage on my own. You carry on...'

Janvi looked at Sahil and wondered what had gone wrong with him. He had changed a lot. Was it just work-related stress or something else? She thought of confronting him but immediately dropped the idea, thinking that it would be a sheer waste of time. She was too exhausted to have an unpleasant argument with him.

Janvi left Sahil in the living room and asked Mahinder to send her dinner to her room. After freshening up, she sat quietly in her room and stared at the tray brought in by Mahinder: bowls carrying chicken curry, *palak paneer*, *dal* and curd along with *rotis* and rice. She kept looking at the tray but couldn't get herself to eat any of it. Thoughts of her mother in the hospital, under drip and with low blood pressure, crowded her mind. Pulling herself together, she decided to finish her dinner because now she knew that in the future she would not receive any help or support from her father, especially when it came to managing her problems and unforeseen challenges. Looking back at her father's business-like tone while addressing her mother's illness, she wondered whether her parents were ever happy together or if, for so many years, they had just put up a façade of happiness and bonhomie. They did it rather skillfully though. Maybe most couples have to learn how to do this.

Next morning, Sunita walked to the car with Janvi's help. She looked drained and frail. On their drive back home, Janvi assured her that she would be up and about in no time, and emphasised that a balanced diet was the key to her recovery. Mahinder had prepared Sunita's favourite chicken clear soup with little bits of celery. Sunita also ate a piece of grilled fish with some vegetables and a slice of brown bread. The doctor had given her a tranquilliser and a few vitamin tablets and asked her to include a lot of protein in her diet to regain her strength. Janvi took charge of her mother's medicines as well as of the entire situation. Sunita had not inquired about Sahil once. Janvi started telling her about his trip to Chandigarh but, Sunita looked at her and said, 'Janu, It's OK. You don't worry, I understand that we all have our priorities. There is nothing to feel disturbed about. We all need to learn how to handle things with grace… you'll understand when the time comes. Could you please take me to my room, I would like to rest a little.'

*****

The medicine shop had a long queue but Janvi was determined to finish buying Sunita's medicines. She had also picked up a few beautiful cotton *kaftans* for Sunita, knowing that she would find them very comfortable to lounge around in. She was sipping her iced tea when she heard Kanika call out to her from across the road. Kanika was her classmate and a good friend.

She hurriedly crossed the busy road circling Connaught Place and ran towards Janvi. Panting and breathless, she caught hold of Janvi's right arm gently and kissed her affectionately. The two friends started chatting about their classmates and who was doing what when Kanika informed Janvi that Anjali had been selected as an air hostess with British Airways. She also told Janvi that Anjali was with her grandparents in Chandigarh and was planning a small get together on her return before she left for her training. Doubt crept up in Janvi's mind when she heard about Anjali being in Chandigarh but, she pushed that thought down and focussed on Kanika and her tales.

*****

Soon, Janvi got busy with college and her classes. She enjoyed Prof. Sharma's lectures and reading the journals and books recommended by her. Almost a month had passed since Janvi had met Kanika in Connaught Place and as she sat in a library sifting through a sociological journal's pages, she recollected Kanika telling her that Anjali was planning a get together before she left for training. Had that get together happened without her? Janvi felt her chest tightening as she thought about the possibility of Anjali, her closest friend, ignoring her completely. She quickly checked herself—Anjali would not ignore her; she might have just postponed the get together. With all these thoughts racing through her mind, Janvi left the library and called Kanika.

'No, Janvi. Anjali couldn't organise the get together. In fact, she also missed her training as she has been really unwell. It's been nearly a month. She was also hospitalised for a week.'

'What is wrong with her?' Janvi asked in a worried and anxious tone.

'Oh, I don't really know and I thought it wouldn't be nice to ask for details from her mother. She was very tight-lipped about the whole situation but, she did mention in passing that it was a bad urinary tract infection. Anjali is still undergoing treatment but she is now back at home. Why don't you speak with her?'

Janvi made some excuse and hung up. She went back to the library but couldn't concentrate and decided to get a few books issued for a week, so that she could catch up on reading in the evenings while spending time with Sunita.

As usual, Janvi found Sunita sitting alone in the living room, looking out of the window. However, she did look better as some colour had started returning to her face. Janvi thought that the little weight gain was also suiting her. She sat beside Sunita on the sofa and held her hand.

'Ma, how do you feel now? Hopefully, a little stronger? I have bought your medicines and also some vegetables and fruits. Please let me know if you need anything else. I can pick them up on my way back home from college this week.'

Janvi knew, by the air and the feel of the house, that Sahil had left for one of his frequent tours. Sunita didn't mention him and Janvi decided not to speak about him. It was pointless talking about something which had become a painful subject for her as well as her mother. She thought that maybe Sunita was receiving information about Sahil's whereabouts from his office and that could be the reason behind her stoic silence about him. They were matters between a husband and a wife and Janvi thought it best to leave him out of their conversation.

The week flew by with classes, household chores and errands and looking after Sunita. Janvi was happy that she had got the chance to look after her mother. A new understanding and a trusting and respectful relationship appeared to be blossoming between her and Sunita. Janvi realised that difficulty and sadness brought people together. An organic friendship seemed to be developing between the hitherto estranged mother and daughter. The doctors had hinted that Sunita might be depressed and Janvi was worried that her depression might turn acute. She wanted to suggest that Sunita start seeing a psychiatrist who could help her, but she couldn't muster up enough strength to say this. She decided that it would be wise to let everything be, and this matter could probably be discussed at an opportune time later.

On returning home from college one day, Janvi changed into her tracksuit as usual and was ready to leave for a walk, when her phone rang. Without checking the number, she casually picked it up and heard a male voice with deep baritone address her. He introduced himself as Prashant Garg, Anjali's father. Janvi had met him once at his house, about two years ago, during Anjali's birthday party. He seemed very decent and soft-spoken. Courteously, he inquired about her mother and asked her whether she was enjoying college. Congratulating her on her excellent board result, he mentioned that Anjali had also cleared the British Airways interviews and would be leaving in a week to join work. He added that he was organising a surprise party for Anjali and was calling to invite Janvi. He promised that he would call back to give her the details about the venue but for now, he just wanted to know whether she would be in town on the day of the party. Janvi confirmed her attendance and thanked him profusely, saying that she would await the details about the venue.

That night, Sahil suddenly came back from his tour. Janvi found him in the living room when she returned from her walk. He looked quite tired and appeared to have lost some weight.

'How was your trip, Papa? You look quite tired, would you like some tea?'

'No, it's OK. Mahinder already gave me tea. I have been home for an hour now. How's your mother? I went to her room but found her sleeping.'

'She is doing much better. Recovering well and eating well too. I'll go in for a bath and join you for dinner in a while.'

Mahinder laid out the dinner quietly. Out of his care and concern for Sahil, he had prepared a wonderful chicken soup with vegetables, which Sahil loved. Recently, dinners with her father had become unusual—full of fake pleasantries and meaningless small talk. Sahil asked her about her college and she asked him about his work. Sunita was also up but she had asked Mahinder to serve her dinner in her room. Mahinder was wheeling the trolley out when Janvi, sensing a chance to get away, got up and said that she would carry her mother's dinner, and that Mahinder should look after Sahil.

Janvi took the trolley to her mother's room and sat down with her to give her some company while she ate. Sunita didn't inquire about Sahil at all. She asked Janvi about her classes and took out a bundle of two thousand rupee notes to give to Janvi. She said that Janvi would need money to buy her medicines and other household things. Janvi assured her that she should not worry about the house at all.

'I'll fetch the fruits and vegetables day after. I need to submit a rather lengthy assignment to Pooja Ma'am tomorrow and would have to study in the departmental library to complete the assignment.'

That same night, Prashant called Janvi at 11pm, which she thought was a rather improper time to call. He said that he had called to invite her for Anjali's party the next evening at 7 pm in a hotel next to their house. Janvi wrote down the address and said that tomorrow would be very difficult for her, but because the party was for Anjali, she would come directly after college. He also offered to pick her up but she declined the offer as Mangal would be around to drop her.

Janvi worked till early hours of the morning and was able to complete a large part of the class assignment. She jumped out of bed at 8 am as she didn't want to get late for class. Then, she remembered that she had to attend Anjali's party in the evening and decided to wear a peach-coloured dress with a very delicate cream lace and embroidery detailing at the waist. She kept her pearl and diamond string necklace in her bag and, without eating her breakfast, jumped into the car and rushed to college. She was able to make it in the nick of time. Professor Gupta was very particular about punctuality.

Janvi had underestimated the time she would take to complete Pooja Ma'am's assignment. She looked at her watch and panicked because it was already 7.30 pm and she would take at least another 20 minutes to complete and submit the assignment. She also realised that she had not told Sunita about Anjali's party. She decided to call her mother from the car, on her way to the hotel. As her mind raced with these thoughts, Sunita called. Janvi told her mother that she was still in the library and after submitting her assignment, she had to attend a party. Before she could complete what she wanted to say, Sunita hung up saying that she didn't want to disturb her further and to let her know if she got really late in returning from the party. Sunita was not worried because Mangal was driving Janvi to the party and was relieved that he would be around.

On reaching the hotel, almost 45 minutes late, Janvi found Prashant in the lobby, sitting on a sofa. He must be waiting for people, Janvi thought guiltily and walked up to him, apologising for being late. She asked him where Anjali was and if the party had already started. He started walking with her and told her that they have to go to the fifth floor banquet hall, where quite a few of Anjali's friends had already gathered. He said that Anjali was on her way and had no idea about the party. In fact, he added, he was waiting in the lobby for Anjali only. Janvi said that he should wait for Anjali and she could go to the fifth floor by herself. However, he insisted on escorting her to the banquet hall and accompanied her in the elevator. He stopped the elevator on the third floor and asked Janvi to follow him as he stepped out. Janvi was confused but came out to the corridor. Prashant started walking and told her that he had booked a room for Anjali and had kept a beautiful bouquet of flowers in that room and since Janvi was one of Anjali's closest friends, it would be nice if she handed it over to Anjali. She could carry the flowers and he would take the cake, which was also in the room.

'OK, Uncle. Let's do that. I must say you have really done a lot of planning.'

' Yes, I just want to see Anjali happy.'

When they reached the room, he opened the door and asked her to come in. Janvi went inside and looked around. It was a nicely done-up, rather large room. The room had a coffee table and two chairs placed near the window. There was also a writing table with a delicate wooden chair and a smart brass lamp with an off-white raw silk lamp shade. The bed occupied the largest area and was neatly made up.

However, Janvi couldn't see the flowers or the cake and wondered where they were. Then, she heard a double click on the main door and turned around to see Prashant standing in front of the door. He walked inside and sat down on the chair behind the writing table. Then, he asked her, or rather ordered her, to sit on one of the chairs in front of him. Janvi felt uncomfortable and asked him about the flowers and the cake, so that she could help him carry them to the banquet hall.

He leisurely lit a cigarette and while blowing smoke in her direction said that there was no party and no one was coming to the hotel. Janvi could feel her legs shaking. She could sense that something bad was about to happen and ran towards the door. But, Prashant was quicker and blocked her way. He told her to go back to the chair and sit as he had something important to tell her. When she didn't move, he dragged her and pushed her back towards the chair. Janvi looked up and saw his face red with rage.

He was seething with anger when he started speaking, 'I had planned to kill your father. But then, I decided to spare his life. Now, once my plan comes to fruition, he'll live like a dead man. But, before that, I want you to know who your father is—

he is an evil man and a rapist. He raped my daughter a year ago. He spoilt her life and her career! Did you know that she aborted his child three months ago? She was hospitalised battling for her life and could have even died if the doctors hadn't saved her. I can't believe he was sleeping with my underage daughter for almost a year! A year! But, what else could you expect from a disgusting person like him. He doesn't even spare a girl who happens to be his own daughter's friend!'

He rambled on as Janvi sat there, dumbstruck, trying to absorb the gravitas of the situation. The flickering doubt that had housed in her mind since she had seen her father with Anjali at the restaurant on the day of her results started to take shape. Prashant took a couple of deep breaths to calm himself, then spoke, 'He had met Anjali in your house and set his eyes on her. He stalked her, hounded her, day and night. The poor girl was so frightened that she hid everything from us. But, after almost nine months, she told her mother. She had a major nervous breakdown after which I finally came to know about her ordeal. I have called you here to tell you that I am going to inflict a lot of pain on your father; you can get the details from him later. You just be prepared to manage your mother and his business because he won't be in a position to do anything for the rest of his life. You can leave now. I have told you whatever I thought was necessary to convey. I refuse to answer any questions and would not like a conversation. I also would not like to meet you ever again. And, you better tell that scum of a father you have to stay away from my family.'

Janvi instinctively knew he was not lying. She also knew that he would never see her again. She picked up her bag, opened the door quietly and left. On the ride back home, she realised that her world would no longer be the same, that she would no longer be the same. She reached home to find Sahil in the living room, having a heated argument with someone on the telephone. He hung up when he saw Janvi and expressed his surprise at seeing her back from the party so soon. He casually asked about all her friends and then stealthily inquired about Anjali. Janvi just stared blankly at him, disgusted with everything she had learnt about him, and without responding, went into Sunita's room.

Janvi found her mother sleeping, but even in the dark she could see the frown lines etched on her face. At that moment, in that sleeping woman, she saw a wronged wife who was very different from the loving mother she had known for the last 17 years. Janvi would be 18 in another four months but it almost felt like she would be turning 38. The night when she had met Prashant, had heard him speak about her father, had experienced his pain and wrath—that one hour had aged her prematurely. In one fell swoop, she lost the zeal of her teenage years, her youthful happiness and zest for life. A large part of her 'self' died in that hour.

She lay awake the whole night, tossing and turning, her mind full of jumbled-up thoughts. Surprisingly, she did not shed a single tear. The blow was so strong that it left her numb. She reflected on the reality of her parents' relationship. She wondered whether Sunita had been suffering for the last 20 years. Had her mother kept quiet not to keep her marriage going, but to hold the family together, for Janvi's sake? Was this not the loving home, the safe haven that she imagined it to be? Or was it just an opulent house filled with useless knick-knacks? Her thoughts moved to her father, had he struck a 'deal' with his own wife to give her money every month for her supposed 'needs' and for Janvi's future? Or maybe he was actually investing in his own future, protecting himself from disrepute and social disgrace by projecting the image of a happy and hard-working family man?

Janvi's thoughts ran riot. Her mother's face filled with pain and anguish flashed before her eyes. She knew that Sunita was married at 20, had three miscarriages and then, after nine years, gave birth to Janvi. She wondered maybe she was not a child born out of marital bliss. Maybe her mother had been raped by Sahil repeatedly? She pondered about their relationship over the last few years. Hadn't she noticed the growing distance between them? Maybe it was because Sahil was always chasing some young girl or the other. Whatever their relation had been in the past, one thing was clear now—Sunita was her responsibility. She would be by her mother's side as long as she was alive. Maybe, like her, Sunita had lost a large part of herself too, over the years. Can she revive her again? Janvi thought that this was highly unlikely. And revive her for what, and for whom? For her father? What should she do about him? Should she confront him with the shameful truth she has recently learnt? Get him behind bars? Move out with Sunita and start a new life with her? But, where is the money to do that? She won't be able to give her mother the comforts of this home. At least in this house, they have physical comforts and financial security. People rightly say that money solves a lot of problems—it does provide confidence and a sense of control.

With such thoughts racing through her mind, Janvi suddenly felt claustrophobic. Breathing heavily, she walked out of her room and went to the back veranda. It was a dark, moonless night. Janvi paced up and down the veranda, inhaling deeply, and then sat in the spacious cane armchair under the fan. She thought about her upcoming birthday. She would soon turn 18, which is just the beginning of a long journey of adulthood. 'However, sometimes it takes just a moment for a decade or two to pass by,' she mumbled, ruefully. The psychological impact of knowing her father's truth was so powerful and electrifying that the elements of her thoughts and feelings smashed into bits and pieces and crushed like glass. The only alternative left for her was to pick up these splinters and start a different life. Even at 18, one's entire perspective on life could be altered forever. For a fleeting moment, she thought about Prashant and his proclamation of revenge. But, even at her young age, Janvi knew that revenge was an indicator of violent emotions that resisted the complete acceptance of a new altered reality. She realised that her new reality demanded a different kind of emotional management. She needed to process all her violent emotions sufficiently, thereby allowing logic and wisdom to take over and discover relevant solutions and responses to this altered reality. Unlike Prashant, Janvi, with her new psychological age of 38 years, was showing signs of a mature mellowness. Too much had happened in the course of that night. Janvi returned to her room mentally exhausted and snuggled against the pillows, falling asleep instantly.

Next day, Janvi decided to attend college regularly and not think about anything else. There was too much to study and prepare for before the examinations. She made a resolution to do well in class and in the examinations. Prof. Sharma met her frequently and even told her that she was happy to stay back late and help her. Janvi was grateful for her encouragement and guidance. Spending even 15 minutes with the professor provided her with amazing clarity about various concepts. Janvi enjoyed reading through the recommended research publications and articles suggested by her. She would go to the library on Saturdays in order to stay away from home and any possible interaction with Sahil. Even though the frequency of his tours had increased, he still managed to be home on Saturdays and Sunday afternoons. Janvi avoided all conversation and interaction with him and while he understood that something was wrong, he didn't have the courage to ask Janvi or Sunita about the clearly visible changes. His interaction with Sunita had virtually stopped. She hardly came out of her bedroom, where Mahinder served all her meals. From her balcony window, Sunita could hear the BMW engine revving up which meant that Sahil was leaving for work. So, on some mornings, when she heard the engine and knew that Sahil had left, she would come out of her room and take a slow stroll in the back veranda. She didn't even seem to have the strength to go down the steps which led to the back lawn and the meticulously manicured garden, which just a few months ago had been her pride and joy. The domestic staff understood that there was tension and strain in the Sharma household but they were discreet and maintained a respectful silence.

Janvi spent more and more time in the library. She had completed most of her reference work and would pick up other interesting research publications and spend the evenings browsing through them. One Friday afternoon, while she was in the publications section, she happened to come across a number of articles which contained socio-psychological researches on homicide and rape; articles which were written by well-known faculty members from various universities in India and abroad. She asked the library staff to issue five such research articles. She decided to read these in the coming weekend.

When she returned home, she found that dinner had already been laid out for Sahil and her in the dining room. Sunita was eating her meal in her bedroom, as usual. Perforce, Janvi sat in her chair at the dining table and kept the bundle of publications on the other end of the table. Sahil was almost finished with his meal. He looked up and said, 'I notice that you come late from the university these days. Do you have extra classes?'

Janvi, without looking up, continued eating and wondered whether she should answer him or not. She finally decided to respond and, in an indifferent tone, told him that she spends her extra time in the library.

Sahil finished his meal and, pushing his chair back, got up from the dining table. He walked to the basin, washed his hands and while wiping them with a towel, he walked back, in an unhurried pace, towards the bundle of papers kept on the table. He sifted through them casually, picked out the article on homicide and rape, and glanced through it. Then, with perceptible anxiety and discomfort, he told Janvi that she was too young to read this kind of stuff. Controlling her anger, Janvi looked straight into his eyes and said, 'If girls my age can get raped by men your age, I can surely read about it. I don't think there is any problem at all.' She snatched back the article from his hands and stormed to her room. Sahil remained standing alone, shocked and uneasy.

On Sunday, when Janvi asked Mahinder to give her some coffee, Mahinder muttered that Sahil had left for a week-long tour. He said that Sahil was going to Chandigarh and after that to some other place whose name he couldn't catch. Mangal came in and asked Mahinder for the keys to the Mercedes. On seeing Janvi, he smiled nervously and stood with his head down like a boy of five who had been punished by his teacher in school.

'Why do you need the keys to the Mercedes, Mangal?' Janvi asked, sipping her coffee.

'Oh, I have to pick up Shahnaz Madam who goes to Chandigarh with Sir. She comes here every month,' he left it at that. Janvi listened to him and realised that things were more complicated than what they appeared to be. How did it matter, anyway? Taking her cup of coffee, she walked into Sunita's room.

It was just another Monday morning for everyone else but for Janvi, it felt very different. In fact, Janvi felt different since that miserable day at the hotel. Adding 20 years to one's life in a single day is no mean achievement even though the change had its genesis in irretrievable tragedy. Her thoughts, as had become routine, travelled back to Anjali and her father. She wondered how thousands of tragic lives go unnoticed in this world. Trauma, murder and rape are reported daily in the print media and aired on television. However, what these reports miss are those people who fester in homes that have exceptional outer beauty or those who have physical comforts but their spirits are wounded deeply. Then, there are those families that boast of immense material wealth but know that morally, they are bankrupt. The only way they can manage this moral bankruptcy is by being completely insensitive to it. Janvi had begun to understand this dissonance. Believing that there is a principle of natural justice, she had taken the decision to let nature take its course. She, as a single individual, couldn't possibly handle this complexity alone and was certain that destiny would play itself out anyway. Her mother slept peacefully as the morning sun filtered into her room through the lovely lacy blinds. At least she seemed to have accepted her fate and continued to scrape whatever smiles that were left over from a life that perhaps should not have been this difficult.

As Janvi moved towards the door, she saw Mahinder standing in front of her trying to mutter something. He seemed to have lost his voice. Mangal appeared and explained that Mahinder was in a state of shock. Mangal informed her that Sahil had met with a terrible accident while driving to Chandigarh and had been rushed to a hospital. He was in a critical condition with severe head and waist injuries. Janvi listened to the news in stoic silence. She couldn't shake away the feeling that subconsciously, she was expecting something like this to happen. She sent Mangal to the hospital with the requisite money and instructed him to stay there till he was needed. He called the next day to convey that Shahnaz had succumbed to her injuries and had passed away an hour ago. Her parents in Jammu had been informed and they were on their way to pay their daughter a final visit. On the other hand, Sahil was in a deranged mental condition as he was rendered paralysed waist-down. Janvi listened to Mangal's report, feeling sorry for Shahnaz.

*****

Five years have passed since that fateful day. Janvi has been managing her mother as well as the affairs of the company.

She has appointed a team of professionals to take care of the family business. Sunita's life is divided between her trips to the doctors, meditation classes and the occasional kitty parties. She has finally seemed to have found her will to live. Sahil is being attended by nurses who stay in the two guest rooms next to the west lawns. Janvi scored exceptionally well in her graduation and post-graduation examinations. She topped the department in both the examinations and also stood third in the university merit list. She has enrolled for her PhD under Professor Seema Chauhan, a renowned academic and a good friend of Prof. Sharma. Everyone in the department believes Janvi's topic of research—personality and the family and cultural socialisation variables for rape of young girls by much older men—to be very relevant. Janvi chose this topic because she wanted to understand why her father did what he did. She wanted to get into the psyche of her father and men like him.

Janvi has already submitted a few critical points that her research on rape has led her to. She noted that rape is described as sexual assault or violence. But, it was also a manner through which unprocessed anger or lack of empathy for women gets expressed. Early signs of this behaviour often begin to appear in adolescence and devolve around narcissism and ineffective management of anger and tantrums. These behaviours, Janvi learnt, are also deeply rooted in the lack of self-respect and self-worth especially when the male child has a history of facing rejection in his family and in the peer group. Parents, therefore, were partially responsible for the development of violent aberrations in their child's behaviour. In India, the way a male child is brought up can be significantly related to the development of these aberrations. The male child is also made to feel superior and more powerful. Psychologically, he is very often made to feel that women must give him what he desires. And if what he desires is not given with consent and willingness, then he has the right to take it by force. Older men raping teenage girls vindicate their power, which comes from their social position and wealth, and also their decreasing physical attraction.

Her research is progressing well except for interruptions caused by her visits to a psychiatrist for depression. She often has to take a week off to wean herself off the drug-induced drowsiness. Janvi has also decided to stay single and look after her mother and the family's properties. She has cut all ties with Sahil and informed the lawyers as well as her mother that she will not perform his last rites.

2

Enabled for a Purpose

Her name was Shakuntala, but she was lovingly called Shakun by her family and her employers. Her family worked as domestic help in the house of a famous political family of Madhya Pradesh—Rai Sahib Raj Bahadur Singhji of Bhudeshwar. Her maternal grandmother had served, for nearly five decades, as a nanny to the four children of Rai Sahib.

The royal family owned several acres of land, some mango orchards and a few lakes in and around Bhudeshwar. Their *haveli* was the epitome of opulence. There was material wealth strewn all over—massive verandas, high ceilings, exquisitely carved pillars of mosaic and marble, shining brass and copper pots and utensils and huge silver candle stands. Every room looked majestic with the most artistically woven carpets and *durries*. The parties thrown by Rai Sahib were always lavish and he took personal interest in deciding the menu. In fact, it was a known fact that many generations of *haveli* cooks had been trained by the best chefs of the world.

The origins of the Singh family could be traced back to Bihar and Bengal. Rai Sahib's great-grandmother was the beautiful and coquettish fifth daughter of a very rich *zamindar* of Murshidabad district in West Bengal. Her name was Promilla. The lady had been brought up in great wealth and made this widely known among the members of the family she had married into. She had also brought in a retinue of servants from her father's home who exclusively looked after her, her clothes and the set of rooms that were allotted to her and her husband in her father-in-law's *haveli.* Promilla pampered the families of her staff and treated them far better than the other staff in the *haveli*. Hence, over decades, Promilla's personal staff had become spoilt and arrogant. Shakun's family had also come with Promilla, from her father's side. Shakun's family members were now the third and fourth generation of domestic help working for the Rai Sahib.

Shakun was the only girl in her family; Shakun's father was a good-for-nothing wastrel surviving on the largess of his employers. Her mother was a chronic patient of tuberculosis and therefore led a secluded existence. Her maternal grandmother still worked in the *haveli* even though she was nearing 80 and was losing her vision gradually. Shakun and her family lived in the staff quarters but, she was in and out of the *haveli* frequently, assisting her aging grandmother. As a result, she got to watch the ways of the *haveli* from close quarters. Many times, she imagined that she too has become as lucky as the girls of the royal family and a charming prince has entered her life to take her away to a beautiful palace in a faraway land. While she was busy daydreaming about a beautiful future, she didn't realise that her present was about to change... drastically.

A girl child in uneducated and comparatively poor families grows up in the shadow of its male members. Decisions about her destiny and life are mostly made by fathers, grandfathers, uncles or elder brothers. Even the mother is most often a mute spectator. Most girls and women in India experience the pain of losing their freedom around the time they hit puberty. At first, it is the freedom of physical mobility. It is not easy for girls and even women to move and travel freely outside their homes. In rural India, the situation is even worse; girls and women are also asked to stay away from certain sections of the house where the menfolk congregate to meet other men to socialise or discuss matters pertaining to the village. The zest for life, any possibility of exploring the world outside and joyfully interact with its people, is curbed and curtailed in childhood itself. When young girls see their brothers, who are of the same age, enjoying this physical freedom, the pain and sadness of missing out on life and its opportunities create self pity and feelings of inferiority. Brothers, given a chance, also don't mind rubbing it in and conveying, at every step, that because these girls have not seen the outside world, their understanding of things is not as good as theirs. In this situation, women begin to lose confidence in their own self, in their ability to deal with the world, and they begin to succumb to the influence and the pressure exerted by the male members of the family. This becomes a vicious circle and perpetuates a culture of extreme dependence. So much so, that many women lose their self confidence and tolerate all kinds of atrocities inflicted on them by the men in their lives in exchange for the food and shelter they provide.

The same was about to happen with Shakun. She had been going to school for precisely three years when it was decided that learning household chores like cooking, sewing, stitching, etc. was more important. And then, just like that, her name was withdrawn from school. That afternoon, Shakun had sat under the *neem* tree in the courtyard and cried without anyone noticing her plight. When Shakun turned 13, her skirts and blouses were distributed among the other young girls of the staff quarters. Her brother escorted their mother Shanti to the market to pick up plain sarees for Shakun. Her father also got white and black waist-length blouses with long sleeves and high neck stitched for her. The colours of her sarees, the style of the blouses, where she will sleep, whom she will meet, how she will speak—everything was decided by the elder males of her family. She encountered a completely different world. As a young girl of about four or five, Shakun would often sit with Faizu, the *haveli* tailor, and was amazed with his deftness with the black hand-operated sewing machine. She admired his art of cutting and drafting, sewing and hemming and smocking, and how he converted a piece of cloth into a beautiful garment for the ladies of the royal family. Faizu would tell her tales of the British *memsahibs* and their beautiful gowns and the delicate laces that he put on their clothes. But one morning, her father called her and reprimanded her saying that she was a grown woman now and it doesn't look nice when she sits with Faizu and talks to him. She was forbidden from even stepping into the veranda where Faizu sat for years. Faizu was as old as her grandfather.

*****

Rai Sahib's daughter, Vijaylakshmi was an affable and pretty girl. She was called Lakshmi because when she was born, a lot of wealth came into the family. Rai Sahib won two major landownership cases that the family had been fighting over for the last two decades. After winning these cases, the family acquired a lot of property which led to weeks of rejoicing in the *haveli*. With the arrival of their pretty little angel, their happiness had increased manifold. In fact, the first lot of money from the court case was handed over to Rai Sahib on the day Lakshmi was brought into the *haveli* from the nursing home. This was one of the reasons why her arrival in the family was considered lucky and a blessing. In spite of all the love and attention showered upon her by the entire family, Lakshmi grew up to be a happy, courteous and considerate girl. She befriended all the young girls growing up with her in the staff quarters, Shakun being her closest friend and confidante.

When Lakshmi had seen Shakun for the first time in a cream coloured saree with a blue border and a high-neck blouse, she was visibly shocked.

'Shakun, why are you wearing a saree?' she asked confused.

Before Shakun could respond, Shakun's grandmother responded rather coldly, 'Baby Sahib, from today Shakun will only wear sarees. She is a big girl and her father feels that frocks and skirts don't look nice on her now.'

'Oh Dayiju, she looks so uncomfortable in a saree. How will she run while playing seven tiles with us? How can she run in a saree?'

'She doesn't need to run any more. No games for her now. Do you know that, for one week, she has been cooking the evening meal for us and she is learning very fast. Her father is very happy with her progress. She will be a big help for her ailing mother too.'

'But, look at me. I am her age and I don't wear sarees and I will not wear a saree till I get married, and even after marriage I will continue wearing skirts, blouses and trousers.'

'Oh Baby Sahib you are Rai Sahib's daughter. With us, it's very different. I beg you please don't put these ideas in Shakun's head. Her father will be very angry.'

Lakshmi looked at Shakun, she had a very sad expression on her face. When Dayiju moved away with the clothes to the dressing and the powder rooms, Shakun whispered to Lakshmi, 'Let it be, Baby Sahib, I'll come to you in the evenings and you can teach me Hindi and a little bit of English too.'

'Why will I teach you? Aren't the teachers at your school good?' Lakshmi asked, sprawling on the bed.

Shakun hesitated before muttering, 'I can't go to school also. Baba has said that I should learn household chores as they are more important.'

Lakshmi was about to say something offensive about Shakun's father but one look at her friend's solemn face and she decided to not give her any more grief, 'OK, Shakun. I'll teach you. We can also listen to the Binaca Geet Mala on Wednesday evening. So, be happy.'

Shakun was a plain-looking girl, dark complexioned and with very ordinary features. However, she had a cheerful presence and was a very obliging person. She would willingly do any work which was given to her. She particularly loved to spend time with Lakshmi and was very meticulous about her work. She dusted Lakshmi's bedroom to perfection and polished all the brass and silver decorative items in her bedroom until they glittered like diamonds. She would also water the plants and did her best to keep them green and fresh. Whenever she found that the gardeners were neglecting the plants, she would pull them up and force them to prune the plants, give them the required fertiliser and water them regularly. Once Lakshmi had told her that plants remained healthy if one played soft music in the area where they were kept, if one talked lovingly and gently to them and flowers responded positively to human touch too. Shakun, since childhood, had a strong desire to learn and experiment. She was naturally curious about Lakshmi's suggestion and decided to try it out. Thus, that day onwards, Shakun would hum to the plants whenever she was all by herself in Lakshmi's bedroom making sure that no one noticed her indulging in these activities. If people saw her doing this, they would definitely think that she had gone crazy.

*****

Shakun watched Lakshmi intently as she emerged from her dressing room and glided into her bedroom looking like a painting. She was wearing a pink skirt with a white and pink embroidered blouse. She looked beautiful and there was a glow which Shakun, being observant and perceptive, noticed for the first time on Lakshmi's face. She wondered what could be the reason behind this beauteous radiance. Shakun couldn't muster up enough courage to ask her. After all, she was Baby Sahib and in a way, her employer and mistress. She would definitely take this as insolence and misbehaviour on her part.

Shakun couldn't help but stare at her. She kept on looking at Lakshmi till Lakshmi felt self-conscious and asked her, 'Why are you staring at me, Shakun? Do I look funny or bad?'

'No no, Baby Sahib. Actually, I can't take my eyes off you. You look very beautiful today. In fact, most beautiful! I have never seen you look so beautiful.'

'Oh, maybe it's the colour of my dress.'

'Maybe...'

Shakun muttered something else which was inaudible and ignoring her, Lakshmi switched on the large black GEC radio and tuned into Radio Ceylon. It was 8 pm on a Wednesday, Binaca Geet Mala would start any moment now.

Lakshmi sat on the sofa next to the radio and Shakun was on the carpet, literally sitting at her feet. They listened to the entire programme. The Hindi film music of the 1970s was very melodious and the lyrics were written by well-known poets who had mastered both Hindi and Urdu, and their spoken and written Hindustani was also beautifully structured and very expressive.

'Baby Sahib, why don't you get married now? People say that you are very intelligent and are doing very well in your studies. You have studied so much. Now is the time to settle down. There will be so many boys keen to marry you. Do you like someone?'

'Oh Shakun, you ask too many questions! I want to study more, travel and see the world and then work, perhaps in Delhi or Bombay or it could also be London. You know we have a very big mansion there, just like this *haveli* and there are many staff members who look after it. Whenever we go to London, we stay there.'

'Oh Baby Sahib, you are so lucky. God has blessed you with everything. Dayiju says that if you did good in your previous life, you are blessed with wealth and good family in this life. Doing good in this life is also important.'

Then, after a pause, she asked, tentatively, 'Will you teach me a little, Baby Sahib, when you have time in the evenings?'

'Yes yes, we can start from next week. I'll get you a book, a copy and a pencil.'

*****

Winter was gradually setting in Bhudeshwar. There was an exhilarating nip in the air. Leaves were springing up in the meticulously pruned rose plants and the stately Rukmini Devi, the mistress of the *haveli,* was delighted; she loved her rose garden. Lakshmi knew that soon, the roses would be in full bloom and the kitchen garden, at the back, would be laden with fresh vegetables. The whole *haveli* looked forward to these winter vegetables; carrots, turnips, cauliflower, cabbage and big gleaming leaves of spinach were so inviting. There was so much variety to cook from the crop of vegetables which grew in their huge farmhouse. The kitchen would be inundated with potatoes, coriander leaves, beans and tomatoes. There were at least a hundred guava trees in the farmhouse. Rai Sahib loved guava jelly and the guava cheese which was personally made by Rukmini Devi every year. He also distributed large amounts to his doctor and lawyer friends, and quite a bit was also sent to ministers in the Madhya Pradesh government.

While Rukmini stood near the large French windows, which gave her a picture-perfect view of the garden, Dayiju, standing next to her, said, 'Bai sahib now Shakun has become responsible and dependable enough to help you in making the guava jelly and cheese .'

Rukmini greeted this idea with a beaming smile and told Dayiju that she had already started thinking about Shakun's marriage and the support which will be provided from the *haveli*. Dayiju bent and touched her feet, blessing her lovingly.

Dayiju was a short, dark woman with a leathery complexion and sunken eyes. She was losing her vision gradually from progressive cataract. Rukmini and Lakshmi were both very keen on a surgery for her, but Dayiju was not mentally prepared for it. The doctor had given them six months to convince her of the advantages of an operation. Whenever Lakshmi got an opportunity, she gently broached this topic with Dayiju and promised her that she would be by her side in the hospital till she was discharged. Dayiju appreciated Lakshmi's concern and said that she had heard from elders that these things should be done during peak winter because healing is better in low temperatures. She said that she would be ready for the surgery around Christmas. This was partly an excuse to escape from the pressure being put on her by Lakshmi for the eye operation.

Rai Sahib looked after the *haveli* staff very well. Before winter set in, he would visit the staff quarters for inspection to see that the doors and windows locked well and the roof tiles were intact. Any damage in the roofs would allow the winter chill to creep in, thus making the nights unbearably cold. Rai Sahib, being a kind and considerate employer, didn't want the young children and infants to bear the brunt of the winters and fall sick. The poor were highly vulnerable to pneumonia and lung infections. He, on a regular basis, distributed warm clothing, bed linen and quilts for all his staff. There were two doctors attending to the staff, performing regular check-ups, administering required medical aid and, if the need arose, arranging for hospitalisation of the ill. Therefore, life for the staff in the *haveli* was very comfortable and also slightly cocooned. It was Rukmini Devi who kept them on their toes and balanced her husband's kindness with discipline and responsibility. The *haveli* ran under her leadership.

*****

Suddenly, Shakun's marriage had become the talk of the *haveli* and amongst Rukmini's friends circle. Anything related to the people of the *haveli,* be it the help, became a topic of discussion in Bhudeshwar. After all, the people of the town also needed something meaningful to engage with. Dayiju had mentioned sometime ago to Rukmini, that it would be important for them to marry Shakun to someone from their community. Dayiju had led an extremely tragic life. Her three sons and their wives had passed away in the last 17 years. She knew that the community felt that her family was cursed and if anyone welcomed Shakun as their daughter-in-law, she would bring bad omen to the family. Dayiju didn't want this stigma to be attached to her family forever. If Shakun married into the community, and then was happy and her family prospered, this negative perception of the family would be removed. Rukmini understood her dilemma and assured her that Shakun will find a nice boy in her own community and Rai Sahib and she would research the antecedents of the family before her engagement. They would do everything to ensure that no mistake was made by them in this aspect. Dayiju bent to touch her feet, as she always did, to convey her gratitude and happiness.

Winter was setting in speedily, providing a splash of colour in the garden. The kitchen garden was full with all the vegetables sprouting and spreading their aroma. Lakshmi loved to eat the raw vegetables and was in constant arguments with the gardeners who got annoyed when Lakshmi plucked them, as the crops were still in their infancy. Lakshmi and Shakun took a round of the garden practically every day and as the gardeners couldn't admonish Lakshmi, they would indirectly express their annoyance by scolding Shakun and warning her not to indulge in any activity which would harm the crops. Both the girls would giggle and pluck vegetables as soon as the gardeners were out of sight.

On one such evening when Lakshmi and Shakun were taking a walk, Shakun suddenly stopped and with her head bent, and an expression of sadness on her face, asked Lakshmi, 'Baby Sahib, do you think I am very ugly? People in the family are worried about my marriage. I know they think that no boy is going to like me because of my looks and dark skin.'

Lakshmi was a little surprised by the suddenness of this question, and also felt embarrassed responding to her. However, she knew that she had to respond with restraint and transparency, 'Shakun not all girls who get married are as beautiful as the gorgeous Waheeda Rehman. But, they still get married and are happy. You have a pleasant face and a nice figure. You are a good person and that adds to your personality. All these qualities will endear you to your husband. He'll be a very fortunate man. You'll make a wonderful wife and mother, don't worry at all. '

Shakun smiled and thanked Lakshmi for her kind words. Then, she reminded Lakshmi that it was getting cold as it was already past 7 pm and that Lakshmi should go indoors to avoid a chill. Shakun and Lakshmi parted ways as Shakun had to reach home and prepare for dinner because it had become her responsibility to cook and serve dinner to the family by 9 pm. Feeling happy with Lakshmi's assurance about her marriage, Shakun braced herself for her evening duty. She reached home and saw that her mother was comfortably tucked away in the quilt and her father was sitting quietly in the veranda smoking a *beedi*. Shakun decided to cook a vegetable dish with cauliflower and green peas, and an egg curry which her mother loved, with some *rotis* that she would serve with curd and pickle. She stopped chopping the cauliflower and decided to light the firewood and put the eggs to boil, as this would save time and speed up the process. It took her 15 to 20 minutes to get the *chulha* going, and then more to prepare everything else.

She could hear her mother cough from her room and wondered why, despite the many medicines that the family doctors gave her, her coughing bouts continued. Needless to say, her appetite had practically vanished, and it was with great difficulty and after a lot of persuasion, that Shakun could force her to eat one *roti* and two tablespoons of rice. Shakun knew that her mother had really suffered. She got married to a man who never cared for her. His sense of responsibility was abysmal and he was a self-centred man. He depended entirely on Dayiju and Shakun's salaries, and lived at the mercy of Rai Sahib's family. Rukmini Devi also disliked him and wondered why Dayiju didn't ask him to leave her daughter years ago. 'Could have got your daughter divorced and married her off to someone decent,' she always used to say.

'These are matters of destiny Bai Sahib and who had control over one's destiny. Not even Raja Dashrath could prevent Lord Ram's exile!' Her grandmother used to reply with a sigh.

Shakun's mother refused to eat anything for dinner. Shakun was worried and touched her forehead and found it burning hot, she was also sweating profusely. In winter, this kind of perspiration was not normal, so she went outside and mentioned this to her father. He said that people break into a sweat when they have high fever and then got busy lighting his *beedi*. Shakun decided to give her the medicine that Doctor Sahib always gave when her mother ran a high temperature. She picked up a glass of water and walked up to her bed. Shaking her gently, Shakun urged her to have the medicine. Her mother looked at her with large, vacant eyes. She was repeating a word that Shakun couldn't understand. She moved closer to her mother and heard her say, 'Prashant'. He was Shanti's second child, a son whom she lost a few years ago. He had drowned while they were crossing a river near Mandla, on their way back from the wedding of a relative's daughter. The child was about five years old. At that time, Shanti had lost her mind and had gone into deep depression. She seemed to be regressing now.

Shanti kept looking at Shakun and beckoned her to come closer to her. Shakun sat on the bed and caressed her mother lovingly. Shanti told Shakun, 'Always look after Rai Sahib and Rukmini Bai Sahib. They are like your parents and have showered so many blessings on you. Never misbehave with them and don't leave them.' She took the medicine and then went into some kind of a semi-conscious slumber.

Shanti passed away in the wee hours of the next morning. While Shakun was inconsolable, Dayiju neither spoke a word nor shed a single tear. She sat near her daughter's body looking stern and dazed. Time and time again, she would look up to the sky with questioning and angry eyes. There was a glint of vendetta in her grey eyes and her lips had tightened near the corners of her mouth in firm determination.

Rukmini Devi, along with Lakshmi, came early in the morning and placed a wreath of white roses at Shanti's feet. Members from the staff quarters were coming one by one to offer their condolences. A few relatives came from Bhudeshwar also. Dayiju just nodded her head whenever a relative would say something. Shakun sobbed quietly in a corner. She looked at her mother who had a peaceful expression on her face and looked serene and dignified. She would frequently go to the dead body and remove the flowers strewn all over her mother's face and hair.

Suddenly, there was a stunned silence in the air and Shakun could hear the footsteps of the Rai Sahib; he had a distinct gait which she recognised so well. In all her years, she had never seen Rai Sahib come so close to where they lived. He bent low so as to avoid hitting his head on the wall above the door and entered the room where Shanti's body was kept. He carried a velvet bag in his hands which he gave to Dayiju, touched her feet and walked towards Shakun. He held Shakun by the hand and asked her to follow him outside, to the veranda. A number of people, who had come to offer their condolence, sat there. Rai Sahib asked everybody to sit comfortably because he wanted to convey an important message to them. When all the women, men and children had found a place to sit, Rai Sahib stood up to speak. He looked at Shakun, straight in the eyes, and said, 'I am saying this with utmost humility and would like this truth to be respected by one and all. The fact that Shanti would die so early, and so young, is difficult to believe and accept. She had been ailing for quite a few years and her condition suddenly deteriorated. Shakun has lost her mother but I want the world to know that she has a father who loves her dearly.'

Shakun heard someone scoff at the last part. Everyone knew that her father didn't care about anyone, except himself. Rai Sahib took a deep breath and said, 'I am her father and Shakun will always have my support and love. Rukmini Devi and I would look after her as long as we are alive. I am leaving some money with Dayiju and will let Shakun decide what she would like to do with it in the memory of her mother. She can donate the money to an orphanage or have a *shanti path* for the departed soul or donate the money to an ashram. I leave the decision to Shakun.'

Shakun was bewildered at what Rai Sahib had said and couldn't understand this sudden burst of affection she felt for him. She felt extremely touched and moved. Thanking him, she bent forward to touch his feet when Rai Sahib moved away and said that daughters should never touch their father's feet, because they represent Ma Durga. Saying this, he said namaste to the whole gathering and hurriedly moved away. As soon as he left, people encircled Shakun and began praising her and showering their blessings on her. It was not uncommon for *zamindars* to father many illegitimate children and everyone, with no other choice, accepted it silently. She moved to where her mother lay and cried hiding her face in her saree. Shakun's father came and stood beside her and kept looking at her. She heard him say to an elderly man standing next to him, 'We didn't know that we had Laxmi in the house all these years.' Shakun didn't like the grin on his face. It was very sinister and calculating. She understood what was going to happen in the future.

Shakun went to Dayiju and asked her if what Rai Sahib had said was true. Dayiju told her that Rukmini Devi was Rai Sahib's second wife and was much younger than him. His first marriage lasted for 18 years. Shanti was the maid and a close confidante of his first wife, who succumbed to tuberculosis. The first wife had borne no children. It was believed that Shanti contracted tuberculosis from Rai Sahib's first wife and being young and extremely healthy, she overcame the disease at that time. During the time when the first Bai Sahib was ailing, Shanti virtually lived in the *haveli*. Rai Sahib was attracted to her and Shanti eventually bore Rai Sahib's first child, that is, Shakun. Rai Sahib's happiness saw no limits as he had longed for a child for two decades. In a hurry, Shanti was married off to the man who the world regarded as Shakun's father. Rai Sahib, being an honest man, had confided in Rukmini and had told her that Shakun was his child from Shanti. Rukmini being a magnanimous and kind-hearted woman accepted this with grace and always had a soft corner for Shakun.

Shakun didn't know how to react. She consciously pushed all her feelings deep into the dark recesses of her mind and concentrated all her energy into saying a final goodbye to her mother. Throughout the funeral, Dayiju didn't even lift her head to get a glimpse of her dead daughter. Shanti's body was draped in a red saree and someone put a red bindi on her forehead. Surprisingly, she looked stately in death as if she had attained the freedom, which she craved for all her life. Finally, she looked like the mistress of this *haveli*, being the love of Rai Sahib and the mother of the first heir to his stature and wealth.

The sight of her only daughter's dead body was too much for Dayiju to bear. With Shanti's death, she had lost all her children. What a life! She was surrounded by so much material wealth, but in abject poverty emotionally. She often wished that God would never give anyone the kind of life He had given her. Seeing one's flesh and blood pass away in front of one's eyes, one by one, is the worst thing that can happen to any mother. Dayiju was convinced that the Almighty was angry with her for her past karma and was punishing her in this life for what she had done in her past lives. She must have tortured many good people in the past to witness one tragic event after another. This was the only thing she could say to herself to keep herself together, otherwise she would have been completely shattered.

Rukmini Devi and Rai Sahib took charge of Shakun in many silent and subtle ways so as to help her in addition to upholding the *maan* and *maryada* of their family. Shakun was asked to look after the central hall upkeep where Rai Sahib and Rukmini met their important guests. The central hall was adjacent to the office of Rai Sahib. He reached his office regularly at 10 am and spent a good three to four hours attending to the *haveli* administration, his land matters, responding to queries from villages and responding to other political and social matters.

Rai Sahib could also see Shakun from his office when she was cleaning the central hall. He saw a lot of resemblance between Shakun and his own mother. His mother was a plain looking woman, a little on the darker side but carried herself with a quiet, assertive dignity. Shakun had the same forehead and hair parting as his mother, and her arms were well shaped and graceful. His heart became heavy when he thought of Shakun's future. After all, his blood ran through her veins and he could not bear the thought of her being married into a lower caste family with no money, and especially to a man like her foster father who would do nothing and survive on the earnings of the womenfolk of the family.

He decided to speak about this to Ghanshyam*ji*, who looked after his financial and personal matters and whose counsel he always took when there was a complicated family matter or a sensitive, emotional issue. It was Ghanshyam*ji* who had advised him to offer some money to Shakun on Shanti's prayer meeting and also to keep some money and land aside for Shakun, which he could pass on to her at a later date. He also asked him be discreet and not tell anyone.

'It would be wise not to mention this to anyone yet, including Rukmini. Money and property have a tendency to create many unforeseen complications if not managed at the right time and by the right people,' he had said.

Ghanshyam*ji* had been with Rai Sahib for over three decades and was a man tested and tried for his impeccable honesty. 'Ghanshyam, do you think we should approach a decent middle class Rajput family for Shakun's marriage? I shudder at the thought of her being married to someone like her foster father.'

Ghanshyam*ji* had a shocked expression on his face after hearing these words from Rai Sahib and, in a matter of fact tone, said, 'Never make such a mistake, *huzoor*. Rajputs aspire for equality if not improvement in their social status and their power equations. They will never bring a half-*shudra kanya* into their family. They would be happy to bring a Brahmin girl because this enhances their status and value as a family. Even if they take in Shakun for money, which you will naturally give in plenty, they will stop valuing her the moment they hear about her illegitimacy or caste. Please do forgive me for being so blunt but I had to say this to you, lest out of goodness of your heart, you missed out in perceiving the dark aspects of this matter, *huzoor*. Indian society is very complex and artificial with so many false and nonsensical projections and facades. I know you and I understand all this at our age and experience but, still do not.'

Rai Sahib kept quiet and didn't respond to Ghanshyam. Some of his words did hurt him deeply. He realised that even if it was the truth, it was difficult to gulp down one's pride especially if it had to do with one's own children. He had a last fleeting glimpse of his child before he returned to his wing for the family lunch and siesta.

The winter was intensifying and Dayiju's aches and pains were increasing. Shakun had never seen her so quiet. After Shanti's death, Dayiju had requested Shakun to wear her mother's sarees which were still intact even though a little faded. It took Shakun a week to sort out Shanti's belongings. It was astonishing to discover her possessions. Shakun could never imagine that her mother had such a collection of gold ornaments. Seeing her excitement, Dayiju whispered, 'Your mother had buried a trunk which contained silver utensils and ornaments which she had received from the *haveli,* on the behest of Rai Sahib. All the expensive sarees that she possessed had come from the *haveli* on different festivals and functions, mostly through Ghanshyam*ji* and a few from Rukmini Devi.'

She began to speak about Shanti and told Shakun how Rai Sahib continued to love Shanti till she passed away, 'All her medicines came from the *haveli* and Rai Sahib would keep a close watch on her treatment and any medication that she required. He had quiet conversations with her whenever he had an opportunity to be with her alone. Shanti had lost interest in life after she was married off to this good-for-nothing man.'

Dayiju was convinced that Rai Sahib still loved Shanti and that he would continue loving Shakun too. But, Shakun couldn't understand what kind of love was this? She had heard rumours that they were planning to marry her off and she was convinced that her in-laws, once they came to know that she was Rai Sahib's illegitimate child, would make her go through a lot of misery. What protection would he give her then? She was convinced that in reality, he just wanted her to go away so that there was no future embarrassment caused to him and his family. He must be anxious about Lakshmi's wedding too. You never know who could bring up this issue and create problems in the family, which might impact important things like Lakshmi's wedding. Such is the way of the world!

Even though, initially she had felt affectionate towards Rai Sahib, now she had developed a hint of negative feelings for him, mostly for not formally acknowledging the presence of her mother in his life, while she was alive. She had realised that women were helpless and vulnerable. Her mother, a young and simple girl, must have fallen into this trap of so-called 'love and false promises' made by the young handsome son of a Rajput family, which was so well-to-do and politically powerful. She resented the fact that he got away so easily, leaving her mother distraught and pining for his love and care, all her life. Shakun was angry and found her respect for Rai Sahib waning.

A couple of days later, Shakun sent word through Dayiju to Rukmini, that she would like to be on leave for about 15 days. She needed some time to get the house in order, after Shanti's passing away. She had also planned to do some *jap* and *tap* for her departed soul on the advice of the *purohitji* who visited the *haveli* every day for morning and evening *pooja*. Moreover, she also wanted some time for herself. Rukmini agreed and conveyed this to Rai Sahib, who was a bit surprised and even worried. He understood that Shakun was making an effort to stay away from him as well as the *haveli* to reassess her life and its various events. Maybe she was trying to seek answers about the troubles that Shanti underwent. Intuitively, he didn't feel too good about his thoughts and became apprehensive that Shakun might take some drastic steps for her future, which could cause trouble and anxiety for other people.

Life takes a lot of twists and turns. One fleeting and transient emotion can lead to major unpredictable changes in life; one small step can cause major upheavals. We keep waiting for major events to happen and yet, even a word has the power to sow the seed for an unforeseen change. Rai Sahib's one word, 'father' had opened the floodgates of change in Shakun's young heart. He had struck so many good and bad strings. Before he had uttered that word, she was a legitimate child of a poor man.

After he had said that word, she became the illegitimate child of a rich man. He had changed her status in life completely. He had destroyed her identity for whatever it was worth. It was very easy for him to proclaim his fatherhood in the presence of so many people. But, what he didn't realise was that his one word would change the image of her mother and will seal her fate forever? What magnanimity was he trying to establish? What responsibility will he take from now onwards? Nothing, she was sure. Except that he would dole out some more money, humiliate the memory of her mother and hurt her even more. Shakun, in her anger and hurt, decided not to continue working at the *haveli*. 'When Dayiju would return, I would hand over the money given by Rai Sahib and ask her to distribute it amongst the poor. I don't want anything to do with him or his money,' she said to no one in particular.

Dayiju came back a little late that evening. Shakun was busy preparing dinner and didn't hear her footsteps.

As soon as Dayiju saw Shakun, she stopped and in a stern voice asked her, 'I didn't say anything in the morning but what is the need for this long absence from work?'

Shakun thought that it was unnecessary to give Dayiju long explanations, and continued cooking the meal for the night.

Dayiju again asked the same question to which Shakun said that she was not feeling too well and therefore thought of staying back home. Dayiju said that there are certain rules of the *haveli* and the basic rule to adhere to, is to inform the employer beforehand if one is taking leave or is absent from duty.

Shakun said, 'I will keep this in mind for the future, if such a situation arises again.'

Dayiju shook her head and walked away. She was aware that Rai Sahib had done a great favour on them by publicly announcing about Shakun's birth. She wanted Shakun to not displease either Rai Sahib or Rukmini Devi with her insolence as it could create unpleasantness for everyone involved.

There were a total of 27 staff quarters but there were some families, like the family of Ghanshyam*ji,* which occupied two quarters because the number of family members was large. He had three sons, out of whom two were married with children. They stayed in a separate quarter. The three unmarried daughters stayed with Ghanshyam*ji* and his wife and maintained the old Rajput tradition of *purdah*. His two quarters were also differently constructed from the rest as Ghanshyam*ji* had a higher status amongst the other staff members. The remaining staff quarters were occupied by the housekeeping and kitchen staff, along with the people who worked in the garden. There was a sense of discipline and decency that the families maintained and Rai Sahib was quite proud of the way the staff conducted themselves. There was no record of any scandal as far as the *haveli* staff was concerned. The families of the staff members mingled with each other during festivals and other functions, and the women enjoyed a lot of camaraderie. It was one large happy group despite differences in caste affiliations, wealth and status in the *haveli*.

Ghanshyam*ji*'s youngest son, Raghuvir Singh or Raghu, was 25 years old and was pursuing his PhD in sociology. He had a brilliant academic record and was highly admired in the university among the students and teaching faculty. Everyone in the *haveli* also held him in very high regard. Apart from his intellectual capabilities, he was very soft spoken, treated the young and the old in the *haveli* with a lot of respect and carried himself with great dignity and humility. His brothers loved him a lot, as did the entire family which had lots of expectations from him, the load of which he carried with a quiet acceptance.

Raghu was attached to Shanti and her death had disturbed him a lot. Whenever Shanti cooked something special like a *kheer* or fish curry, Raghu would be invited and fed. His mother knew that he had eaten at Shanti's home because on that day he would skip practically all the meals at home.

Raghu had been closely noticing Shakun after Shanti's demise. She looked depressed and had withdrawn herself. Most of the time, she sat in the dark and dim room that Shanti occupied during her illness, or was busy cleaning up the house. He was also aware that she was not going to work in the *haveli*, anymore. He had never spent any time with her before. His interactions with her had been limited to a simple hello and sometimes inquiring about Shanti's health. He had never indulged in any lengthy or meaningful conversation with Shakun all these years. In fact, he had kept a discrete distance from all the girls in the staff quarters. He had seen Lakshmi Baby Sahib a couple of times, and in his 25 years, had not been inside the *haveli* even once since children or families of staff members, unless they explicitly worked in the *havelis,* were strictly kept off bounds; strict boundaries were maintained.

One evening, Shakun had cooked *dal* and vegetables for dinner, and would be serving that in an hour. However, the *rotis* still had to be prepared and the fire in the stove needed to be kept lit and strong. She brought more wood, which was stacked up outside the house along the right wall, covered with a polythene sheet lest they got damp by rain or the dew at night. She shoved extra pieces of firewood in the burner and blew some air onto the pieces of wood, through a cylindrical pipe called *phukni*. As Shakun got busy with lighting the fire, she had no inkling that a corner of her saree had caught fire. The saree was woven from a synthetic material called *kela* silk. She had taken out this saree from Shanti's possessions that were kept in the large aluminium trunk.

Shakun decided to keep some extra pieces of firewood back in the stack, and as she came out of the room onto the veranda, her father sitting at one corner of the veranda, noticed her burning saree. He leapt up, screaming at her. Shakun panicked and turned her head backwards. She caught the sight of her burning garment and, in panic, started running. As she ran, the flames became stronger and started spreading to the other parts of the saree. Before she could pull off the saree from her body, her legs had been scorched by the flames and parts of her arms had sustained deep burns.

Shakun slumped to the ground; the skin of her legs peeled off like the skin of a ripe banana. She looked dazed and felt excruciating pain with burning and itching sensations all over her body. In no time, Rai Sahib, Rukmini Devi, Lakshmi and other staff members arrived. Raghu had also rushed to the scene. Her father brought out a sheet from the house and covered her. Rai Sahib instructed the driver to take out his Mercedes to drive her to the Civil Hospital. He was preparing to follow in another car. Raghu and her father jumped into the Mercedes and drove off. Dayiju slowly walked into her quarters, lay on her bed, shivering, and closed her eyes. She appeared to be giving up. Having lost her daughter just a week back, she knew that she could not fight any more, she couldn't handle the death of another beloved. She was prepared to surrender completely to destiny and didn't have the energy to comprehend and question what the future held for her. She went into a deep silence and closed her eyes. Rukmini, who was just outside her room, saw her walking inside and was worried about her condition. She called for the family doctors who arrived promptly on the scene. They took Dayiju's blood pressure and checked her pulse rate, and informed Rukmini that things were under control. 'People from that generation are made of a sturdier stuff,' mused Rukmini. Although Dayiju was unaware of her actual age, she appeared to be about 82–83 years old, but could be older. Rukmini asked God to give Dayiju a long life.

Shakun was in the hospital for about a month. Her legs below the knees received major burns. There were also burns on her hands and on the right arm. There was no danger to her life except that she would not be able to move around at all for a month, and had to be nursed. The home care arrangements were taken care of by Rai Sahib's family and office, and her low fat and low salt diet was organised by the *haveli* kitchen.

On Shakun's return from the hospital, Rai Sahib and his entire family and a number of staff members came to see her. They assured her of a speedy recovery and showered their affection on her. Dayiju teared up a little to their expression of emotion and assurance. However, Shakun perfunctorily thanked them and seemed a bit aloof and reticent. This was noted both by Rai Sahib and Rukmini. Lakshmi not only noticed it but was amazed. She described Shakun's behaviour as downright rude and expressed her disapproval strongly. She told her parents that she would refrain from visiting her again till she received an apology for this horribly rude and unbecoming behaviour. Rai Sahib and Rukmini were a little perplexed at the change in Shakun's behaviour. They attributed it to the shock that she underwent because of Shanti's death and then this incident. But, both of them believed that she needed to be confronted and counselled, and also made to understand that this negative behaviour will not be tolerated at all.

Raghu visited Shakun almost daily to enquire about her health and to check the medicine stock. He would also shop for her medicines and other things like milk and fruits. Shakun's condition was improving gradually, but she was still far from wearing proper clothes like a *salwar kameez* or a saree. She wrapped a light cotton muslin cloth that reached above her knees and wore a loose shirt on top. Dayiju kept reminding her to cover herself with a thin *chadar* whenever they had visitors like Raghu. Dayiju was in a dilemma about Raghu's frequent visits. She felt relieved that he had taken charge of so many things but was not sure how the *haveli* staff was viewing this sudden development of friendship and bonding between Raghu and Shakun. She was sure that Ghanshyam*ji* would not be happy about it at all, so she deliberately started avoiding him lest he brought this up with her and made some lewd and uncalled-for remarks about Shakun and her family. She also knew that Ghanshyam*ji* was fiercely caste-conscious and was arrogant about the fact that he was a high-caste Rajput.

One evening, Shakun was sitting in the veranda, combing her long hair when Raghu came in with some guavas. As Shakun's hands still had some open wounds from the burn, she was struggling with the comb while disentangling her knotted hair. When Raghu saw her struggling with the comb, he asked her to give him the comb, 'Let me comb your hair. You will hurt your hands and they will start bleeding.'

'No no, it's ok. I will manage; it will only take a little while longer than before,' she smiled.

Raghu got up and said, 'Oh, come on. If I could pick you up and take you to the hospital, I can surely touch your hair and help you comb it,' he got up from his chair, took the comb gently away from Shakun's hands and began combing her hair. It took him about 10 minutes to disentangle the knots and comb Shakun's hair properly. Then, he made a fairly decent single plait and tied a black ribbon at its end.

Shakun was embarrassed with all the attention but liked Raghu's concern and care. Raghu noticed that Shakun, even though plain looking, had lovely, thick, black hair, a glowing unblemished skin and a face that radiated with goodness and determination. . Returning home, he couldn't keep his thoughts away from Shakun. He realised that she had a subtle, quiet dignity which grew on him.

Raghu's and Shakun's meetings became longer. Shakun shared a lot about her life with Raghu. 'I would like to study, Raghu. But, where is the money for school, and later for college?'

'Why? You don't need to regularly attend school. You can study at home and then appear as a private candidate for your eighth, tenth and twelfth standard board examinations.'

'But, I'll need tuitions at home. I believe tuitions are very expensive.'

'I will give you all the tuition that you need and you can buy me a good book once in a while.'

Shakun's tuition lessons with Raghu began in real earnest. They even planned out a time table. Raghu insisted that come what may, Shakun had to adhere to the time table and complete all the tasks that he gave her to do, every day. Raghu discovered that Shakun was a quick learner with a good grasp over numbers; her comprehension was also good. She enjoyed her classes and was keen to read beyond the prescribed syllabus. Dayiju didn't approve of the tuition classes and the fact that Raghu was in their house every day. She was convinced that this kind of physical proximity could create other complications.

A month had passed since the tuition classes began. Shakun, health wise, was progressing well. Her burns were healing and Shakun had begun to move around the house. The *haveli* doctor came and carried out regular check-ups; he was highly satisfied with her progress.

Dayiju noticed that Rai Sahib and Rukmini had stopped inquiring about Shakun. Lakshmi too never brought up Shakun's health issue with her. This was very perturbing for Dayiju as she was depending on Rai Sahib and Rukmini for financial support for Shakun's wedding in the future. Dayiju was worried and this had begun to impact her health negatively.

Ghanshyam*ji* was aware that his son Raghu had become a regular visitor to Shakun's house. He felt proud of the assistance that Raghu was extending to Shakun in her learning journey. He admired Shakun for the fact that she took tuition in the open veranda in front of her quarters which encouraged other young girls to also join in. All the other families were quite happy that not only Shakun, but the other girls had also begun to concentrate on their studies. 'Raghu is such a big help!' he continuously heard from one family or another. In fact, some young boys from the staff quarters also requested him to ask Raghu if they could, from time to time, be included in the classes too.

Many elders from the staff quarters offered Raghu fees for teaching their children. Raghu vehemently declined these offers and conveyed to the families that he was very happy to provide his support for the education of children and felt that this was his responsibility and privilege.

Rai Sahib also heard of this laudable service being provided by Raghu to the children of the staff in the *haveli*. Rukmini and Lakshmi praised this effort by Raghu as well. The family also approved of how Raghu and Shakun managed this with utmost dignity. Dayiju even heard Rai Sahib commenting that the children had made him proud and thanked the Rajput blood that ran through Raghu and Shakun's veins.

Raghu's tuition classes continued steadily. Shakun was picking things up fast. But, she required some extra help in English and geography. Raghu gave her tips on how she can study and cover a lot of syllabus on her own. He wanted her to sit for the eighth standard boards in a year, or at least in the next 18 months. Raghu was also concentrating on his own studies and was certain that he would be able to obtain the UGC scholarship that he had applied for, more so because the head of his department had sent a strong recommendation to the UGC committee for his selection. All the faculty members in the department felt that he deserved the scholarship on sheer merit.

Rukmini was certain that after the burning incident, it would be difficult to find a good match for Shakun. 'Dayiju, have you spoken to anyone in your community about Shakun's wedding? Do they know about Shakun's burns and the fire incident?'

'Yes, Bai Sahib, they all know about the fire incident by now. Our community is not very big, we are all related to each other, someone's daughter or granddaughter has married into someone else's family. I spoke to some people about a marriage proposal for Shakun. I have been very disturbed lately, and therefore have not followed up.'

'I wonder how difficult or easy it will be to find a boy in your community now, especially after the fire incident. Shakun is doing the right thing by studying; she should be equipped to be financially self-reliant. No one can say what plans destiny has for us.'

'Bai Sahib, Shakun works very hard on her lessons. I heard her say the other day that she feels quite confident about appearing privately for her eighth standard board examinations.'

'Oh, that will be very good. Raghu is also working very hard with her. He is a brilliant student and a very nice boy, just be careful about his visits.'

Lakshmi was quietly listening to their conversation. She looked up and saw Dayiju a bit surprised to hear the last remark made by Rukmini. When Dayiju walked out, Lakshmi asked, 'Why did you say that, Ma? What is wrong if Raghu goes to Dayiju's place to teach Shakun?'

'There's nothing wrong in his teaching Shakun but their being together everyday might lead to something else, which might become a big problem for Ghanshyam*ji*'s family. As you are aware, they are upper caste Rajputs.'

'Oh Ma, the times have changed. No one really bothers about this anymore.'

'You are very wrong. In India, caste identity is a reality and caste sentiments run very deep. Even the educated have strong caste affiliations. If you don't believe me, ask your father how he feels.'

Lakshmi listened to her mother and wondered about the nature of the complexity of the Indian society. She realised that her parents were very caste-conscious and were quite arrogant about being upper caste Rajputs. She was surprised that even after being highly educated and widely travelled, they harboured these beliefs and biases. It was already the late 1960s and many technological innovations and breakthroughs were happening in the world. Movies had become technicolour and cooking gas was found in a number of kitchens in the country. Even the human race had landed on the moon, and these people still believed that Brahmins were better than the Rajputs and that the Rajputs were the only people who could rule well.

Holi was around the corner and so were Shakun's board examinations. This was the first Holi after Shanti's passing away. Mothers have a presence that fills up the house as well as one's life. They not only occupy physical expanse but also fill up the emotional, mental and spiritual spaces. After they go away, nothing remains the same again. Mothers are best friends and well-wishers; they are confidantes and safety valves. Their perceptiveness is unparallel—they can detect hunger and ambition with the same deftness and accuracy. They can be soft as the finest cotton and as hard as steel. They can be spiritual gurus and their guidance and coaching give their daughters life skills which assist them to face the many ups and downs of life. When a mother passes away, especially for her daughter, in a general sense, a culture and a spiritual legacy is taken away forever. The void which a mother leaves behind, no one else can fill. Shakun felt a vacuum, an emptiness, on that morning of Holi. However, she wanted to celebrate the festival in the same way as her mother would have celebrated.

She decided to prepare a few snacks and some sweet *gujiyas*—a typical Holi delicacy. She began to organise herself for the day-long cooking when Dayiju forbade her to go anywhere near the stove and the firewood burner. In all these months, all their meals were being supplied from the *haveli* kitchen. Dayiju felt really indebted to the support provided by Rai Sahib and Rukmini Devi. She was sure that whatever Shakun wanted to cook would come from the *haveli*. Raghu came in when Dayiju was speaking about their food coming from the *haveli* and agreed with her totally. He told Shakun that her examinations were only a fortnight away and it would be extremely foolish on her part to take a risk with her health. Shakun gave up her plan to cook and decided to spend a little time with Raghu to clear out a few doubts. Dayiju got ready and left for the *haveli*.

Raghu was in love with Shakun. He had realised this about two or three months ago. Her dignity and determination attracted him. She had been through so much at such a young age. There was an earthy quality in her which was difficult to ignore. She represented women from the soil of India—natural and strong. He liked that she was who she was and never pretended to be otherwise. Without a speck of make-up on her face, she glowed with an inner serenity and a courageous acceptance of the challenges that she had faced, with aplomb.

Raghu had given himself away many times when he was with Shakun. She understood his feelings for her and admired him for his decency. He maintained a civilised distance and saw to it that their interactions always took place in the outside veranda which was completely visible from the *haveli* as well as from the other staff quarters.

The date of the board examination drew close. Shakun was nervous but determined to go through them with positivity and hope. Whenever she faced a problem, especially in English and geography, she would send a message to Raghu through children of other staff members who lived near her quarters. He would come over and help her immediately. She didn't visit his house, and had never done so in the last year seven or eight years. The last time she went to his house was to invite the family for a *puja* that Dayiju had organised during the *navratras*. The family had not come but they had sent Raghu to attend the ceremony. He stayed with them for almost three hours and Dayiju had sent *prasad* back with him for the entire family. Dayiju, she was sure, must have felt bad but accepted it with grace. Shakun thought that this was also a sign of maturity and comes with age. It is part of the understanding of the ways of the world.

Shakun's examinations were a mixed ride. Some papers went very well, some not so well, and in some papers, she faced some difficulty. The English paraphrasing exercise was particularly bad. However, after Shanti's passing, no difficulty appeared to be insurmountable. Death of a loved one, especially one's own mother, could create a certain daredevil attitude. It could also be a sign of depression, wherein either nothing seems to be very important or everything feels like the end of the world, in a certain way. She expressed this feeling to Raghu one evening. Listening to how she felt— numb at times—Raghu looked worried. He gently suggested, 'Sometimes crying out your feelings or even sharing them with someone you trust could be helpful.'

'I don't want to bother you and become a nuisance for you. As it is, you have so much on your plate, ' she said and changed the topic.

Raghu was awarded the UGC scholarship and this made his father and the entire family very proud. Rai Sahib and his family were also very happy. On the day the scholarship was announced, Rai Sahib, while sitting in the garden and sipping tea, said to Rukmini, 'I have been, for quite a few days, thinking about something and didn't know how you would react after hearing what I have in mind. Nonetheless, I may as well know how you feel. Why don't we speak with Ghanshyam*ji* about Raghu and Lakshmi? They would make an extremely handsome couple. Raghu is eligible in all respects and Lakshmi, I feel, would be very happy with him. I think Lakshmi also likes him. We could buy a bungalow or build one in the land which is vacant on the north-west end of the *haveli*. Lakshmi and Raghu can stay there. Or we could construct a large bungalow which could accommodate Ghanshyam*ji*'s entire family, and a separate set of rooms could be constructed for Raghu and Lakshmi.'

Rukmini had a broad smile on her face and she, in unsuppressed excitement, said, 'Oh, I am so happy to know that you have been thinking on similar lines as me. In fact, I have been thinking about this for a long time. I have also mentioned this to Lakshmi and she is not averse to the idea, except she would like to graduate before getting married, which will be next May or June. You can mention this to Ghanshyam*ji* and take his consent. I think that the family also has to agree. I don't think there will be an issue from Raghu's side. He is an obedient and a family-oriented boy. We can even do some small ceremony to finalise the alliance.'

The journey of life does not take a straight and simple road. It takes a road which has many twists and turns and one cannot always predict what lies on the other side of these twists and turns. Ghanshyam*ji* was not prepared to hear what Rai Sahib had to say about his desire for Raghu and Lakshmi tying the knot. He was bewildered but at the same time, he felt great pride for his son and was very happy to know that Rai Sahib and Rukmini Devi could even think about such a liaison. He immediately gave his consent and assured Rai Sahib that his family, including Raghu, would be extremely happy with this decision.

Ghanshyam*ji* met his wife at the gate of his house. He was beaming with joy and his hurried steps conveyed that he had something extraordinarily important to disclose. He asked for Raghu and was told that he was with Shakun. Raghu was summoned back immediately. Ghanshyam*ji* wanted to give this news to the entire family together and therefore waited for Raghu to return and join the family in the hall.

Raghu left his tuition class early and joined his family in their living room. As soon as he entered the room, Ghanshyam*ji* got up and greeted him with a hug and a light peck on his cheek. Everyone in the family was surprised as Ghanshyam*ji* was an undemonstrative man and was not in the habit of easily expressing his emotions. He hardly hugged or kissed his children and Raghu couldn't remember the last time he received a hug from his father. Nonetheless, there was an expectant atmosphere in the room and the entire gathering felt that there was a piece of great news that Ghanshyam*ji* was about to share with the family.

Raghu tossed and turned in his bed during that night and couldn't sleep till the wee hours of the morning. Rai Sahib's offer was beyond his understanding. How could his father accept it and take such an important decision for his life and future without even consulting with him? Maybe he couldn't say no to Rai Sahib or the lure of money and property may have made him accept the offer. Did he realise what he was committing to? Lakshmi had been brought up in the lap of luxury. Ghanshyam*ji*, after all, was an employee of the *haveli*. His status and lifestyle were nowhere near what Lakshmi was used to. How would Lakshmi adjust to the ways of his family? And, what about Shakun?

Raghu decided to confront his father and his family, and convey to them that he was not mentally prepared for marriage, that he was not thinking of marrying anyone for another three to four years. Moreover, he didn't think it was wise to accept this offer as there were so many differences in background, status and lifestyle between the two families.

At the breakfast table, where the entire family gathered, there was so much cheer and happiness as if they had discovered a huge treasure. Everyone was in a celebratory mood. Ghanshyam*ji*, as usual, after his bath and morning *pooja*, had gone for a walk in the beautiful park outside the *haveli*. While he was on his way back, he was called in by Rai Sahib, which was the reason for him coming late to breakfast. He apologised to the family and begun to narrate the conversation that he had with Rai Sahib and Rukmini Devi, 'Rai Sahib is getting construction work started on the plot which is lying vacant on the north-west end of the *haveli*. He is planning to make a huge bungalow for us and for the newly-wed couple. It will be ready to move in a little before the wedding. He will be gifting the bungalow to Raghu. Many other things related to the marriage were discussed. He also wants an engagement ceremony on an auspicious day in the next 10 days or so, and would like Raghu's consent so the preparations can start as soon as possible.'

Raghu sat with his head down and didn't look up even once while his father spoke. He said, 'I don't understand this hurry and don't like the idea of accepting such ridiculously expensive gifts. Kindly discuss things with me before giving your consent and taking this matter to another level.'

'Are you saying that you are not happy with this proposal?' Ghanshyam*ji* asked in anger and disbelief. His tone reflected mixed emotions and he was certainly not happy to see his son on the verge of refusing such a life-changing gift. His voice was seething with frustration.

'I am requesting you to think through all aspects of such a decision in a dispassionate view.'

'I have considered all aspects and I feel that this is the best thing that can happen to you and our family,' said Ghanshyam*ji*.

'OK, then,' Raghu moved away quietly to his room. Hearing this 'OK, then' from Raghu, the family indulged in a second round of rejoicing at the breakfast table.

Raghu sat alone on his bed, thinking about his decision. He knew it was the right decision; in fact, it was the only decision. He understood the enormity of animosity he, and the rest of his family, would have faced if he had refused a proposal of marriage from the royal family. He also knew that he couldn't say no to this alliance because of Shakun who had, till date, not shown an ounce of interest in him apart from respecting him as her teacher. He sighed and lay down on his bed.

Shakun had wrapped up the preparation for lunch. She requested her father to go to the market and get some raw mangoes, so she could prepare a fresh mint and raw mango chutney that Dayiju loved with her lunch, during the summer.

She pulled out a nice, loose salwar kameez after months and decided to wear it after her morning bath. She had forgotten the feeling of wearing proper clothes in all these months because of the burn wounds on her legs and arms. She was even able to comb her long thick hair and make a plait. She remembered the day when Raghu combed her hair. He had done it so tenderly and with so much affection and care! She wondered whether he liked her enough to be in a relationship with her. However, the next moment she controlled her thoughts and told herself that it was pointless to even think on these lines. He was out of her reach in many ways—caste, money and status being just a few of them. However, the thought itself gave her a happiness which she had never experienced before. His respect for her filled her heart with gratitude and positivity.

Dayiju came in for lunch. She asked Shakun for her clothes and moved slowly to the washroom, which was a little away from the house. It was shared with four other families who belonged to their caste and work category. All these families freed the washroom for Dayiju before lunch, out of respect and regard for her. Dayiju burst into tears on entering the washroom. She had heard about Raghu and Lakshmi's impending marriage in the *haveli* and knew that Shakun will be heartbroken. She didn't know how to break the news of the engagement to Shakun. She thought that the child had gone through a lot in the last six months—her mother's death and then the horror of going through the fire and the burns.

Dayiju silently sat down for lunch besides Shakun's father. Shakun was wearing a salwar kameez and seeing Shakun in proper clothes after so long, Dayiju said, 'Couldn't recognise you Shakun. Seeing you in these clothes after so long!'

Her father jumped into the conversation, 'Now, Shakun will be wearing beautiful clothes. I am sure Rukmini Devi will gift her many clothes for the wedding.'

Shakun stopped serving the *dal* to Dayiju, looked up at her father and asked, 'Whose wedding and what gifts from Rukmini Bai Sahib ?'

'Oh you don't know! I wonder why such news hasn't reached you, Shakun! You are so busy with your studies that you don't have time for such gossip. We came to know about the wedding quite some time ago.'

Dayiju looked at her son-in-law with disgust and said, 'How did you know this some time ago? I came to know only this morning when Rai Sahib and Bai Sahib told me about the engagement. If you've finished your meal, then I urge you to go and do your work.'

Instinctively, she knew that the wedding was between Lakshmi and Raghu. Shakun felt that she would sink into the ground. Dayiju, in an almost inaudible voice, mentioned that Raghu was engaged to Lakshmi. The engagement ceremony was being planned to be held on 15 June and the wedding will be in the month of May or June the following year. Bai Sahib wanted the engagement ceremony to take place before the monsoons set in, as the celebrations would all be held on the side lawns of the *haveli*.

'I am 19 now. If I cleared my eighth standard board examinations, I would try my best to clear the tenth and the twelfth board exams by the time I turn 22. Age wise, I would be the oldest student in college in the first year of my bachelor's degree, that is, if I ever went to college,' Shakun started blabbering. It seemed to Dayiju that her mind was refusing to register the fact that Raghu was getting married to someone else. Shakun continued to eat her lunch in a daze. Dayiju was very pensive and anxious, and was also quiet throughout the meal.

When Dayiju was sipping her black tea with jaggery, Shakun asked her for some money to buy a typewriter. She said that she has been receiving requests for typing notes and other materials in Hindi and English from college students.

'I could do this in my free time. This would serve two purposes—I could earn a little money which will help me pay my fees and I could also procure books that I would require to prepare for my exams. Also, I would perforce have to read what I have typed, which would enhance my knowledge and vocabulary.'

Dayiju had a faint smile on her face. She wondered how human beings find ways and means for coping with their sense of loss. Shakun had lost Raghu and this was not a small loss. She must have woven so many dreams for herself and Raghu.

'Of course, tell me how much it will cost and I will give you the money. Just be happy, my dear daughter,' Dayiju said as she picked up her plate and started walking towards the tap which was installed under the tree. The steel on the sides of the tap had rusted with time. She remembered the tap to be in the same place when she had gotten married and had come to the *haveli* for the first time.

Raghu had disappeared from the scene completely. He stopped visiting Shakun; it was almost a month since she had seen him. Shakun had not shed a tear or even spoken about Raghu or the shock of the news of his engagement with anyone. Raghu, she thought, must have a clean conscience as he had never openly conveyed his feelings to her. How easily men move away from a relationship! She knew how he felt during those days and he knew that the feelings in her were quite intense too. The feelings by themselves impose a tacit responsibility. However, without any evidence through overt behaviour or in explicit written communication, how does one confront, blame or even talk about a relationship? She felt let down and alone. Her self-respect took a knocking. She was neither good looking nor educated. She didn't have the wealth and status to compare herself to Lakshmi. The comparison itself was ridiculous. She belonged to a backward caste and her grandmother was a servant in the *haveli*. The fire had disfigured her legs and arms, and she was sure that the scars would remain for the rest of her life. With this body, marriage with any man would become a problem, and it became gradually clear to her that she would spend her life alone and should prepare herself to be self-reliant.

One of the worst things to happen to any woman is to be let down by a man. It destroys her self-confidence and it could be the source of depression and stress. Being bereft of love and security is not a good feeling at all. When the woman doesn't know why exactly the man has moved away from her, she is confused and humiliated. Pain is the source of this sort of humiliation. Mostly, such women withdraw into their own shell. Pain is borne in silence because deep and real pain eludes verbal expression. It is just felt and exists within the body, mind and spirit. A woman finds it very difficult to forgive a man when this happens to her for no fault of hers. Anger festers with this unforgiving pain, sometimes for a lifetime and steals away from life, lightness and joy. Another name for this feeling is tragedy. A tragic life is where events beyond a person's control play havoc with happiness. A tragic life has to be lived or actually spent, not for oneself but for others, for one's family and the future.

Shakun understood the script of her life and how it would gradually unfold. She seemed to have matured in a couple of hours, her life had changed its course. She fell asleep in the hot summer afternoon, next to her grandmother who had only seen tragedy and loss. Her reticence and restraint explained it all.

Shakun's examinations results were announced the next day in the Hindi newspaper. She had secured above 85 per cent, and in subjects like mathematics and Sanskrit, she had obtained 97 per cent. English was a big let-down as she had managed only a 60 percent, which was not really that bad considering the fact that she had not heard English being spoken or read at home. The paraphrasing exercise was quite difficult and Shakun knew that if she wanted to build a career she would have to work very hard in English language and literature. She resolved to do much better in English and had already purchased a dictionary. She had also decided to read the *Illustrated Weekly* even if she understood only 20 per cent of what it contained. She also decided to start listening to the English news on All India Radio every day. Shakun was given a typewriter by Dayiju two days after her results were announced and it became her most prized possession. Word spread in the staff quarters about this, and many complimented Shakun on clearing her eighth standard board examination. She felt good about her decision to earn through typing English and Hindi content as it would give her the opportunity to strengthen her grammar and vocabulary in both the languages. When Rai Sahib came to know about Shakun's new endeavour, he instructed his office to get all documents typed by her. He and Rukmini Devi had accepted the fact that it would be difficult for Shakun to keep working in the *haveli* because of her physical condition. Rukmini was also relieved that Shakun's confinement to the house would keep a number of possible problems in check. Shakun also spread word in the staff quarters, in the *haveli* and the neighbourhood areas saying that she had time to coach children studying in first to fifth standard in Hindi medium schools. In no time, she had nine kids in her tuition classes and she decided to charge nominal fees from them which their parents readily agreed to pay.

Raghu had become an integral part of Rai Sahib's family. However, he felt that at times Rai Sahib and Rukmini Devi's tone was patronising and instructional. Raghu found this disturbing but managed it well with the specific objective of avoiding unpleasantness and keeping them happy. He liked to spend time with Lakshmi—he found her simple and straightforward; a woman who would like to do something with her life. In no time, she became his friend. However, he also realised that she was spoilt and would not be able to handle things like running a home and supervising the numerous chores of a house. He was worried as to how Lakshmi would adjust with his family. In any case, Lakshmi's parents were planning to build a separate section in the new bungalow for him and Lakshmi, which would make life easier. He was also pleased to know that he would also acquire a large portion of cash and property from Rai Sahib, which would solve a lot of his and his family's problems.

Raghu got busy with his PhD dissertation and his classes. In his mind, there was no conflict or remorse about what had happened with Shakun. He didn't even give it any thought. However, he was glad that he had extended support to her when she needed it. He had heard that she was giving tuitions to school-going kids and earning through typing. He was very courteous with Dayiju whenever he met her in the *haveli* but she seemed a bit distant and aloof. At times, he even caught her looking at him with anger. It was surprising that given his intelligence, he had not understood Dayiju's hurt and disappointment. He had failed to realise that like every human being who has the freedom to dream and think, Shakun had also begun to dream of a future with him.

Goodness is interpreted by most people as a weakness. They believe that worldly success depends largely on guile and competence and goodness doesn't stand a chance. However, in the long run, the combination of goodness and competence is the only option. Shakun had this combination of goodness and competence. She started looking at long-term goals and prepared herself for that run. Shakun had also realised that Rukmini Devi had the guile to succeed only in the short run. She had played her cards well by orchestrating the wedding of Raghu and Lakshmi, and doing away with Shakun. This ploy had become clear to Shakun. She understood that Rukmini had also been humiliated by Rai Sahib when he acknowledged his relationship with Shanti in public and took the first clumsy step in establishing Shakun's legitimacy. What he didn't realise then was that he had unknowingly disturbed the hornet's nest.

Shakun needed tuitions in some subjects and had decided to privately sit for the tenth standard boards in the following year. The syllabus was vast and without guidance, it wouldn't be possible for her to clear a few papers. She began asking families who were sending their children for tuition to her, whether they could recommend someone who would be willing to coach her.

Dayiju was not keeping well. Her complete loss of vision in the right eye was a cause for concern for Shakun. She wondered if it would be sensible to get the left eye tested and get it operated in advance. They needed money for an operation and she wondered maybe Dayiju had saved some money from the amount Rai Sahib had given her during the time of her mother's death. That evening, when Dayiju returned home, Shakun asked, 'Dayiju, do you still have money left from the lot that Rai Sahib gave you when we lost Ma?'

'Yes, most of it. Why ? Do you need it?'

'No, I don't need it personally but I need it for something,' said Shakun.

'What does that mean? You need it and yet you don't need it. I will never understand children of your generation. Just tell me straight,' Dayiju said this with a twinge of irritation. She walked inside to get a shawl as it was raining and it had suddenly gotten colder.

Shakun said, 'I need the money for your eye operation. Your left eye can still be saved.'

'No operation for me Shakun. I won't live for too long and you have decided not to marry. I really have no reason to live any more. I am happy carrying on like this, who knows what will happen tomorrow. I can understand your anguish and pain, Shakun. I would like to see you happy. Your mother was also a very unhappy woman and look at her, she passed away so early.'

Dayiju, covering her head with the shawl, sat on the floor of the veranda. She began peeling green peas and cleaning the spinach for dinner. She liked doing these small jobs at home as it gave her the feeling that she too was contributing to the running of the household. Shakun's father sitting in one corner of the veranda, heard the conversation and unable to control himself, asked Dayiju, 'How much money do you have any way? Why don't you give it to Shakun? She can keep it safely.'

Dayiju picked up the knife she was using to cut the spinach and flung it in his direction. It nicked his forehead and in a second, massive amount of blood began to gush out from a small gash it created. Shakun sprung to her feet and ran to him with a cloth. He began to scream in pain and seeing blood, collapsed and fainted. Dayiju didn't realise what had happened and began to panic. Shakun reassured her that everything was alright and under control. Her father would be all right. Shakun sprinkled a little water on his face and kept dabbing the cloth on his forehead so that the bleeding would stop. It took about 10 minutes for the blood to start clotting. Soon, her father opened his eyes and started groaning in pain. He said that he wanted to lie down. He cursed and abused Dayiju and swore that he would destroy her, and see to it that she has a very painful end.

Shakun, in the darkness of the night, couldn't control her racing thoughts. This man was not her real father. However, he was the husband of her late mother but this didn't give him the authority to touch her money. He didn't have any right over her personal wealth which was given by Rai Sahib. Yet, he had an eye over her money all the time and was continuously eavesdropping. What will he do to Dayiju and after Dayiju, how would he behave with her? These thoughts started worrying her and kept her awake throughout the night. In fact, it was in those few hours that she realised how deeply she loved Dayiju and respected her for her courage and dignity. The poor lady had not seen a single day of happiness in her life and yet, she said that she was living only to see her happy.

Winter was gradually setting in and Shakun was happy that she could sit in the winter sun and do her typing. Her burnt skin was turning back to normal and she was feeling more and more confident each day. She was happy she was getting her old body back.

One day, a man of about 30 met her at her house and said that he would be able to guide and coach her for her tenth standard boards. He said that his name was Arjun Singh Rathore, he had completed his Master's in Economics, and was now planning to sit for the Indian Administrative Services Examinations.

'How did you come to know about me?' Shakun asked with a raised eyebrow.

'One of your students is my aunt's daughter. I came to know about you from this aunt. I admire girls like you who have the courage to battle their way through life,' he said with a smile.

Shakun was amazed at the sudden appearance of this man, who looked princely but was so polite. She wondered why he was offering to teach her, after all. Dayiju told her to be careful and not to agree without finding out more details about the boy and the family. Shakun verified his credentials from his aunt and was told that his family was one of the wealthiest and most well-known Rajput families in that area. Arjun Singh Rathore was the great-grandson of the *zamindar* of Rairupangarh, which was one of the largest princely estates in northern India. She also came to know that Arjun's forefathers had given away their land to Rai Sahib's family for services rendered over a hundred years ago. Before receiving this largess from the Rathores, Rai Sahib's family was not well-off at all and they fell under the category of landless and poor Rajputs who had fled Rajasthan centuries ago, and had settled in the central provinces.

He came again to meet her and to convey that he could begin classes from the following Monday. Shakun couldn't come up with an excuse to stay away from this offer immediately and said, 'Thank you ever so much. But, could you just give me a couple of days to complete an urgent typing assignment? I'll send word to you, as to when you can come and commence the tuitions. I also have to procure quite a few books.'

'Oh, don't bother about the books at all. I have procured all the books prescribed in the syllabus. By the way, I know it is rude to ask a lady about her age, but how old are you?'

Shakun looked quizzically at him and said, 'I am going to be 19 in a couple of months.'

'Oh, so young! Good good. Do let me know when I can come and start your classes. I am not a bad teacher.'

Dayiju was quite worried about the arrival of this Prince Charming on the family scene. After what had happened with Raghu, she was wary of boys of that age and thought that they always have a tendency to take advantage of young and vulnerable girls. She had made up her mind to discover his antecedents and those of his family, and then dissuade Shakun from taking classes from him.

'I will tell her to find a lady teacher rather than these young boys, who always came with hidden motives and agendas,' she mumbled walking inside.

Dayiju was in the *haveli* in the evening and was cleaning Rukmini Devi's room when Rukmini herself walked in and inquired from Dayiju how Shakun's father was. Dayiju could perceive a faint, cynical smile on Rukmini's face while mentioning the words 'Shakun's father'. She knew who Shakun's father really was, what was then the objective of this taunt? Dayiju gulped her anger and hurt, and responded that he was doing quite well.

After a while, Dayiju, seeing an opportune moment, asked Rukmini, 'Bai Sahib you must be knowing the Rathore family who are zamindars and are a well-known Rajput family?'

'Oh Dayiju, who doesn't know them! They are the biggest zamindars of northern and central India. It is an excellent family, highly cultured and they have an enviable reputation.

They have two children, a son and a daughter. Their son, Arjun is brilliant and extremely handsome and their daughter, Meenakshi is beautiful and a very well-brought-up girl. They're a pious and a highly-educated family. We'll always be indebted to them for their support and affection. But, why do you ask about the Rathore family, Dayiju?'

'Oh some people were talking about great families in the region, like your family, and told me that I am very lucky to have spent my entire life with you and Rai Sahib. In the same way, they took the name of the Rathore family.'

'Oh, I see. Yes yes, the Rathore family is a big name in our community. They are also admired for maintaining the highest Rajput traditions and the way they brought up their children. Arjun is a little different. He does a lot of social work and does not believe in caste and religious affiliations. In fact, some people say that he is an atheist, sort of a rebel. People in his family have accepted his thinking and I believe that his father supports him a lot, but his mother keeps worrying about him as he has said, numerous times, that he doesn't want to get married at all.'

Dayiju was quite happy to know these facts about Arjun and his family. After all, even if he meets Shakun and helps her in her studies from time to time, she was now sure that she would be safe with him. However, Dayiju, having seen too much of this world, had the wisdom which prompted her to convey to Shakun that it will be advisable if she maintained her distance from Arjun as there was no commonality and convergence in their worlds and lives.

Winter had intensified and it was already November. Shakun loved winters because so many flowers suddenly blossomed, especially a variety of roses and dahlias. She decided to plant a few winter flowers in the patch of vacant land in front of her house, and thought that it would be nice if they could also plant a small kitchen garden with spinach, cauliflower, cabbage and other winter vegetables. Shakun mentioned this to her father who was smoking a *beedi* and to her utter surprise, he agreed to work on the garden project. The very next minute, he asked her for money to procure seeds, pots and manure for the garden. Shakun was sure that he would give her an inflated estimate and would keep some money for himself. But, she still gave him the money because then he would at least get busy looking after the garden.

The seeds, pots and manure arrived and Dayiju also got excited about the garden. This also made her speak with her son-in-law and the rift between them started to gradually sort out. Shakun's father worked hard in the garden. Many people from the staff quarters complimented him on what he was doing. Shakun perceived a subtle change in his attitude and behaviour. He even began to help in the other chores of the house. He would run small errands, ask Dayiju whether her medicines required replenishment and at times, even walked her to the *haveli* telling Shakun that he was worried about her worsening eye sight. Shakun learnt her first important lesson in motivation—recognition and appreciation are food for the soul. A sense of self-pride does work wonders in changing a person.

Dayiju did not share with Shakun all the good things that she had heard about Arjun, as this could create a soft corner for Arjun in Shakun's heart. Arjun had not visited them for a number of days and Shakun wondered why; she was waiting desperately for the books so that she could begin to prepare for the tenth standard boards in earnest. Shakun decided to wait for a day or two, after which she would ask Dayiju for money to buy a few essential books.

Dayiju was about to leave for the *haveli* that morning when Shakun's father held her hand and began to walk with her. They would chat while they walked, and Shakun wondered about the beauty of this evolving relationship as a result of the garden project. She was already in the garden collecting a few vegetables for lunch. Dayiju and Shakun's father were still at an audible distance when Shakun, louder than normal, asked them whether they would like to eat cabbage, *dal* and a potato and spinach preparation for lunch.

'Yes, that sounds perfect,' she heard someone say. She looked up to see Arjun standing close to her with both his arms full of books.

'I was down with a very bad bout of typhoid and as you know, it leaves a person very weak. I am much better now. However, I am still not back on my normal diet and have been advised by the doctor not to exercise for another fortnight. I have been thinking about you and feeling very guilty for not giving you the books on time, as I had promised.'

Shakun realised that Arjun had lost a lot of weight as a result of typhoid.

'Don't worry, I am a fast learner. I will catch up so you should not feel guilty at all. One's illness is really not in one's control, is it?' she said.

Handing over the books to her, Arjun said that he had managed to procure all the books prescribed by the state educational board, and that he had also bought some good reference books which Shakun might find very helpful for her preparation. Shakun placed the books on the *charpoy* kept outside and asked him for the amount that she had to pay for the books.

'I'll let you know when we are through with your examinations, and the results are announced. Then, we will be in the mood to celebrate. We can start with your tuitions tomorrow. I will also make a schedule for the month. We won't go beyond a month because I don't know when Mr Typhoid or some similar thing decides to revisit,' he chuckled sweetly and left.

Dayiju felt proud of her granddaughter. She knew that she was pursuing an extraordinary goal, given their financial and social situation. Arjun was very respectful and dignified in his behaviour. Even Shakun's father praised him whenever he got an opportunity. Arjun had endeared himself to the whole family. He would come to their house on a cycle, wearing a kurta with a pair of jeans or a pyjama to look as inconspicuous as possible. He had requested Shakun's father to allow him to sit in the room which was open from two sides. This way Shakun and he would not be visible to the others living in the staff quarters, which would prevent gossip.

Shakun's tuition classes were going on well. She was a quick learner and had a good memory. Arjun found a natural curiosity in her as well as an eagerness to put in her best effort. He was a hard taskmaster and didn't waste his time in chitchat. Dayiju was surprised that no one had noticed Arjun's coming to the house. He would normally maintain strict timings—come in at 5 pm and leave by 6.30. Shakun couldn't believe that November was over and Arjun had become so comfortable in his relationship with Dayiju and her father.

Lakshmi's wedding was around the corner. Dayiju was working overtime and Shakun was really concerned about her health. She felt that at this age, overexertion for Dayiju could be extremely harmful. She gently warned Dayiju and told her that her health was of primary importance and everything else came after it.

She replied, 'Shakun, my child, what you say is correct but I have a responsibility to discharge. I have brought up Lakshmi with my own hands.'

Rukmini Devi was excited about her daughter's wedding. Rai Sahib was determined to make the best arrangements possible. He had arranged flowers to be flown in from Pune, *shehnai* players from Varanasi and the best *Kanjivaram* sarees from Madras, that were to be given to the relatives of the bridegroom as well as the bride. Rukmini Devi kept announcing to the *haveli* staff that this would be perhaps the most lavish and expensive wedding of the century in Bhudeshwar. Lakshmi was happy at the way her parents were organising everything with so much interest and affection.

Lakshmi made a ravishing bride and Raghu looked handsome in his sherwani and *safa*. Dayiju couldn't believe that Lakshmi, who was born in front of her eyes, had grown up to be a beautiful woman who was about to become a wife, and then would become a mother soon. She remembered, during her own wedding, a number of her relatives had told her parents that she too looked quite stunning. Dayiju wiped her tears and cried after many years remembering her husband and her dead sons. Arjun's parents also attended the wedding with his sister while he was with Shakun completing a section in arithmetic. He found the ostentatious display of wealth in weddings obscene. Shakun had always dreamt of attending Lakshmi's wedding. Even though, since the last couple of months, they had become distant, still she was sad that she was missing the wedding of her best friend but she knew she couldn't go. She couldn't bear the idea of seeing Raghu as a groom for she had lost all respect for him.

Rai Sahib had made special arrangements for the Rathore family. He and Rukmini Devi were constantly with them and personally served them dinner. The Rathores were given very expensive silver, gold and diamond artefacts and jewellery along with very expensive sarees and suits. Arjun's mother and sister were presented with the most expensive French perfumes. Arjun's mother was quick to understand that this was probably prompted by the desire of asking for Arjun's hand for some cousin or someone. Everything in the world operated on the principle of give and take. Minutes before they left, Rukmini told Arjun's mother, 'Didi, we missed Arjun. We haven't seen him in years. Hope he's well; do give him our love and regards. We have packed his gifts separately.'

Working and preparing lessons with Arjun was fun. However, Shakun also knew that Arjun did not tolerate complacency and laziness, and therefore she was always on her toes and well-prepared. As she got closer to the date of her final examinations, Shakun's stress levels were rising. She couldn't sleep and developed dark circles under her eyes.

One evening, Arjun casually mentioned to her, 'You know Shakun, worrying is useless thinking. In that time, you could be studying, because your worrying is useless.'

They both had a hearty laugh at that.

Holi came and went and for Shakun, time was racing ahead. Her days were packed with mathematics practise, English language paraphrasing, writing out answers for possible and important questions in geography, economics and social studies and memorising formulae for chemistry.

Shakun thought that she had written her tenth board examinations well. However, she was sure that she would fare badly in mathematics and English. Arjun was sure that Shakun would pass with possibly a first division, which she did. He came to meet Dayiju, Shakun's father and Shakun a week after the results were announced and told them that he would be leaving Bhudeshwar for a short vacation. However, his parents would be coming to meet them soon. He declined Dayiju's offer of a cup of tea and said that he was in a hurry as he had to buy a few articles before he left for his holiday. Shakun wondered why his parents were planning to visit them. Dayiju was surprised and anxious, and wondered whether she had done something during the wedding which annoyed them. Shakun's father found Arjun's communication odd and couldn't attribute a logical reason to his parents' plan to visit them. However, none of them discussed their doubts.

Dayiju was ready to leave for the *haveli*. She had finished her breakfast of a *roti* and black tea with jaggery. Shakun's father held her hand and they both walked slowly towards the *haveli*. They had just crossed the vegetable garden when they saw a huge black shining car drive towards their quarter. It stood right in front of their door. Rai Sahib Rathore and his wife got off the car and most respectfully greeted Dayiju and Shakun's father. Rai Sahib turned to Dayiju and said, 'Didi Sahiba, we will take just 15 minutes from you. May we sit in a private space somewhere?'

Shakun's father hurriedly, and with unsure steps, took them to their half-enclosed and half-open veranda. There were two chairs and a *charpoy*. The couple sat on the chairs and Shakun's father and Dayiju sat on the *charpoy*. Rai Sahib Rathore said, 'Didi Sahiba, we know that Arjun gives tuition to your granddaughter, Shakun. He admires Shakun and would be very happy for your consent to marry her. Of course, she should also give her consent. We have had long discussions with him on this. We are equally happy with his choice. He is a spiritual man, not spoilt by wealth and power. He would like to dedicate himself to social service and has found in Shakun someone who would understand him. We would like to endorse his decision to marry Shakun, and bless them.' Bai Sahib Rathore got up and touched Dayiju's feet.

Dayiju was overjoyed that her granddaughter was entering a family of *zamindars* who were even more reputed and powerful than Rai Sahib's family. Her eyes filled with tears at the thought of Arjun, calm and dignified Arjun who had the courage and conviction to see the brilliance of Shakun and proclaim his love for her. Dayiju also knew that Rai Sahibs, especially Rukmini Devi, would not be able to accept their happiness at all. But such is the way of destiny, it takes with one hand and compensates with the other.

When Shakun found out about the proposal, she refused to believe that the Prince Charming she used to dream about had finally come for her. But, then Arjun made her realise that sometimes dreams do come true.

Shakun married Arjun in a civil wedding at Dayiju's quarter on 15 May 1970. A week before that, Dayiju broke the good news to Rukmini Devi in the morning when she reached the *haveli* for the day's work. For a couple of minutes, Rukmini couldn't register what Dayiju was saying. Rai Sahib was at the breakfast table. Rukmini hurriedly went to the dining room asking Dayiju to follow her, and asked her to repeat her words to Rai Sahib. On hearing Dayiju's words, Rai Sahib looked completely astounded. Then, he got up from his chair, walked to Dayiju and said, 'Dayiju, you deserve this happiness.'

A message came from Rai Sahib's office saying that Rai Sahib Rathore was in the *haveli* and wanted to meet him and Rukmini Devi for a few minutes. Rai Sahib and Rukmini Devi welcomed Rai Sahib Rathore in the central hall. Rai Sahib Rathore began the conversation thanking Rai Sahib Bhudeshwar for inviting him and his family to Lakshmi's wedding. He complimented Lakshmi's parents for the immaculate preparations for the wedding, and gave his compliments about how handsome and cultured he found Raghu and his entire family. Bai Sahib of Rathore pitched in from time to time reiterating the same sentiments. Rai Sahib Rathore then conveyed Arjun's decision to marry Shakun, Dayiju's granddaughter. He explained how Arjun had heard about Shakun's fire incident. He had also heard of Rai Sahib Bhudeshwar's declaration that Shakun was his daughter from Shanti. He found Shakun's determination to study very inspiring and had decided to meet her, and if possible, marry her. Arjun, explained Rai Sahib, was democratic in his thinking. He was very well-read and was an atheist. He visited Shakun's house on the pretext of coaching her but had already confided in his parents that, if everything worked out, he would consider himself very fortunate if Shakun agreed to marry him. Arjun found Shakun extremely principled and dignified; all the qualities that he wanted in his wife. He informed them that Shakun and Arjun were married on 15 May.

'Arjun didn't want anyone there except us, Dayiju and Shakun's father,' Rai Sahib Rathore said. 'After much insistence, Arjun has agreed to let us host a small reception on 26 May which would be held in an orphanage in Bhudeshwar.'

The proud parents informed them that he had decided to donate a large sum of money to the orphanage during the reception. They also added that Shakun would be working for the orphans thereafter.

There were about a 100 people in the orphanage for Arjun and Shakun's reception. The newlyweds, with Dayiju, got down from a black Mercedes. Shakun looked pretty and serene in a rust, cream and gold chanderi saree. She wore a single diamond string necklace, a diamond bracelet and a pair of solitaires adorned her ears. Arjun escorted Dayiju to the dais and urged her to bless them and say a few words.

'I don't know what to say. There is an old saying that when sorrow and tragedy is incomprehensible, it is followed by happiness which is equally indecipherable. My dear Arjun and Shakun have given me back the sons I had lost. These boys and girls are my children. Arjun has assured me that the few years of my life that are left, will be spent here with my children... my sons and daughters.'

3

Empowered to Die

Cloudbursts are almost always accompanied with a massive downpour. It was an unprecedented occurrence for April—all roads were under two or three feet of water. Coconut palm trees lay uprooted in many places and in some parts of the village large pools of water, more like ponds, surfaced overnight. However, nature has its own way of completing any process. On these nascent ponds, a few batches of small black and white ducks, typical of any West Bengal rural landscape, began to swim in glee with all their vigour. Everything, from trees to roads to the mud walls of huts, appeared to be cleansed and washed.

Asma had woken up a number of times during the night. Her small thatched hut was leaking at several places. There was hardly any place left for Akbar and her to sleep—the entire floor was wet. She pulled out a torn blanket from the aluminium container that she had carefully stowed away after winter. The blanket was the only warm thing she had. Like she did on most cold days, she gave the blanket to Akbar who folded it twice and slept underneath, while she managed with one of her limited stock of sarees.

Abject poverty cannot be defined or described. It has to be experienced to be understood. Poverty is a day-to-day affair and it often tends to erase the past and the future. The only context and reality is the present. In fact, for the poor, memories of the past are so painful that they are automatically suppressed. And, since the future is all about fear and anxiety, the poor don't like to think about it at all. Their concept of future is the next one hour or, at the most, if perceived from the morning, the evening... nothing beyond that. There is no time for worry or stress because worrying is a time-consuming activity. People living in abject poverty are only involved in urgent activities—procuring food, kerosene for fuel, washing clothes if there is some detergent or soap in the house, taking loans or paying interest on loans, running errands to bring in some extra money which will help them buy medicines for fever, a cold or an upset stomach, etc.

There is no time for cognitive activities like contemplation or visualisation. These activities are for those who don't have to engage in a battle for their survival. When there is no food for lunch, it simply has to be organised at any cost. The complexity of options is not there. Whatever food is obtained after two hours of labour is good enough. Menu cards and recipes are all the luxuries of the rich.

Children of those who live in abject poverty see death all around them, all the time. They learn to accept it with unusual stoicism. Mothers keep dying during childbirth, children die of malnutrition, their fathers and brothers die as a result of liver failure from alcoholism, suicidal deaths occur because of financial difficulties, brides are burnt when they don't bring in enough dowry, and then, there are also deaths from the lack of medical care.

As a result of unexpected showers and the lack of warm covering, Asma had developed severe body ache during the night, and her body felt warm in the morning. She was, however, up and about. Her small and rusted tin container was empty; there was no money in the house. She was ready in 15 minutes to reach the crossing in front of her hut where men and women congregated to be selected as daily wage labourers deployed to various projects. She was sent to work on the highway repair project about five kilometres from the crossing. Fortunately, she managed to get a lift to the work site on a tractor belonging to a person she knew from her village.

Unlike the cool night, the day was hot and sultry. By the time it was mid-afternoon, her stomach was growling with hunger. She drank litres of water to keep her hunger in control. She could feel that her fever had also risen. However, she decided to continue working because a full day's work would give her ₹300 to take back home. At the end of day, she received only ₹150 from the contractor as there was shortage of cash. The contractor told her that she would be given the uncovered amount by the end of the week. She felt a little better as she made her way to the market. Vegetable prices were soaring yet she managed to buy a small quantity of potatoes, onions and garlic and a few green chillies. There was a little flour and about three kilograms of rice in the house. She also bought a small bottle of the cheapest cooking oil available and commenced her return journey to the hut.

After serving a nice hot meal to Akbar, her son who would turn seven in two months, she ate the leftovers. Her body temperature had cooled off a bit; she lay down on a damp sheet on the floor and in no time, was fast asleep. The next day, the same cycle, the same struggle for survival, resumed.

Asma was the elder daughter of a family of Sunni Muslims who lived in a village in the South 24 Parganas district of West Bengal, not far from Akbarpur, where Asma now lived. They were weavers by profession and wove cotton sarees, one of Bengal's most famous exports. Her paternal family was quite well-off but was very conservative and orthodox. Girls were not allowed to go out of the house and they followed the *purdah* system. But, the girls were taught to weave and some even became great experts in the trade. Weaving gave most women the opportunity to express themselves creatively by letting them play with different colours and designs. Asma had become very good in weaving and her talent in new designs using unusual and striking colour combinations was appreciated by a number of saree dealers and stockists in the district.

As a result, her father felt he had an upper hand in her marriage and wouldn't have to shell out a large sum for her dowry. He even told Asma's in-laws that he was giving them a dowry for life as his daughter would be able to earn well through her weaving. The money that she earlier brought into his family would now be all going to her in-laws. They understood his point and didn't ask for much.

Akbarpur was lush and green and had a population of about 5,000 people. Most people were weavers and there was a sizeable Muslim population. Mohsin Ansari was Asma's husband. When she married him, he was a young boy of 22; good-looking and affable. Even though, he seemed a little aimless and lacking in ambition to Asma, she was happy that he didn't have any bad habits like smoking, drinking and gambling and he also kept away from prostitutes, whose numbers were steadily increasing in Akbarpur and the neighbouring villages.

The prostitutes came from diverse caste and religious backgrounds. Some even came from the neighbouring state of Bihar as there were a lot of moneyed people in these districts, who were mostly engaged in saree and *chadar* weaving. A large number of families in these villages were also engaged in making cooking utensils with brass and copper. The Bengal brass and copper utensil traders shipped a lot of these utensils to Bihar, where these utensils served an important part of the bridal trousseau.

Mohsin's friends had shared with him that the government keeps conducting workshops and awareness camps on a disease called AIDS, which is mainly transmitted by the prostitutes to men who have direct intercourse with them. His friends were quite aware of AIDS and how, once infected by the disease, it's a battle against early death as there was no cure for it.

The incidences and deaths from AIDS were galloping in these districts. Many families had members suffering from the disease but, out of sheer shame and embarrassment, they would not disclose the information and, at times, they would even avoid medical treatment.

Mohsin was the only son of his parents and Asma's mother-in-law Zubeida was quite possessive about him. The moment she had entered the house, Asma could feel the hostility and lack of warmth in Zubeida. She, however, decided to maintain a cordial and respectful distance. Mohsin's elder sister was married with grown-up children and lived in the Ganga Sagar area of Bengal, which was not very far from the Canning district.

Mohsin had once told her that these quaint names of districts and roads were the legacy of the British Raj. 'There was a road in Akbarpur which led to an English medium primary school established before Independence, which was still called Queen's Road. A number of village elders had different and interesting stories to tell about the road. Some even believed that Queen Victoria gifted this school to the village and travelled on that road for the inauguration of the school, hence the name.'

Asma conceived Akbar two months after her wedding. Mohsin's parents desperately wanted a grandson, so Asma was quite relieved when she gave birth to a son. Zubeida's attitude towards Asma gradually became positive, especially after Akbar was born. As days passed, she became obsessively attached to Akbar and would hardly let Asma handle him. As Akbar grew, Zubeida became more and more possessive. She bought a number of good luck charms and tied some around his waist, some around his neck and a few she would keep under his mattress. She would not allow Akbar to go out and play. He was a fair-skinned child which made her feel that people would curse him out of sheer jealousy. Akbar's food would be cooked by her and she would spend lavishly on his clothes and toys.

Sikandar, Mohsin's father, had made a name for himself in that area as a master craftsman—his sarees and *chadars* were highly appreciated for their colours and designs. The texture and the quality of his products were among the best in that area. However, in recent years, his health had become an issue. One day, while he had taken a dozen sarees for washing in the pond, which was a few yards away from his home, he felt giddy and fainted. He was rushed to a government hospital and was diagnosed with diabetes, high blood pressure and a cardiac dilation. After the incident and medical diagnosis, he was advised a lifestyle of less physical exertion, a reduction of his work load and, of course, continuous medical treatment.

Mohsin had not learnt weaving. He had a lacklustre academic record and dropped out of school after failing twice in his high school examination. He continued doing odd jobs like painting of roads, or helping a group of electricians during Durga pooja for the lighting of pandals and roads. Sikandar was worried about him because he didn't see any sense of responsibility in him and didn't know how he would financially support the family in the future. He was convinced that Zubeida had spoilt him and was also making attempts to do the same with Akbar. Akbar was five when Sikandar passed away. It was a big blow to the family in many ways. He was the head of the family and was the sole bread earner. He had not asked Asma even once to take to the loom and start weaving, even though there were weeks during which he had to literally drag himself to work because of his failing health. After Sikandar's passing, there was no money in the house for Akbar's regular medical check-ups. There was barely any money for rations and vegetables.

Two years before his death, for the first time in his life, Sikandar saw his family sleep on an empty stomach because the stock of rice had been exhausted. He couldn't bear the pain and foresaw the possible financial plight of the family in the future. There were no savings. His earlier savings and money from the loan that he had taken were all spent on his daughter's wedding. For years, he continued paying off the interest on the loan which he took from the sahu. The loan only got repaid two years before his death. Sikander was a self-respecting man and hence didn't ask Asma to take to the loom even in these financially difficult times.

Asma finally took to the loom after a week of Sikandar's passing. Mohsin was completely unconcerned about how the family should organise itself for survival and what he should do to shoulder the financial responsibility of the family. Looking at the bleak atmosphere at home, he started spending more time out of the house, eating his meals with his friends and returning home late only to sleep. Zubeida assisted Asma by cooking and washing utensils and clothes. Asma put in almost 12 hours on the loom everyday and would weave quite a few sarees in that time. She also had to network with the dealers and the stockists, and soon began visiting their *addas* in a *burkha*. Initially, Zubeida would accompany her but after a few months, Asma could handle the negotiations herself.

Money that came into the house was not as much as Sikandar earned, but it was enough to cover the expenses of meals and a few medicines that were required. There was, however, no money for new clothes and sweetmeats on Eid and other occasions. Asma would give all the money she earned to Zubeida and would only keep a meagre amount for Akbar's occasional demands for a kite or a toffee, and for her own soap and hair oil. Lately, Asma noticed that Zubeida would exhaust the weekly revenue from the weaving of sarees and *chadars* very fast and would complain that Asma was not handling the financial negotiations with the traders well. Asma often suggested that Mohsin could do the negotiations so that she would have more time to weave. This way, she could also manage to do some cooking or other household chores. Zubeida would ignore the suggestion and snap back saying that Mohsin was very bad with managing money, and she would not like money to go directly into his hands.

As weeks and months passed, the financial condition of the family worsened. Asma had seen Mohsin taking money from Zubeida on a number of occasions. Zubeida would pass on the money to him quietly and if Asma questioned her, she would either deny it or provide a long explanation saying that she had to send some money to the grocery shop from where she had purchased cooking oil or some other item.

One evening, Mohsin returned home absolutely drunk. Asma got into a fight with him and asked, 'Where did you get the money to drink so much?'

He snapped back, 'You keep your bloody mouth shut, you bitch! You go to the stockists and dealers and God alone knows what you do there. That is the reason why they pay you so handsomely for the rubbish that you weave. You think that you will run my life. Look after your son, I am sure you don't even know who his father is. There are so many of these men who you keep visiting.'

Unknown to them, Akbar had heard his father saying this to Asma. At night, when Asma was lying next to him, Akbar asked her about the men she met and sold sarees and *chadars* to. Asma was shocked at the question but told him not to ask these questions as he was too young to think about all this.

Mohsin began to drink very heavily. He would drink in the mornings and started borrowing money to buy his alcohol. One day, the vegetable vendor complained to Asma about Mohsin's mounting debt with him. The grocery shop owner also piped in saying that had also lent him money which he had not returned since the last eight months. Many people also mentioned that Mohsin would avoid them and not respond to their messages related to the repayment of loans. Asma also noticed that Mohsin was rapidly losing weight as well as his appetite. These symptoms could be of Aids because of his frequent visits to prostitutes or signs of a failing liver. He had started drinking uncontrollably. He had stopped eating completely and if he didn't drink, his legs would pain. He couldn't even hold a glass of water because of a frightening tremor in his hands. He had not ventured out of the house because of the constant fever he would suffer from. On top of all this, he had withdrawn into a shell and would spend most of his time sleeping.

Zubeida didn't have the courage to confront Mohsin. As years passed, her obsession had turned into some sort of paranoid disorder. Any criticism of Mohsin would upset her beyond logical reasoning as she was still fiercely protective about him. In the past also, she would give all her attention and energy to fulfil the demands of Mohsin, often at the expense of neglecting Sikandar.

Mohsin's debts accumulated for quite a few months till one night when there were about 9–10 men, standing outside their house, shouting and asking him to open the door. Both Zubeida and Asma got up in a fright and Zubeida walked up to the door and opened it. They were all men they knew from the village accompanied by one or two younger men with tough, well-built bodies who appeared to be from another village.

Zubeida insolently asked, 'What do you want? Why are you disturbing us at this time of the night? You don't have mothers, sisters and daughters in your house? Do you think it is good behaviour to disturb women at this time of the night?'

Kedar Nath, the vegetable vendor, said, 'Zubeida sister, we respect you and would not have disturbed you, if it were not for your son, who is a good-for-nothing man. He has borrowed large sums of money from us and refuses to pay us back. In all these months, we have not complained to you because we respect you. But now, Mohsin has begun to abuse us and is blatantly refusing to pay back all loans. We have a responsibility towards our families too.'

While Kedar Nath was explaining this to Zubeida, Mohsin got up and stumbled towards the door in a drunken state. Seeing the group of men, he lost his temper and, in very foul language, asked everyone to go back. Threatening them and telling them that he had decided not to pay back the money, he slammed the door and was trying to lock it from inside. One of the tough men in the group broke the flimsy door into bits by pushing and slamming it twice. He entered the room and dragged Mohsin out of the house. He was beaten black-and-blue. After 10 minutes, they left him sprawled outside on the road, bleeding from his head, mouth and nose. His spine was smashed and he had sustained fractures in his left arm and left femur. The two women, for almost half an hour, sat crying and cursing him. Then, they pulled him inside the house, wiped his blood and left him in one corner of the room, not realising the extent of his injuries. In the morning, Mohsin didn't move when Zubeida called him. He didn't respond to Asma either.

Mohsin had passed away during the night. Possibly he died of AIDS that his friends kept warning him about or it could also have been liver failure because of his excessive drinking habit or maybe he just succumbed to his injuries—Asma didn't know. She, not surprisingly, didn't shed a single tear. She had cried innumerable times during the last so many years; her life couldn't have been more miserable. Zubeida broke down completely and was never the same again. She lost interest in life and fell ill. There was no money for her medical treatment. She ran a fever and developed a constant cough. There were days when she would not even brush her teeth. She kept groaning and moaning. Her eyes were sunken and watery; they looked like pools of pain and longing. A sensitive person could read her life's script by just looking into the depths of her eyes. There were so many shades of emotion which would glide past her eyes, in every passing moment. She too died in her sleep one day, and was buried next to her son.

Akbar had witnessed two deaths by the time he was six and a half. Poverty lives with death more than life. Therefore, people who are poor take death in their stride and don't make too much noise about life. Both are just facts to be faced and managed. The simplicity of this nature of understanding is stark and humbling.

Asma took to the loom again. She was determined to work hard and wanted to send Akbar to a good school in the village. She wished she had the money to send him to the English medium school on Queen's Road. However, she knew that it would be out of her reach because the monthly fee was very high. Then, there would be other additional expenses like uniform, books and fees for different activities in the school. There were other schools that were not as expensive but Asma had made up her mind to admit Akbar in a school which would give him a good education.

She thought of Kedar Nath who was Mohsin's childhood friend. The day Mohsin was thrashed by the group, it was only Kedar Nath who had tried to save him. He was the only person who had tried to describe Mohsin's irresponsible attitude to his mother with some patience. It was only when Mohsin got abusive that the situation went out of hand leading to Mohsin's serious injuries and subsequent death.

She went to Kedar Nath and asked for his help. He took Asma to a government school and introduced her to the principal who was a god-fearing man. He understood Asma's plight and, for a very nominal fee, admitted Akbar to the nursery section of the school.

In most villages, government schools are bereft of even basic infrastructure, the same was the case with Akbar's new school. There were neither libraries nor qualified teachers. In fact, the teachers remained absent from their classes for a number of days in a month. Many a times, a few classes were held just prior to the examinations. There was a lot of hanky-panky in attendance and in money matters. Petty corruption was rampant, making the life of the poor even more difficult. As a result of this, even talented children ended up not receiving the attention and guidance that they so justifiably deserve. Asma knew that education was the only way out of physical, mental and emotional misery. She had to do something to educate Akbar. At the same time, she had to be an example for him so that he doesn't go the way his father went. She was a worried and anxious woman.

Asma sold off practically everything in the house for a pittance and spoke to Kedar Nath about renting out the two-room house that was left to her after the death of Mohsin's parents. During Sikandar's illness, almost all the gold ornaments were sold off, including those that her father had given her for her wedding. Zubeida had even sold Asma's gold nose stud, which was a symbol of her marital status and legitimacy, to the village sahu. However, Asma had noticed that Zubeida hadn't sold her own nose stud, which she continued wearing with an air of defiance.

Asma managed to retain the loom as that was her lifeline. With a few utensils, some torn and mended clothes and a few tins of ration, she shifted into the small hut which Kedar Nath had provided her as a temporary shelter. From the meagre rent of the rooms she managed the daily requirements of the house as initially her weaving didn't fetch her enough.

When people saw Kedar helping Asma, they started talking about his intention and even gossiped that something was going on between him and Asma. Young widows have to bear a lot, not only sorrow and responsibility, but also humiliation and open attacks on their self-esteem and reputation.

'This has been the way of the world from time immemorial. It will not change and it cannot change,' said Kedar Nath to

Asma when she mentioned to him what some village people were saying about his visits to her hut.

As Asma settled into her new life, she realised that there were so many things to be completed within an hour in the morning. She had to drop Akbar to school which was a good half a kilometre away from where she lived. On returning back home, she had to cook something for herself and take it to the site where she worked as a labourer. The threads and other material for the sarees and the *chadars* were not available during the monsoon and therefore Asma had decided to work on the road site during this season. She was not in very good health and, from time to time, would suffer from bouts of vomiting and would throw up large quantities of bile. She had no money to consult the doctor who sat in the market in his small clinic every evening. Kedar Nath, who came to see her every second or third day, suggested that she see the doctor at least once and take the medicine which he would suggest. He offered her a small amount of money and assured her that he would take it back from her when she is paid by the contractor, lest she felt small and embarrassed. Kedar Nath took her to the doctor who examined her with great care and also reduced his fee. Asma was convinced that Kedar must have told the doctor about her dire and dismal situation. Out of pity and sympathy, he must have reduced his fee for her which was a good gesture on his behalf and she felt grateful, but quite small. This and other previous incidents, when Mohsin was alive and immersed in debt, made her realise the importance of self-respect. She decided to pay the doctor his complete fee after she was back from work, the following evening.

Decisions taken during times of difficulty appear to be inconsequential but are actually life-changing. The resolve for independence and freedom is adopted in these day-to-day challenges. These decisions alter our cognitive perspectives and the manner in which we perceive ourselves, our lives and this world. The change is always from inside to outside—something in the way the heart feels and the mind thinks must change to respond to the world differently. The way we begin to define ourselves, impacts the way the world defines us. It is never the other way round. Changes that take place in this sequence are long-lasting.

The same happened with Asma. She felt strong throughout the day and even had the confidence and the courage to ask the contractor for the complete money she was owed. Feeling upbeat with the extra ₹150, she walked to the shanty clinic and paid the doctor his total fee.

Mohsin's death had taught Asma some cruel facts about the world at a young age. During Sikandar's illness, her parents and other members of the family had visited her. After that, her family distanced themselves from her. The first lesson that she learnt was that her parents would not take responsibility of a widowed daughter and her son. They would, however, look after a daughter-in-law and her children. A daughter has to be looked after by her in-laws or by herself. Even if the daughter is given shelter by her parents, she must earn to preserve her respect and dignity. She should do this for her children. Money and wealth are not easily shared. Emotional support evokes more pity and sympathy than trust and confidence. Asma didn't inform her parents about her financial difficulties. She had made up her mind to work and earn well so that she was able to support Akbar and his studies.

It was a resolve that made a difference to her thinking and the way she approached the problems that came her way. There was one single purpose in her life which was a source of inspiration and gave meaning to all her actions—the happiness, well-being and the success of her son. There were times when she caught herself being too involved with Akbar. His happiness in little things mattered disproportionately to her. If he found the vegetables tasteless, she would compensate by running to the grocery shop, buying a few eggs and making an omelette for him. Kedar experienced this first-hand one evening when she had called him to repay a portion of the money that she owed him. Kedar had joined them for dinner and was about to compliment her on her culinary skills when Akbar began to complain about the vegetables. Asma left her half-eaten plate of food, rushed to the grocery and came back with eggs that she proceeded to make, her own hunger forgotten.

It is commonly observed that during widowhood, a woman goes through various negative emotions. Some women learn to deal with them and move on. Many women suppress these emotions and begin to suffer from physical ailments of stomach and joints, as a result of the suppression of negative energy. A few just cannot handle these emotions and begin to suffer from mental and emotional disorders, the root cause of which can be the feelings of guilt, shame, resentment and sorrow.

Kedar, being a friend and a self-appointed mentor and counsellor, didn't want the same to happen with Asma, so he decided to spend a little time with Asma and explain to her how her being strong will be good for Akbar in the long run. She had once confided in Kedar Nath about how she felt responsible for Mohsin's death, 'Bhaiya, there are times when I feel that perhaps I was responsible for his death because widowhood was written in my destiny. My husband could have died because of me. I keep blaming myself and feel sad and depressed.'

'You have to accept that you were not responsible for Mohsin's death; it was his destiny. Similarly, Akbar destiny's is his own and you were neither responsible for everything that has happened to him nor for might happen to him in the future. Akbar would figure out his life by himself. If you do not distance yourself from him, you would create problems for him and his future,' he said softly.

It was a dark night, damp and warm, and they were sitting on two rocks outside Asma's hut. Kedar shared with Asma his limited understanding of the *Gita* in which Sri Krishna tells Arjun that all mankind keeps walking through the rounds of births and deaths which are determined by their karma. It is the karma of the individual that makes one's destiny and impacts the chain of life and death. No other person has anything to do with this, not even the mother in whose body the foetus grows.

The *Quran* or the maulvis in her village never spoke about this perspective, thought Asma.

'Kedar *bhai*, we don't believe in this. After death we either go to heaven or to hell. No one says that we come back to this earth again and again. Our good actions take us to heaven and bad actions take us to hell.'

'Yes, yes, Asma *behen*. It is the same thing. Mohsin's drinking took him to his death. God has given everyone a mind to think, he succumbed to his bad habit. You are not to be blamed. You tried your best, you wanted to save him, his health and your home. So, why do you suffer from guilt? It is this guilt that causes you tension which leads to frequent vomiting bouts. Even doctor *sahib* was saying the same thing. Don't spoil Akbar, you have not taken his father away. It was the doing of his father and it was his destiny. Now, if Akbar grows up to be strong and able, he will make his life. You must help him to do this by being strong yourself.'

Asma didn't say anything then but this conversation had lodged itself somewhere deep in her mind.

Kedar's affection for Akbar and Asma was taking deeper roots than he was aware of. In Akbar, he saw his dead son who would have been Akbar's age today. He lost him to dengue which went undiagnosed and therefore untreated. After him, three daughters were born. One passed away two days after her birth and the two other girls, one three years old and the other barely one and a half, stayed with him and his wife Kusum. He had dreams to educate them so that they could stand on their own feet. Seeing Asma, he sometimes, during the night when sleep eluded him, shuddered to think what would happen if the same events were to take place in his daughters' lives and what they would do if they were not educated. Thus, he liked doing little things for Asma. At times, he would bring some leftover vegetables from his shop for Akbar and Asma and feel happy to see them eat green peas, cauliflower, cabbage and spinach. He knew that the prices of these vegetables were soaring every week and Asma couldn't afford them herself.

*****

One day, after leaving Akbar at school, Asma noticed a lot of activity in the village. There was a huge *peepal* tree in the central circle of the village, adjacent to the market and the small panchayat hall. A number of village elders from the *julaha*, weaving community, to which Asma too belonged, were congregating in that area. The most vociferous member of the group under the *peepal* tree was Firoz Ansari, a prosperous weaver who had requested for the panchayat meeting. He was there with his friends and a few relatives. Firoz was about 55 years old, had given up active work and was only engaged with the supervision and the financial management of his saree business. He had a number of looms and had about 25 weavers working under him on a daily basis.

Firoz complained to the panchayat about the growing relationship between Kedar Nath and Asma. Kedar Nath was already present under the *peepal* tree and Asma was summoned by the panchayat to be present. Asma was about to leave for work and hence she requested to be excused. The panchayat was relentless and forced her to attend the meeting.

Firoz, in front of the gathering, said, 'I have observed and not only me, but a number of other people have observed, that there is a relationship between Kedar and Asma. Some *chakkar* is going on for quite a few months. We would not allow a Muslim widow to be enticed by a Hindu married man. This would lead to a larger conflict in the ensuing months. This has to stop immediately. Both Kedar Nath and Asma owe us an explanation, an apology and a commitment that they would stop this nonsense immediately.'

Kedar Nath was visibly livid. He looked at Asma and said, 'Asma *behen* do you have anything to say? Or should I speak?'

Some random passerby interjected, 'Don't use words like Asma *behen,* you scoundrel.'

Asma kept looking down and in a calm and controlled manner, she informed the panchayat that the allegations hurled at her and Kedar Nath were completely baseless and were a bunch of lies, 'Kedar Nath was known to my late husband and after his passing, he has been helping me by giving me a hut to live in and introducing me to the village doctor when I was not well. He also gave me a little money, which I have been paying back, time to time. This money was used to restart my weaving work. He is the only person who bothers to find out, on sheer human grounds, about me and Akbar. No one else from the village is concerned about us at all. Whenever Kedar visits my hut, we sit outside for not more than half an hour, in complete visibility. And I give you my word that this would also not happen again. However, I would be grateful to the panchayat if it would explain to Firoz and the other men that I would not tolerate their overtures anymore and would personally request the police and other officials to intervene if such a matter arose in future. Now, I am leaving to resume my work at the construction site.'

*****

While returning home, she bought a few vegetables from the lady who sat by the highway. Her vegetables were a little expensive as she mostly sold them to the rich driving past in their shining cars. Asma had taught Akbar to light the lamp as soon as darkness descended upon the village. She saw the light of the lamp from a distance and was relieved to know that Akbar had safely returned from school.

She noticed that people had started maintaining some distance from her since the incident at panchayat. Kedar Nath had not come towards her hut for weeks. She was happy that he had accepted the verdict of the panchayat, which was in fact her verdict, and was handling it maturely.

Asma had been close with her mother's younger sister, Reshma, who used to visit them sometime. Reshma *Khala* had once advised her to lead a low-key life and not to be seen or heard in the village. She had asked Asma to keep to herself and only go out of her house when she really needed something.

'A single woman should not be seen nor heard. Silence and invisibility were her strengths,' she always used to say.

This advice came back to Asma and she had made up her mind to maintain a discrete distance from everyone in the village, keep to herself largely and immerse herself in work so she had no time left to think about the social dynamics in the village. If Firoz showed up again, she would quietly inform the police or even travel to the collector's office and discuss the case. She knew that she had to be sensible in these matters as she had to look after the safety and security of Akbar.

Akbar was growing up fast and had begun to take responsibility of the small errands in the house. He was also concentrating on his studies. Many times when Asma returned from work, he would keep some water and puffed rice ready for her knowing that she would be very hungry after the day's gruelling physical labour. Asma had commenced her work on the loom. Durga pooja was approaching fast and she knew that women from Akbarpur and the neighbouring villages would be purchasing a lot of sarees for the occasion. As a young child, Akbar felt sleepy after 10 pm but since his mother worked on the loom till after midnight, he would slink in close to her and sleep on the floor. Many times he reminded her that so much physical exertion was not good for her, that she would develop fever and then his doctor uncle would have to give her a big painful injection.

Complete immersion in work and a large meaningful sense of purpose can convert a major tragedy into a challenge, which requires courage to be managed well. Her insight that the world does not provide financial help when one is in great trouble, and that loss and pain have to be borne alone, facilitated Asma to focus on her work and her son. She was surprised to notice that her health improved, maybe because of her resolve and hard work. Almost 16 hours of continuous work was not telling on her physical health at all. In fact, she felt energetic and her earnings were also increasing with every passing month. She was also creating varied designs and colour combinations for the sarees that she was weaving. Sales were good and she was able to repay Kedar's loan.

Asma was hardly seen in the village. It had kept prying eyes and gossip away and Asma could concentrate on her work with tremendous focus. Her work output was increasing by leaps and bounds and her income from the sale of sarees had become substantial. Akbar started teaching her the Bengali alphabet and numbers and in no time, Asma could read and write. She remembered how she had been in school for only three years. The memories of school came rushing back as she continued to read and write. She progressed well with Akbar's tuitions. They also had a lot of fun together in the evenings when Akbar sat down with his homework. Sometimes, Akbar would also give her suggestions for various designs and colours for her sarees.

Reshma *Khala* came to visit Asma one evening and told her about a lady who was in the saree business in Kolkata.

'I have heard that she is planning to expand the business and is looking for weavers who could meet the increasing demand for woven sarees, and were capable of learning and innovating new designs. I think you should meet her in Kolkata. I could get the lady's address and telephone number, if you want,' she said.

Reshma and Asma left for Kolkata with Akbar. They met Geeta Gupta who lived on Rashbehari Avenue where she had a large warehouse and a showroom as well. Asma was amazed to see the large range of sarees and the variety of exquisite weaves. She had carried samples of her work and Geeta *di*, as Mrs Gupta was called, liked her work.

'Your work is neat and some of the designs are very unusual. So, tell me, how many looms do you have and how many sarees can you supply in a month?' she asked.

Asma said that she worked on just one loom and then, while sipping the tea which the showroom staff served them, she related her story briefly.

Geeta *di* liked something about Asma; she was a self-made woman herself and was prepared to risk a small sum of money with Asma.

'I could provide you funds for four looms but the problem is, who will work on these looms?' she asked.

Asma thought for a moment and then said, excitedly, 'Places like Katua, Krishnanagar, Canning, etc. have a large number of women who know how to weave sarees, *chadars* and fabric. I will organise some women from there to work with me on the looms. I would also leave my work on the road construction site and devote all my time to weaving. My work will definitely make you proud Geeta *di*.'

On returning, Asma communicated to many women that they would get regular work from Kolkata for weaving sarees. A number of them came to Asma and expressed their desire to work. In no time, she had partnered with eight competent women from other villages who joined her team and started working on the orders from Kolkata. Asma was happy to see the quality of the weaves these women produced. They were willing workers and had the capacity to put in long hours of work. The first order from Geeta Gupta was executed before time and the designs as well as the quality of the sarees were appreciated by her. This was a big encouragement for Asma; she also noticed Akbar feeling proud and confident.

One evening, while Asma was working on the loom, Akbar walked up to her and said 'Ammi, can I also help you on the loom? I want to learn how to do this.'

Asma looked at Akbar's small, tender hands and suppressing her tears, said, 'You are too small, Akbar, to do this work. You should concentrate on your studies and when you grow up, you can decide what you would like to do.'

Without saying anything, Akbar walked away and got busy with the ball and bat that Asma had not seen before. Asma watched him play and asked him, 'Where did you get this from, Akbar?'

'Ammi, my best friend in school gave the bat and ball to me to play with. I will return the set to him next week.'

Mohsin's face swam in front of his eyes. Asma didn't want Akbar to follow in his father's footsteps. She, emphasising a few points, told him, 'Akbar please don't borrow anything from others. We'll buy the set tomorrow and you can return the set to him when you are in school. We should only use those things that we can afford to buy ourselves. Borrowing things is not a good habit.'

Asma told Akbar to sit on the loom and start learning how to weave. 'This loom is yours. I know you are interested, therefore, from tomorrow Afsari didi will teach you weaving.'

The evenings turned very enjoyable for both Asma and Akbar. They would both sit on the loom and weave the most beautiful patterns in exquisite colours. Akbar's interest in the art of weaving was growing each day. Even in school, his mind would wander off thinking about the evenings, and the designs and colours interspersed with his mother's storytelling. She would relate interesting incidents of her childhood and, like many mothers, shared a lot about how a good life could be led with the right values and intent.

Geeta *di* had become a significant part of Asma's life. Apart from a vendor-customer relationship, they shared a personal bond which Asma valued a lot. Normally after the business transaction was over, Asma would have a meal with her with some fish curry and rice, which was a distinct part of Bengali cuisine. Asma's earnings were gradually but steadily increasing. She would continuously receive feedback and support from Geeta *di* for improving the quality and the finish of the weave. She also received immense encouragement to innovate and come up with new designs. At times, Geeta *di* would also be highly critical and stern with her feedback. However, Asma could always decipher her underlying concern for Asma's improvement and well-being.

Reshma *khala* kept visiting Asma and had grown very fond of Akbar. For Akbar, she was the elderly grandmother figure whom he missed. He had faint memories of his paternal grandparents and didn't know his mother's parents at all. Soon, Akbar turned 13 and was doing well in school. His interest in weaving, fabric designs and colours was very obvious. He had mentioned, on many occasions, to Asma that he would like to become more serious about this work. Geeta *di* understood Akbar's passion and advised that he should complete his tenth standard board exams and then move to Kolkata to pursue a degree in the craft, fabric, design and textile area. There were many institutions that ran formal educational courses in the subject but this kind of education was expensive and Asma would have to plan for it much in advance.

Reshma *khala* came visiting on a Sunday knowing that Akbar and Asma would return from the looms a little early. She had brought a kilo of chicken with her and cooked a delicious chicken curry. After dinner, Akbar sat with his books as he had to finish his homework. Asma and Reshma cleaned the utensils and arranged the bed for the night. It was still early to sleep so Asma decided to talk to Reshma about the thoughts that were weighing heavy on her mind.

'Khala, can I talk to you about something very important which has been troubling me for quite a while. At times, I feel depressed and very anxious,' Asma said.

'Certainly,' said Reshma, 'It's good to share your troubles with someone you trust. It lightens your mind and dispels your confusion by identifying what actually needs to be done.'

Asma confided in Reshma that she was living with a lot of guilt and shame after Mohsin's death. She blamed herself for not saving his life. She knew that she was not responsible for his drinking and the tragedy that followed, but somehow these thoughts didn't leave her in peace. She also felt that Akbar felt let down by her. He had not said anything to her but she had sensed this many times in his questioning eyes. It always seemed that he wanted to know what had exactly happened between her and Mohsin, which led to his drinking and death. She also shared how she felt let down by her own parents and siblings, and she was not sure whether she would be able to continue her efforts to earn more and support Akbar's studies in the future.

Reshma listened to her in total silence and encouraged her to tell her everything that she wanted to share. With tears welling up in her eyes, Asma continued, 'Reshma *khala*, I want to die. No, please don't misunderstand me. I am not talking about suicide. I want to destroy the diffident, guilt-ridden and depressed Asma forever and I know that I can do this.'

Asma related to Reshma what Kedar Nath had once shared with her—even after death people are born again and they return to the earth to commence life in another body, live in a different family and assume another identity. The chain of birth and rebirth depends upon the individual's own actions or karma. She said that no other person can influence this, 'Our karmas have the power to determine our destiny. We can make our own destiny.'

She paused and took a deep breath, 'I don't want to wait for my death to be born again. After having worked for so long and having faced so much in life, I feel enabled and empowered to change my own destiny in this life itself. But I know in order to do that, I have to die first—the old fearful and guilt-ridden Asma has to perish.'

She urged Reshma to help her execute a plan. She wanted her own grave to be dug where she would bury her wedding photograph. Then, Reshma would get the grave properly cemented with her epitaph engraved on the cement.

'I want the epitaph to read—Asma decides to die while she lives but while she continues to live in the same body, she is reborn in spirit and strength as Akbari. This is the grave of Asma, the disempowered woman.'

Reshma couldn't believe her ears. She told Asma that no religion allows this. Contradicting her, Asma said that Kedar Nath had told her that in Hinduism when a person takes *sanyas*, he or she lights his or her own pyre. This is followed by assuming a different name and identity, renouncing the family and the world. The person thereafter progresses on the path of spirituality. Asma pleaded with Reshma, 'I have thought about this very carefully. I have to take my own life with my own hands if I have to move on.'

Asma and Reshma discussed Asma's plan till three in the morning. It was a life-changing conversation for both of them. After that night, their lives changed drastically.

Asma's grave was dug in the graveyard where her husband was laid to rest. The wedding photograph was lowered into the grave, and it was later cemented by Reshma. Then, she engraved the epitaph with immense trepidation. That night, Asma slept peacefully after a long time. The next morning, an empowered spirit rose from the ashes of a troubled past to face the new day with courage and confidence.

A week later, Akbari called Geeta *di* to tell her that on account of certain spiritual reasons, she has changed her name from Asma to Akbari. She also conveyed to her that she was ready to increase her work manifold and that, after two years, Akbar would also start playing a more active part in her trade.

'Apart from Akbarpur, I have started looking for loom-space in Katua and Krishnanagar too. I want to organise weaving centres in as many villages as possible. I request you *di* for more work and whatever support you can offer in terms of funds, learning opportunities and inputs for problem-solving,' she said.

Geeta Gupta was happy to become her guide and mentor.

*****

Kedar Nath had greyed considerably but he had the same warm eyes and the self-effacing demeanour. He stood in front of a huge black iron gate. On one side was a shining brass plaque which read 'Akbari Ansari and Akbar Ansari'. On the other side of the gate, another shining brass plaque read 'Karma'. Kedar Nath pressed the bell and passed his card to the security card, saying, 'I want to meet Asma*ji*.'

The guard replied, 'No Asma*ji* stays here. This is the house of Akbari Madam and Akbar Sir.'

As he said this, a long navy-blue car drove near the gate and a young man, very good-looking and expensively dressed, leaned in from the window and asked the guard what the matter was. The guard responded by saying that there was a gentleman who wanted to meet some Asma Madam.

'I told him that this is not her house,' the guard declared.

The young man, on hearing this, got down from the car and walked up to Kedar Nath. He recognised him immediately and touched his feet. Akbar escorted Kedar Nath to the main door of the house and pressed the bell. He informed the staff to call Akbari and requested Kedar Nath to wait in the drawing room.

Excusing himself, Akbar explained that he would have to leave as he had a flight to catch to Paris.

Kedar looked around the drawing room while waiting for Akbari. He couldn't believe his eyes when he saw the expensive décor of the room and the sterling silver and expensive crystal strewn all over. The chandelier in the drawing room and the one in the dining area, which could also been seen from where he sat, were exquisite. He wondered how Asma and Akbar managed all this. Tea was brought for him in a silver tea service and the staff, walking around, were all dressed in white and gold uniforms. There were biscuits and sandwiches served with the tea.

Asma looked ravishingly beautiful as she emerged from the passage on his left. Kedar rose and said namaste to her. She smiled and walked to him and said that she was very happy to see him after so many years. Requesting him to sit, she inquired about his family. There was a minute-long silence between them and then Kedar asked, 'Who is Akbari, Asma?'

Looking at him a little enigmatically, Akbari said, 'I am Akbari. Asma is no more, she died many years ago.'

'How did this happen, Akbari?'

'Asma made it happen. She had to rise like a phoenix from the ashes of her past. The phoenix can only rise if there is a larger purpose. Akbar is my sole purpose. You know, he is now married to Reshma *khala's* daughter. Their children study in London. We have a business there too. *Khala* travels between Dubai and Kolkata. She looks after our Dubai house.'

Kedar saw a tattoo of a bird on her arm. He remembered seeing the same tattoo on Akbar's arm.

It was a phoenix.

4

Platform Number Six

No one could ever imagine that a girl could be called 'Platform Number Six'. This is the real story of such a girl, and there are many such girls in shelter homes all over India, who are rescued from railway platforms where they are thrown within hours of their birth, often by their own mothers and fathers.

I happened to meet one such girl at a shelter home, a number of years ago. Make no mistake, shelter homes, contrary to what their name might imply, are not really homes, rather they are places where tragedy, loss and pain fester. Most shelter homes are cruel places where young children go through unspeakable horrors. However, a few of them are better than the rest which completely depends on the people who are running it. I went to a shelter home that fitted into the latter category. The team which ran this shelter home was decent; they were dedicated to the cause of helping poor girls. The team was affectionate and caring towards these girls.

The shelter home was near a railway station and smelled strongly of detergent and Dettol. There were two large halls in which classes were held and all the girls were assembled in one of them when I first visited. There was a young woman, with a pleasant face which exuded positive energy, making them recite a poem. I noticed that some girls were in their teens while others had not even crossed the age of 10. A few girls looked bored and some parroted the poem after the young woman, almost as a chore. However, there was only one girl who appeared to be enjoying, but she was also very restless. She caught my attention not because of the poem she was reciting but because of the chaotic energy which was oozing from every part of her body. She had rough, matted hair that seemed to have been bleached golden by the sun. She wore a faded blue shirt and a pair of white pyjamas. The image of her wild eyes darting everywhere still lingers in my mind and I have been haunted by it ever since.

However, when I expressed my desire to document her story as she had made an indelible impression on my mind, I was told that I could not do so as there was an ongoing case filed against the NGO, which was running the shelter home. Nevertheless, I persevered and managed to trace her down. I had many conversations with her, but, she never spoke at length. I filled in the gaps as much as I could and finally I had a story—the story of Nutan, who was called Platform Number Six, a young girl who was only eight years old when I met her.

*****

'Platform Number Six' was written on the cover of her file. I was told that she was rescued from the railway station's sixth platform. She didn't have a name that she knew of; it was much later that I found out that her name was Nutan. When she was brought to the shelter home, she was already six years old. Imagine living without a name for six long years! How were people addressing her on the platform where she lived or existed or survived? When I asked these questions, I was merely told that there was no need to have a name. She was known as 'that girl' and that's what people generally called her. How would a name make a difference to her life on the platform, anyway? She lived alone without a family's identity and even protection. To me, it seemed like living in the wild. She was perhaps perceived as an animal, like the numerous dogs and cats, continuously looking for food and a place to sleep on the platform. Maybe she was just a moving object or a source of nuisance, not even worthy of pity.

I met and spoke with a number of people during the years since I last saw Platform Number Six in the shelter home. I couldn't forget the wild tortured emotions in her eyes when she spoke about the platform which made me follow her story with an obsessive persistence. I remember someone telling me that her parents had thrown her on the platform when she was a few hours old. This is a wild guess, of course, based on years of witnessing such abandonment of little girls by their parents or relatives. I spoke to a few people, even though I was told not to. I realised that what happened to Nutan had happened to many girls on the platform... and it would keep happening in the future, throwing children on the platform will never completely stop.

After talking to him, I understood that these children are usually born out of wedlock or they are unwanted children born to extremely poor parents. Since the girl child is perceived to be more burdensome, a greater number of girls are thrown onto the platform compared to boys. Sometimes, it's the father who makes the decision on his own and throws the child away, telling the mother that she gave birth to a stillborn. Sometimes, the mothers are pressurised to throw away the child because of social stigma, especially in cases when the child is illegitimate. The children are also thrown by parents who have recently separated or divorced because single parents don't always have the stamina to bring up the child by themselves. In some cases, the child is unwanted because of lack of love for the spouse, for the child itself or because the economic and social situation do not allow them to raise a child.

Actually, looking more deeply at this issue, it is possible that the real challenge is of self-worth and self-esteem. The child is perceived to be a part of the self which has indulged in sex with a partner who perhaps is disliked. Disliking oneself or one's sexual partner leads to the abhorrence of the outcome of the sexual act, which is the child. The child, therefore, is thrown away because it is an outcome of hatred. The act of sex which leads to this violence is raw, banal and instinctual. Some might even say that it borders on insanity. Men and women who engage in this behaviour have not seen life through its positive dimensions of endurance, empathy, nurture and unconditional love. They perhaps have not received it from their parents and therefore can't give it to others, not even to their own flesh and blood.

The throwing away of the child is a homicidal act and is equivalent to the murder of the child. People say that when infants are thrown on the platform, the possibility of their survival is not even 5 per cent. They die out of starvation or dehydration, or they are bitten by stray dogs or other animals, maybe even snakes. Sometimes, they are injured and hurt by vehicles or even people walking on the platform. A number of infants develop pneumonia because of the cold and die right there.

The platforms of Indian railway stations are places of great complexity and contradiction. The narratives of railway stations can only be understood and captured by those who have spent a lot of time there. What is apparent is very far from the real truth. It is only recently that railway stations have improved their infrastructure. Now, a lot of them have better services available in terms of food, beverages, magazines and newspapers and other goods. Today, the sanitation and maintenance is much better and far different from what it was like two or three decades ago. There is also improved security and safety and the response of the central government to problems and difficulties is much speedier. There is an unspoken acknowledgment of the fact that passengers are customers and, therefore, all attempts are being made to effectively manage the aspirations and the demands of these customers. However, railway stations are still seats of rampant crime, starting from prostitution to drug peddling to theft and hooliganism. Corrupt practices on the platform have not been completely eradicated.

Thus, children who manage to survive amidst all the crime and corruption of body as well as the mind till six long years, like 'Platform Number Six' aka Nutan, are the ones who are destined to live. They must have been lucky to receive sustenance and support from someone. According to people on the platform, that someone in Nutan's life was an old, sickly beggar woman who believed that people would give her more money seeing the plight of the infant. She told everyone she met that she had saved this infant girl, but she didn't have enough money to feed her and provide her with the required medical care. As expected, people gave her money, generously.

The beggar woman kept Nutan for two years but once Nutan started to walk, she could no longer manage her and refused to run behind her. The woman knew that if she left her strategic seat, near the exit gate, she would lose a large chunk of her earnings. Thus, at the age of three, Nutan became used to aimlessly walking around the platform, picking up an overripe banana thrown on the floor or drinking juice from the cans thrown in the garbage heap. She also became clever in the ways of procuring food for herself. Sometimes, a tea shop owner would give her biscuits and a slice of bread; at times, a good-hearted traffic policeman or a security guard would take her for a walk outside the platform. However, they would always bring her back to the place where she slept, which was under a wooden bench along the wall near the retiring room.

The staff in the retiring room had given her some torn sheets and towels. A few female staff members also helped her defecate and, once or twice a week, gave her a soap-bath and changed her clothes. Stealthily, they would include her clothing in the bundle of sheets and towels from the retiring room that were sent to the laundry for washing. That way, she would have clean clothes to wear.

When I had asked Nutan about her growing up and living on the platform, she had said, 'It was very different from here. This place is very boring, that place is full of people; there were trains coming and going, noise and activity. I didn't know how time passed. It actually flew.'

'Where did you get your food from?' I had asked.

'Oh, there was a lot of food. I got some from the food court and the vendors. Some I picked up from the vendors when they were not looking, some I stole from the passengers. And some, of course, came from the garbage heaps,' she had replied nonchalantly.

Nutan had lived on platform number six all her life. That was the only kind of existence she knew. I remember being awed by an unmistakeable look of longing in her eyes when she spoke about the platform, her home.

While growing up, children thrown on these platforms would generally visit other platforms in search for food, money or company. One girl named Kiran was visiting platform six when she happened to spot Nutan and developed an instant liking to her. She took Nutan under her wing and moved to platform six the next day. She even found herself a place to sleep under a wooden bench near the retiring room.

In fact, it was Kiran who had named her Nutan. One day, she heard a woman passenger call her daughter by this name and liked the sound of it. So, she asked that lady what it meant. The woman replied that it meant a new thing, something that was fresh and unspoilt. Then, the woman asked her what her name was and Kiran told her. The woman told Kiran that her name meant the first rays of the morning sun. That day, Kiran had wondered who had kept this name for her. It must have been Mausi, she thought. Who else could it be?

During their numerous talks, Kiran told Nutan that she didn't remember anything of her life till she was about four years old. Everything was a blank before that time and she had no memories to recall. The only thing she remembered was a burning fever and a dark, fat woman pouring water on her head from a tap. Then, the woman took her to her shanty near the station where she kept her, fed her and even got her medicines. She also made Kiran do small household chores like sweeping the floor, getting water, etc. Kiran did these chores happily because the woman gave her food to eat and a place to sleep. She soon grew fond of the fat woman and started calling her Mausi.

When Kiran grew a little older, she asked Mausi how she found her. Mausi replied that she found her in a railway compartment when she was doing her 'night business'. She said that Kiran could have been abandoned or lost, she didn't know for sure, but she never informed the police because she wanted to keep her. Kiran didn't know what to make of it, she was just grateful that she had a full belly and a roof over her head.

Kiran, who was as inquisitive as any kid her age, had also asked Mausi how infants survived on the platform without their mother's milk. Mausi, by that time tired of her constant questions, had snapped back and said, 'Why? Is mother's milk only available in the house of *memsahibs,* you wretch? It is available in plenty on the roads and on platforms and in the colonies where the poor live. In fact, it is more readily available there than in those huge bungalows. There are many women—the beggars, daily wage labourers, prostitutes or street walkers—who happily feed these unwanted children in return of some money. You know, they also sell their milk to the hospitals.'

Kiran listened to her wide-eyed, trying to understand the ways of the world. Mausi laughed at the look of wonder on her face and said, 'But, you must have been fed by a prostitute!'

Even though, Kiran didn't understand what Mausi meant, but this narrative of Mausi did explain to her that she must have been fed by some woman, maybe even Mausi herself, and that's why she had big bones and a strong body. Later, sitting with Nutan, this conversation would play in her mind and she would realise that Nutan must have been fed by many beggar women on the platform too. The aged beggar woman who raised her initially must have given money to the younger ones on the platform to feed Nutan. The ways of the platform never ceased to amaze Kiran.

Over the course of her stay with Mausi, she observed that many men came to the shanty at night and left in the morning. On a number of occasions, Kiran had also seen men sleeping on the same bed as her Mausi. One night, Mausi casually asked her to sleep on the bed with a tall man who had a thick black beard. Mausi told Kiran that she was not feeling well so Kiran would have to do whatever she could to please him. Thus, that night, at the tender age of eight, Kiran was initiated into prostitution. In the morning, the man gave Kiran a 50 rupee note—something she had never held in her hands before. Mausi smiled and told her that she could buy anything that she liked from that money but, afterwards, whatever money she earned, she would have to give a share to Mausi. Kiran just stood there numb. She was hurt, more mentally than physically. The whole experience made her feel dirty, in some way.

Looking at Kiran's stoic expression, Mausi shook her head and spoke, 'See, everyone has to work for food and shelter. Consider this as your job. The less you think about the nitty-gritty of the whole thing, the happier you would be. Now, go and buy something pretty for yourself.'

Soon, Kiran started to earn all by herself. She stayed in the shanty with Mausi till she was 12 years old and then she was asked by a pimp named Ralim to join him at the small brothel he ran near the station, catering to the carnal needs of the porters, rickshaw pullers and daily wage labourers of all the platforms. Kiran, knowing that this would provide her with an opportunity to earn much more than what she managed with Mausi, willingly joined him.

Kiran lived with Ralim for almost three years and during that time, she contracted various venereal diseases. He would take her to the nearby government hospital and when she felt a little better, she would always go back to the trade. Maybe it was for the want of money or maybe there was some feeling of security which came from being in the company of other prostitutes and pimps. There was a kind of camaraderie and a weird bonding in this life of crime and degradation.

Sex workers, especially the ones who have grown up in this trade, don't find their world alien or morbid. They have not experienced any other world. The principles of the trade are simple and clear—the best ages to work in the trade are between 16 and 35 as this is the most active and productive time for women, sexually. Girls are formally initiated into the business and the most gifted girls, in terms of beauty and prowess, are the most successful and like in all other businesses, nothing succeeds better than success. Innumerable support services thrive around the trade—procuring clients, housing and maintenance, apparel and cosmetics and even medical services. Red-light areas are self-contained townships; they are power centres governed by successful prostitutes and the underworld who use them as nexus between their other notorious businesses. The police and the politicians themselves provide support and perpetuate their crime. This is a very real world. We don't like it, so we denounce it and attack it. But, people who are inextricably involved in this world live well and find their happiness within it. From the outside, we assume that they are not happy, because we think how can one be happy living such a life? But, they don't know any other life. In fact, they would find our lives highly pretentious, devoid of action and pleasure, perhaps even facetious.

If there is more fragility and less security, more loneliness and more fear in their lives, there is also romance and emotion, relationships and commitments. Even though these relationships might be largely transactional, but, the people belonging to this world will not easily opt for a different life.

Kiran, who had also grown up seeing Mausi service her many clients, adjusted comfortably to this new world. She was matured for her years; she had also developed physically because of the work she was involved in. She ate well to keep the curves and contours of her body in correct shape because she knew that in her trade, her body was all that mattered. That is why when she found out that she was pregnant, she quickly aborted, twice, and learnt how to use contraceptives. After her numerous trips to the hospital, she also picked up a basic understanding of AIDS. After that, she refused to have intercourse without contraceptives and her clients readily agreed because her skills of 'customer servicing' and pleasure-giving were widely known on the platforms as well as all around the railway station. Kiran was an expert at providing all sorts of entertainment to her clients which earned her more money than the other girls. In fact, some pimps from outside the city had even come inquiring about her and whether she was willing to travel for additional clientele. Hence, Ralim started keeping a close watch on her and ensured that she was kept away from the roving eyes of other pimps.

After some years, Ralim allowed her to spend time on the platforms because that way she could interact with porters, passengers and other vendors and maximise his business. Kiran carried on her trade in abandoned railway coaches or in a two-roomed space which Ralim had rented out in the lane just outside the railway station. But, slowly Kiran started liking sleeping on the platform as it allowed her the chance to be away from the claustrophobic one-roomed or two-roomed shanties which the other girls shared with Ralim. It gave her some open space and more fresh air to breathe.

It was during one of those days when she was looking for customers that Kiran spotted Nutan, a sprightly girl, of maybe four, with the hair the colour of the sun. Kiran had a scheming mind, she hadn't come this far in her profession by just being beautiful. One night, as she lay under the wooden bench with Nutan, she decided that she would look after Nutan till she was 8 years old and then initiate her into the trade like she had been. And, Nutan would also help her with the cleaning, cooking, and washing in the little shanties where she conducted her 'night-business'.

From the next day, Kiran took charge of Nutan in all respects. She would bathe her in the washroom of the retiring room and even cleaned her up after her bowel movements in the morning. She also commenced Nutan's toilet training and vehemently told her not to urinate in her undergarments. Nutan, like an obedient child, would accompany Kiran on her morning rounds of the platform as well as of the areas outside the station. While Kiran would disappear in abandoned bogies or slink into dark corners with different men, Nutan would patiently wait for her, biding her time by playing with the trash all around her. Kiran genuinely felt that since Nutan had joined her, her work had increased manifold. Nutan was the new lucky charm in her life.

Kiran and Nutan adjusted well with each other. Kiran knew that the more she took care of Nutan, the better her growth would be and soon she could also start participating in the trade and begin earning. Kiran thought that if Nutan is as lucky as her, once initiated into the trade, she would quickly pick up the ropes. Kiran had understood that once Nutan entered the trade, it would be difficult to extricate herself as the racket operated systemically through a network that started with the pimp, went around the police station and included the vendors and porters on the platforms and even shops and small private establishments outside the station. The tentacles of this entire system were strongly intertwined with other criminal activities.

Two years flew by and Nutan was now almost eight years old. However, Nutan was attractive and looked mature beyond her years. She could have been well over 10 as the beggar woman, who had claimed to raise her, wasn't sure. After spending time with Nutan, Kiran was in two minds about Nutan's early initiation into the trade. Kiran had realised that Nutan was a sensitive girl even though she came across as blunt and brazen. On numerous occasions, she had asked Kiran why she met so many different men, or let them come into their house and sleep with her. Kiran never knew what to answer. So, whenever there was a client at night, Kiran would ask Nutan to sleep over at another shanty or, if all the places were occupied, she would have her sleep in one corner of the bathroom. Kiran would leave a red light on in the bathroom and sitting under that red light, Nutan would, initially out of curiosity and later in anger, watch the entire episode play out before her.

Once, she asked Kiran why she did what she did. And just like how Mausi had explained to her, Kiran explained it to Nutan, 'It is just like a job, something I have to do so I can buy food and clothes, etc.'

Over time, Nutan became used to these nightly activities as well.

People who knew Nutan described her growing up with Kiran as a sort of apprenticeship before her initiation into the world of crime and violence. Nutan, on her part, had not seen any other life. Her entire world revolved around being street-smart, living on the railway platform, looking to procure food and other goodies and get by one more day. She also spent a number of hours with the porters, many of whom had grown fond of her. However, she was oblivious to the fact that many of those friendly porters, or *bhaiyas* as she called them, were keeping an eye on her for themselves and kept asking Kiran when she would organise Nutan's first night.

Seeing the restlessness of the men around Nutan, Kiran started planning. One day, Kiran took a round of the market which had shops selling sarees, ready-made blouses, petticoats, salwar-kurtas and ladies' undergarments. She identified all the good shops for women's wear. She also found shops which sold cheap cosmetics, ribbons, hair clips and hair bands. She wanted Nutan to look as beautiful as she possible could for her first night. That night, Nutan asked her about pickpockets and how they operated. She inquired if she should learn the skill and begin to pick pockets. Kiran, astounded by the conversation, forbade her from even thinking about picking pockets. Nutan had never seen Kiran so angry. Her eyes begin to pool with tears. Kiran with a sigh took Nutan's face in hands and whispered, 'You are meant for larger things, my child.'

Baddu—a member of the underworld real estate criminal gang which operated near the railway station—was also one of the many admirers of Nutan. Baddu was a well-built man of 26. He enjoyed wrestling and was a member of one or two wrestling *addas* near the station. He drank heavily, smoked *charas* and visited prostitutes regularly. He also shouldered the responsibility of his mother and two younger sisters willingly. He was waiting for his sisters to get married and had conveyed to his mother that he would only marry once they were settled.

He had first seen Nutan, as a little toddler, running at platform number six. Many times, porters and the other members of his group would take her outside the platform for a chocolate or a banana. On these occasions, Baddu would see this little girl with golden-brown curly hair and wheatish glowing skin with a defiant air about her. He liked her constant gibberish and would miss her if he didn't see her for long.

When he didn't see Nutan for many days, he inquired about her and found out that Nutan had been 'rescued' by the shelter home. That day, he vowed to bring her back. He had already developed a dislike for the team of the shelter home. According to him, they were encroaching on his rights as well as his trade and had no business picking up girls from the platform and taking them to the shelter. He suspected their motives and was convinced that in the garb of conducting education and music classes, the shelter home itself was involved in all kinds of illegal activities. Baddu, with the others of his gang, filed a case against the home saying that the shelter was allegedly engaged in prostitution. Soon, because of the case and lack of funds, the home closed down its shutters. Nutan was back where she belonged. As a result, Kiran also became friendly with Baddu even though he was a client of another sex worker.

It was a cold winter morning. The morning *azaan* was being recited from a mosque which was near the railway tracks. Baddu was a Hindu but he had many Muslim friends who would attend the morning prayers. He would accompany them to the gate of the mosque. The *dhabas* would open by 5.30 am and start serving tea. Baddu would leisurely sip his morning cup while his friends were inside. The *dhaba* owner and his helpers were Baddu's buddies since many years. He provided them security and protected them from the police, and so he could eat and drink anything from the *dhaba* for free.

That morning, Kiran, shivering because of the uncharacteristic cold, asked Nutan to get her a cup of tea from one of the *dhabas*. Nutan stepped out and realised that it was murky outside. The fog was coming down, thick and grey. The smoke from the chimneys was also adding to the bleakness of the morning. However, lit cigarettes and *beedis* could be spotted from faraway. Dogs had woken up and were expectantly wagging their tails while gathering at the roadside *dhabas* to eat the leftovers from the previous night.

Winter mornings near the railway station were considered omens of ill luck for many. Nutan, completely unaware of what was awaiting her, slowly approached the *dhaba* for tea. Baddu was leaning against an auto rickshaw parked near the *dhaba.* He was smoking a *beedi* and holding a steaming cup of tea when he saw Nutan walking towards the *dhaba.* He had been physically attracted to Nutan for a long time and decided that today was the day.

Walking along the left edge of the road, Baddu managed to creep behind Nutan. Without wasting a second, he leapt forward and caught her by her waist, twisting her towards him. Then, he whispered, urgently and aggressively, to walk with him quietly and not raise an alarm. She was shocked and did not utter a word in sheer fright. Baddu clutched her hand in his vice-like grip and began to walk fast. He instructed her to match his pace. Once they reached the crossing from where one lane led into one of the platforms, he asked her to walk in front and climb on to the first dark coach that was parked in the yard ahead. Nutan nodded and started walking.

After about five minutes, both Baddu and Nutan were standing inside a pitch-dark general coach. Baddu began to hurriedly disrobe her and ordered her to lie down on the floor. He told her that since he liked her he didn't want to hurt her or be rough with her. But, if she resisted, he would not hesitate to get what he wanted with force. Nutan, again, nodded mutely. After half an hour, Baddu left her in the coach and told her to be there the next day, at the same time.

Nutan was bleeding profusely, when she, with trembling hands, started to put back her clothes. She climbed out of the coach and started walking towards the *dhaba*. A beggar woman noticed her and whispered to her to cover herself as her kurta was soaked with blood. She gave her a torn stole which Nutan tied around her waist.

When Nutan returned after almost an hour with the cup of tea in her hands, Kiran was livid with anger. But, before she could say anything, Nutan showed her the blood-stained kurta. Kiran paused for a moment and said, 'Baddu did that, right?'

Nutan just nodded.

'I knew it,' she whispered. Even though she was annoyed with Baddu, she understood that it was pointless to get into any conflict with him as he was an integral part of the organised mafia. She swallowed her anger and said, 'Anyway, did you like it? Now, you are also initiated. Let's celebrate today. He won't share you with anyone else, you don't have a choice.'

Nutan trusted Kiran's wisdom and followed her advice blindly. She followed in Kiran's, whom she considered her mentor, footsteps. Soon, she became known in that area, and also beyond it, as one of the most attractive and skilled women available for the strong and the moneyed. She practised the trade with courage and finesse, and grew more attractive with time. She was the queen of all the platforms but platform six was solely hers as it was very close to her heart. Baddu became her pimp as well as her lover. Kiran gradually left her own clients and managed Nutan's money and other comforts.

5

Flames of Greed

Flames of untutored greed are hellish. They consume reason and logic and convert the heart into a cauldron of hatred. Samnabad, a fairly large village in the district of Ratanpur, Uttar Pradesh, a few kilometres north of the river Ganga was burnt to ashes during one of the most violent riots between two religious communities—the Hindus and the Muslims—almost a decade and a half ago. It was a horrific time and the after-effects were still visible on many faces in the village. The older men and women were badly impacted but the worst hit was the young generation, the hundreds of boys and girls who stayed in the village. Some survived but many didn't, succumbing to the physical and emotional wounds of the aftermath. It was one of the worst examples of human cruelty ever witnessed in that region.

A lot was written in the newspapers and a number of social and political analysts presented their erudite and wise explanations and reasons as to why and how the riots took place. They explored the major reasons behind the nightmarish incident and what made it subside. They even questioned the people who were involved and were to be largely blamed as well as those people who intervened to bring things back to normalcy. The analyses contained views on the roles played by the political parties, politicians, big and small businessmen, the coal and sugar mafia, their powerful dons and of course the centuries-old rivalry between Hinduism and Islam which, in all the complex intellectual analyses, was identified to be the main reason for the riots. They extrapolated that there was an immediate need to promote *bhaichara* between these two religious groups for a peaceful and sensible future.

Sahiba was not educated and therefore was unable to read the articles on the riots that continuously appeared in newspapers and magazines. However, she listened to the conversations taking place between the village elders, month after month, when they congregated under the banyan tree in the centre of the village, near the panchayat hall. Some said that the politicians were to blame, some blamed the sugar mafia and its powerful goons and others felt that these incidents kept happening every three to four years because of emotional and social tensions between the two religious communities.

Women hardly voiced their opinion which made it seem that they had no opinion to voice. As always, they suffered in silence because from their childhoods they had been told that good, decent women are seen, that too a little bit, but never heard.

Sahiba wondered why it was so difficult to see, understand, accept and say the truth. She was 35 years old now and when the incident took place, she was just 20; old enough to understand the truth but not its intricate intellectual dimensions. However, she knew the truth and didn't consider it worth her while to spend hours discussing it with the people of the village. Instead, the truth had prompted her to act and having done that, she had spent the following 15 years of her youth in jail serving a life imprisonment sentence. This is the story of Sahiba and the social and political archetypical rivalry between two religious communities in a nation where it has been festering, unchecked, for centuries.

*****

The houses of the Sharmas and the Mushtaqs were adjacent to each other. While one was a Hindu Brahmin family headed by

Madhusudan Sharma, the other was a Muslim one with Anwar Mushtaq at its head. Madhusudan and Anwar were very close friends and the families practically lived together. The houses had a boundary wall running along the inner courtyard which was low enough to allow members of both families to have conversations with each other and exchange delicious food. The children from both families could be seen running in and out of either house, and outsiders could hardly discern which child belonged to which family.

Anwar was the personal assistant of the chief secretary of the Ministry of Tribal Welfare. All the officials thought very highly of him and fondly addressed him as Anwar *Bhai*. He had served many ministers and all his seniors admired him for his honesty, his cheerful disposition and his obliging and positive attitude. There were five years left for his retirement, to which he was eagerly looking forward. He had plans to work, in his individual capacity, for the poor and the differently abled, especially women and children. He knew the tribal belt very well as, throughout his career, he had travelled a lot and was in touch with the community which the ministry served. He had struck personal and close relationships with village elders and members of a few well-known NGOs which worked tirelessly in that area. A number of them were keen to have him in their teams after he retired.

Anwar Mushtaq had brought up his children with liberal and democratic values. He encouraged his two sons and two daughters to study and obtain professional degrees. The elder son, Watan was almost 21 years old and the younger one Mehfuz was 19. Zubaida and Zahida were his very pretty twin daughters, who were still in school. His wife Noori was an extremely cultured and soft-spoken lady completely dedicated to the family, her husband and children. Watan had obtained a bachelor's degree in civil engineering and was applying for jobs in companies all over India. He had done well in his final examinations and was sure to get a good job. His father was also helping him by using his contacts in the government and in the corporate sector. Quite a few times, he had requested his father not to use his influence as far as he was concerned.

One evening, he finally told Anwar, '*Abba*, I would be happy if I got the job on my own merit. I know you are taking the route of *sifarish* because of your concern and love for me. But, I find it humiliating and it will make me lose my self confidence.'

Anwar looked at him with pride and said, 'No, no. I am not undervaluing your intelligence at all. But, we have to be realistic. So many well deserving boys are rejected because they have no one supporting them. I was only mentioning this route if there is a need. *Insha'Allah* I am confident that you will do well in your interviews.' Anwar was also uncomfortable with the thought that he might have to take help his son get a job. Like Watan, he disliked the *sifarish* culture prevalent everywhere but, he also knew the realities of life.

Mehfuz was studying for his graduation and aspired to qualify for the Indian Administrative Services. He was a bright boy and was also religiously inclined, tending to be a bit ritualistic and orthodox. He was close to his maternal uncles who were traditional and fanatic Muslims. Anwar hardly ever interacted with or visited his in-laws as he found the atmosphere in Noori's side of the family very oppressive.

Noori was keen to get her daughters married immediately after they completed school but Anwar insisted that they must be given the opportunity to attend college, like their brothers. He added that if they wanted to teach, he would encourage them to get a B.Ed degree so that even after marriage, they could work in a school. He believed that women should be able to stand on their feet and have the capacity to earn.

The Sharmas were not very well-off. Madhusudan Sharma eked out a very modest living through his work as a *pujari* of the nearby Ram Mandir. He also did *poojas* in the homes of people on special occasions like *Diwali*, during weddings and sometimes he offered prayers on behalf of families during a *katha*. His wife Kusum belonged to a family of *pandits* from a nearby village. They had two daughters, Madhumalti and Madhubala, and a son whom they had named Krishna Murari. They didn't have enough money to send the daughters to school and were managing their son's education by enrolling him in a government school.

Madhumalti or Malti, as she was called by all, was 15 years old and had been to school only for six months. Whenever she saw Zubaida and Zahida in their immaculate school uniforms in the morning, she would develop a lump in her throat and would commence on a self- pitying trip. She was friendly with both the girls and had managed to learn a little reading and writing from them. She could count and write up to a hundred and sign her own name. She was attached to her father but a little distant from her mother as Kusum would hardly speak with her, which she found rather surprising. Her mother, she felt, was more attached to her sister and her brother, of course, was the apple of her eye. The only conversation between her and her mother would be about work or related to household chores. She realised that she had ended up becoming a surrogate mother for her younger siblings and was gradually being loaded with more and more household responsibilities. So much so, that the entire burden of cooking and washing utensils had fallen on her shoulders. Kusum would chide her whenever there was a little delay in the preparation of meals or in the cleaning and washing tasks.

Malti had a beautiful figure, flawless skin and thick black hair. But, one day as she sat brushing and oiling her hair, her mother taunted her saying that girls of her age should be simple and not be concerned with their looks. As a result, she started neglecting herself completely.

Bala, as Madhubala was affectionately called, was her mother's favourite and extremely spoilt. She would talk back every time Malti asked her to do something and would not even lift a finger when it came to preparing the meals or helping in the kitchen.

Malti started avoiding her mother as well as her sister and believed that the most minimum interaction with them was best for her mental peace and happiness. She would wait for Madhusudan to return in the evenings and would cook something special for him like *pakodas* or a nice sweet *halwa*, or if nothing was available, she would fry peanuts and puffed rice and serve it to him as a snack with his evening tea. He would look at her lovingly as she sat next to him and asked him about his day. Madhusudan had a habit of lying down for an hour after his evening bath. Since his work needed a lot of walking, Malti would quietly slip into the room to massage his legs or oil his hair. Kusum resented Malti's closeness with her father and felt that Madhusudan neglected the other two children.

Watan had grown up into a cultured and a sober boy. He was sensitive and very courteous. He maintained extremely cordial relationships with everyone in the neighbourhood, especially with Madhusudan and his family. As he grew up, his visits to the Sharma house became less frequent as he respected the difference in their cultures and norms. He had also been noticing that Malti and Bala had started staying indoors. They would hardly be seen outside the house and barely in the corridor. He caught glimpses of the two girls now and then, but had not really seen them or interacted with them in a few years. Moreover, his engineering studies had taken him out of the village and, in the last four years, he had hardly spent any time in Samnabad. It was only now that he was spending time at home and with his family.

Watan had written almost five applications to different companies asking for a job. He decided to visit the post office so that he could mail the applications on time. He was aware that for every vacancy, there would be thousands of applications. Then, there was the political pressure and people pulling strings. This had become the common practice across the country. After posting the applications, he was returning home on his cycle through the narrow lane which led to his house when he saw Malti limping towards her home. He stopped and asked her what the matter was. Malti said that a couple of days back she was walking barefoot in the courtyard and had stepped on a sharp shard of broken glass which she hadn't noticed. There was profuse bleeding and she had to visit the doctor who had to take out bits of glass from under the skin. The doctor had given her an injection and some medicine. The pain however, was still persisting.

Watan brought her back home on his cycle. They spoke a little about their lives and he was struck by her beauty and dignity. He liked her presence. Throughout the day, Malti's face would sneak up in his mind and he thought that whenever he married, he would like to marry a girl like her. He remembered that he had heard very good things about Malti from his mother as well. Noori had praised her many times and had also mentioned that Malti appeared to be a bright girl who showed a keenness to learn, but because of the family's financial situation, she could never attend school and be formally educated. Malti's sense of responsibility, her dedication to her father and her culinary capabilities were also immensely appreciated by Noori. His mother had mentioned many times, in passing, that any family would be proud to have a daughter-in-law like Malti.

Since that day, whenever Watan saw Malti, he felt drawn towards her. When he discovered that Malti goes to the courtyard in the mornings to pick up the washed clothes, he made sure that he too would be on his side to catch a glimpse of her and exchange pleasantries. The frequency of these interactions kept on increasing. One day, he was delayed and noticed that Malti was waiting for him. It was then that he realised that Malti too looked forward to their meetings and had started liking him.

A couple of days later, around noon, Watan saw Malti walking in the courtyard, looking towards his house with a brass bowl in her hand. Out of curiosity, he came out to the courtyard and as soon as she saw him, she signalled to him to come closer. When he walked up to her, she handed over the bowl and said, shyly, 'Noori *chachi* had mentioned that you like paneer cooked with green peas. So, I prepared it for lunch. I just want you to have some of it.'

Watan thanked her and smiled. He stood there for a while staring at her beautiful face. He could see that she was shy and blushing, but looked very happy. Watan sat in the veranda and ate it all. As expected, it was delicious. He realised that he was growing very fond of her and maybe this was the beginning of a love that Malti, too, was reciprocating.

The following morning, he walked across to Malti's house on the pretext of returning the bowl. Seeing no one around, he whispered urgently, 'I would like to meet you somewhere quiet in the evening, perhaps in the small park to the left of our houses.'

Malti was about to ask him the reason for the meeting but before she could even utter a word, he moved back into his veranda. That evening, when they met, Watan said, 'I have been thinking about you a lot and always imagined to be with a girl like you. In fact, it will be wonderful if we think about a future together. I am sure we will be very happy.'

Malti looked at him lovingly and whispered, 'I feel the same way. I know that we'll be very happy together.'

Watan and Malti kept meeting a number of times in the following fortnight. Then, one evening, Watan told Malti that he had received an offer from a Delhi-based company and had to appear for an interview.

'I would have to leave for Delhi soon but the entire trip would take me about three days, after which I would be back in Samnabad and wait for the decision of the company,' he explained.

Then, he casually mentioned that he had discussed about his desire to marry her with his mother, who had asked him to wait till he got a good job.

'When the Delhi job is finalised, I would come and talk to your parents about our marriage,' he said in a matter of fact tone.

Malti was in a state of shock when she heard this. She was practically tongue-tied. Recovering quickly from the jolt, she gently reminded Watan about the difference in their religions, 'I don't see any possibility of my parents agreeing to this proposal easily.'

'I don't see any problem. Parents always want their daughters to marry into a family where they would be well looked-after and respected. On this count, I don't think your parents would have any problems with my family. They have seen me grow up and I am sure they like me as a person.'

Watan was optimistic about their marriage. He was sure that Sharma uncle wouldn't say no to him. He didn't smoke or drink, kept good company and was responsible. He was well behaved and courteous towards the village elders and the senior family members. Moreover, his mother and Kusum *chachi* were the best of friends and shared everything of importance with each other. He was sure that his mother must have told Kusum *chachi* fairly decent things about him. He had never befriended a girl or a woman and was not in the habit of visiting any place of ill repute.

'What is the issue then?' he asked Malti.

'You are Muslim and I am a Brahmin,' she replied.

'Malti, religion is a matter of faith and every human being has the right to decide who he will worship and how he would do so. Today, I might decide to change my faith and my parents, being the kind of people they are, would not object at all,' He said, full of positivity.

Malti listened to him quietly and said, 'You are absolutely correct in all the things that you have told me. However, my parents are not like your parents even though they are good friends. Moreover, the community that we belong to is that of priests and they are very conservative. They would not only object to our marriage but would also ostracise my family from the *samaj*. My extended family would also cut all ties with us.'

Watan asked her for a solution and about her feelings for him, 'Tell me Malti, are you willing to go through all these difficulties to be with me or are you considering marrying someone else to avoid facing the resistance and the challenge?'

Malti was quiet for a long while. Then, she said, 'Your proposal has taken me by surprise. I need time to think.'

Watan was a little disappointed by Malti's response. On reaching home, he thought more about what she had said and found it quite sensible. He decided that the best thing would be to wait for some time. He needed a job first and reach the position where he could shoulder the responsibility of a wife and running a home. He wanted to be like his father, with the same commitment for work, similar liberal values and dedication to the family and all others in the community.

*****

The good news came from Noori—Watan had been selected for a job by a large public sector engineering company in Delhi, and would be paid a fairly decent salary. He would be posted in Delhi for a few years and after that would be shifted to one of the locations where the company operated from. Anwar, seeing all his efforts and prayers bear fruition, was on top of the world, like any other father. He was sure that Watan would keep the flag of the family flying high. He also believed that

Watan, being a diligent and conscientious boy, would leave no stone unturned to establish himself in his job and build a clean and credible reputation in the company. Noori spent two days cooking Watan's favourite food and even sent some delicious vegetarian dishes for the Sharmas. However, she thought that the Sharmas were a bit hypocritical as far as not eating non-vegetarian food was concerned, 'They would not eat anything that was alive and moving but they would eat vegetables and fruit which also had life but, fortunately for them, didn't move or make noises.'

Also, Kusum would keep asking Noori for leftover fish bones that she would mix in the soil for her rose plants as roses absorbed them and blossomed more beautifully. She found these beliefs and their behaviour towards vegetarianism hugely pretentious. Noori could never have a discussion about this with Anwar because he believed in the saying—each to his own—and being judgmental was not one of the vices he wanted to imbibe. Noori believed that the best thing was to keep her views to herself as she was, as far as her husband and children were concerned, not erudite and wise enough. They had often told her that there was still time which she could utilise to her benefit by appearing privately for her matric examination and then, she could even decide to pursue further studies. They said a whole new world would unfold for her. She, however, thought that the world did not have enough tests to test her coping mechanisms. Noori was a worldly-wise woman.

Watan returned after three months from Delhi to celebrate Eid with the family. The Sharmas were invited for the celebration and both Madhusudan and Kusum looked very happy with Watan's achievement.

On the occasion of Eid and Watan's success, the Mustaqs gifted new clothes to the Sharmas. Malti and Bala looked beautiful in their *gharara-kameez* and the long *dupattas*, which were Eid gifts from Noori. Krishna also looked handsome in a beige *sherwani* and *churidar*. Kusum had received a beautiful *banarasi* half-cotton and half-silk saree in a lovely shade of mauve with gold, ochre and sap green embroidery. *Panditji* was wearing a steel grey *sherwani* and a white *churidar*, and looked very much a part of the family. Watan stood in a corner of the hall where the celebrations were being held, looking very handsome and confident. Malti deliberately kept away from him all night.

During the celebration, Madhusudan mentioned to Kusum that he wished Watan was a Hindu boy, so, he could have asked for his hand for Malti.

'It wouldn't even have mattered which caste he belonged to,' he said with a smile.

Kusum cut him short and chided him for thinking like that, 'I would have put my foot down. Malti will only marry a Brahmin boy.'

Madhusudan asked, irritated, 'And, how do you intend to pay the dowry that Brahmin families demand? Where will the money come from?'

'In that case, I would rather have them stay with us for the rest of their lives,' she said.

Madhusudan walked away from the room to avoid a heated argument and further unpleasantness. He knew that they had to participate in the festivities at Anwar *bhai*'s house and needed to be in a cheerful mood for their sake. He didn't know then that soon a 15-minute conversation was going to change everything between the two families.

Three days after Eid celebrations, the Mushtaqs decided to call on the Sharmas. It was past six in the evening when Mehfuz dropped in and told Kusum that his *abba* and *ammi* would like to meet them for a while. Kusum was a little surprised at this formality and told Mehfuz so. She also told Mehfuz that his parents could come over whenever they wanted as their house was always open to them. Mehfuz smiled and said that he would convey her message to them.

Anwar and Noori walked in an hour later carrying a box of sweets, a bunch of flowers and a set of salwar-kurta with a beautiful dupatta. Noori was also carrying a gold chain, four gold bangles and a delicate necklace in her bag. And, Anwar was carrying ₹10,000 in cash in an embellished envelope. This was to be the *muh dekhayi* to be given before they left. Both Anwar and Noori were beaming with happiness.

Anwar, after exchanging pleasantries, asked Noori to keep the stuff that they were carrying on the table in the room. He moved closer to Madhusudan and sat down. He held Madhusudan's hand in his, and said in a loving and respectful tone, 'This is a very happy day in my life. I have worked with honesty and have worked very hard. You know everything about me. I have not hidden a thing from you. Our families have been living together for almost 70 years now. Our forefathers lived like one big *kunba* and we carried forward the same emotion, values and tradition. You have seen Watan grow up and now he is settled in a good job and with the grace of God, has a bright future ahead. I have come to ask for your Malti's hand for my Watan. I believe they like each other. Watan shared this with his mother. We hope you and Kusum*ji* will agree and not disappoint us.'

Kusum got up and left the room in a hurry. Within a minute, all three of them could hear her sobbing and mumbling something. Noori didn't know how to respond to her and therefore kept sitting. Madhusudan, the good man that he was, kept holding Anwar's hand and said, 'Anwar *bhai,* I can't believe that Watan, who is such a handsome and talented boy, likes Malti who is so plain and uneducated. I am blessed to have neighbours like you. Watan is like my own son. I've admired him and I know his qualities of head and heart. Which father would not feel proud to marry his daughter to a boy like him?' He said and paused. He closed his eyes and said softly, 'However, you know that this marriage can't take place. I can't even marry her into another caste, ours is a different religion. I am sure there are hundreds of beautiful and talented Muslim girls from good families willing to marry Watan. And, I know it will not be easy to find good and well-settled boys for my daughters. But, still, I can't agree for this match. I hope you will understand and not take this in the wrong way.'

'Madhu, I knew you would react like this only. It is natural and this decision is certainly not easy. I also know that we will be scoffed at by our own families and not be supported by the community, and even by the people in the neighbouring villages. But, if we are happy, who are they to interfere in our decisions and happiness? This also concerns the happiness of our children. I can give you so many examples of very successful Hindu-Muslim marriages and it is a myth that their children have a tough time adjusting in the society and in getting social acceptance. The world is marching forward into the scientific era, Madhu. You are a man of God and He doesn't teach discrimination, hatred and prejudice. We have brought some things for the *shagun* so that things can be finalised today.'

Kusum came out of the room, her eyes swollen from crying, and anger and irritation written large and clear on her face. She said in a hostile tone, 'You know that these marriages are not welcome in our society; they are not even accepted. After all, we cannot cut off ourselves from our kith and kin. My husband will lose all his work. No one will call him for any *pooja-path* and we will be ostracised from his own family and community. My younger daughter will not find a boy in our caste and my son may not find a girl. We will end up on the road. No one will eat from our hands or even drink water offered by us, and I will be cut off from my family completely.'

She looked at Noori and said, 'You know the same thing will happen to you Noori *bhabhi* and to your children. What will happen to Zubaida, Zahida and Mehfuz? Have you even spoken to them about this because I know Mehfuz will not accept this alliance as he is a conservative boy and very close to his maternal uncles who are orthodox Muslims. How could you even entertain this suggestion from Watan? And why are you insisting on this? This marriage cannot take place. It's very clear to me.'

Noori's face turned crimson. Getting up from the chair, she asked Anwar to stop the conversation as it would lead to an unnecessary argument and was a complete waste of time. They both said goodbye to the Sharmas, picked up the things that they had brought and left. There was a heavy silence in the room and no one spoke for a long time. Malti and Bala laid out the dinner on the same table on which, moments before, the Mushtaqs had kept the stuff that they had brought for Malti. Kusum was seething with anger and was very annoyed with Malti. How dare she do this to them? It was all because of her father who had spoilt her by putting it in her head that she was stunningly beautiful and could marry into a well-off family. Bala and Krishna were not bothered with the events of the day. In fact, Krishna couldn't understand what the fuss was all about. One of his friends' brother had married a Muslim girl. There was a huge drama when he announced this to the family but in the end the family, his parents in particular, came forward and married him off to her.

Madhusudan looked very sad and slipped into a disconcerting silence. Kusum tried discussing the episode with him many times that evening but he wouldn't utter a single word. Instead, he looked at his daughter with great concern and sadness. Finally, not being able to control himself, he walked up to her, hugged her and asked her to accompany him for a short walk. As they walked out of the house, Kusum commented, 'This is all your doing *Panditji*. You have no time to tell the children what is good and bad, right and wrong. You only know how to read out the lessons from religious texts to others; you do not know how to apply it or teach them to your children. You do not have any time for your family. You are such a useless father and husband. This one episode can lead to a major disaster, not only for us but for so many people who live here in Samnabad. Remember that!'

Malti and her father walked along the small tributary that flowed into the Bain Ganga river, which was located a few hundred kilometres from Samnabad. Malti couldn't stop herself and started talking, 'I have hardly met him, father. There is no romance or physical relationship between me and Watan. We both respect each other and have affection for each other, that's it. But, I know that he will understand and not do anything that will bring pain or shame to you or our family. Please believe me. He is a decent man.'

Madhusudan's voice was choked with emotions and his eyes were moist with tears as he spoke with his darling daughter, 'Malti, I too like Watan immensely. However, this is too complicated a matter, my dear child. It won't be taken lightly by the family or the community in Samnabad or the surrounding villages, and neither in our Saryupari Brahmin *samaj*. We will be thrown out of the *samaj*. Apart from my work, which will stop for sure, it won't be possible for me to walk on the streets of Samnabad at all. I am sure your Anwar *chacha* and Noori *chachi* will understand and our relations will go back to normal very soon. Don't lose heart and don't blame yourself for anything. This is life and many things happen. I have immense love for Anwar *bhai* and his children. Perhaps more than what I have for my own brothers and sisters. There is nothing wrong in loving a human being. It is the best thing that happens and it's so beautiful and godly. These are superstitious social beliefs and since we have to live in this society, we have to adhere to them. I really feel helpless. But, you just be patient. Everything will sort itself out. Now, let's go home, your mother will be worried,' he said as he walked back with Malti, his arms around her shoulders.

*****

The Mushtaqs stopped visiting the Sharmas. Watan left for Delhi after a week to rejoin work and Mehfuz and the others got busy with their studies. There was a visible chasm and a certain kind of strain between both the families. It seemed as if they had lost the zeal or the need to feel joyful. Anwar looked lost and Madhusudan had a vacant expression in his eyes. Both Noori and Kusum could be heard snapping at the children frequently. Bala had become uncharacteristically quiet and was over-concerned about Malti. Whenever Malti took more than the usual time to return from the nearby grocery store, she would panic and become restless. Both the families were very unhappy and people in the neighbourhood also started noticing that they had become distant from each other.

Madhusudan's misery was also noticed by Roop Singh Chauhan, who was the richest farmer in the district. One afternoon, when Madhusudan was visiting Chauhan to pay the instalment of a small loan that he had taken from him, he asked, 'The entire village is talking about the growing distance between your family and Anwar *bhai*'s family. What's the matter? Your friendship was an example for the village and the entire district. We praised you and Anwar *bhai*, and the whole village believed that it was the triumph of love over all other things, including superstitions and religious differences. So, what has happened now? Tell me, you can share with me, what is the matter and I will be happy to address and sort out the problem.'

'Roop Singh*ji,* this is very kind of you. But, it is a very personal matter. I am sorry I can't share it. I am certain you can't do anything. In fact, you would agree and appreciate how both the families are handling it. We are not fighting at all, there is nothing to fight about. It has to be handled sensitively, and that is what we are trying to do,' said Madhusudan.

'There is nothing that you cannot share with someone you trust, Madhusudan. I believe that if you discuss and take help from others, you can solve a problem in the best way possible. Never mind, you don't need to tell me today. Any other time is good, if you feel like it,' saying this, Roop Singh took the money and went into his large and impressive house.

Since that fateful evening, Madhusudan hadn't been able to sleep. He had also lost his appetite and was slowly losing his interest in work as well. He kept watching Malti and found her silence and sadness unbearable.

'What if she is never happy with any other man? What if marriage with someone else would make her unhappy? How can I marry her to any other boy?' These thoughts kept him occupied throughout the day. He also noticed that Malti remained inside the house and had stopped going to the courtyard lest she was seen by the Mushtaqs.

Madhusudan was sure that she still thought about Watan. 'Who wouldn't, being the boy that he is? He is like a rock, sober and solid. What bad luck, that religion came between them and played havoc with the destinies of their children.'

Madhusudan realised that till this 'episode' hadn't happened, the thought of religion had never come up between the two families and now it had turned into a big ravine that they can't seem to cross.

*****

A couple of months later, Roop Singh announced the engagement of his elder daughter and invited the entire village for the celebrations. Both Kusum and Noori refrained from attending the function. The daughters stayed back as well; only the fathers and the sons from both the families graced the occasion.

Roop Singh was happy to see both Anwar and Madhusudan, and noticed that the wives and daughters stayed back, but did not comment on it.

Then, seeing the atmosphere of celebration all around him, Madhusudan broke down and decided to share everything with Roop Singh. Approaching him, during the course of the evening, he sought time for a meeting, the next day. Roop Singh nodded, curious to finally find out the reason for this sudden animosity.

*****

The next day, Madhusudan reached Roop Singh's *haveli* at the designated time. Without any preamble, he shared what all had transpired between his family and the Mushtaqs.

'It is not a simple matter, Madhu,' said Roop while sipping tea in his huge courtyard. 'However, it can be solved if it is handled well. It is actually about love and decency. It is about two families who have lived as one for so many years. It is actually the best thing that can happen to any family and our children, but social norms and beliefs cannot be ignored. After all, illegitimate children from Hindu fathers and Muslim mothers and vice-versa are alive and they have also a right to live in this world. What has happened between Watan and Malti is happening all over the world. The societal norms are becoming fragile and weak and will gradually give way to another set of rules and regulations.'

'I really don't know what to do and how to handle this. I also know that I just can't wish it away,' said Madhusudan.

'Do you want me to talk to Anwar? Maybe all three of us can meet and try to find a solution together. The assumption being that we want this to happen without disturbing our reputation in the community, our ties with our families, our job and the future of our other children who will suffer if there is a negative backlash,' said Roop Singh.

'Oh yes, you have put it so well! I know I can depend on you. I will do as you think is right,' saying this, Madhu rose and prepared to leave for his home as it was already dinner time.

Madhu felt a lot relieved as he walked towards his house with surer steps. He was impressed with Roop Singh who was a courageous and a forward-thinking man. He knew Roop Singh would take bold but sensible steps to sort out this situation. And, he had the charisma, reputation and the clout to talk the village, if not the entire district, into accepting his decision.

He asked Malti for food and called out to Bala and Krishna. After weeks, they all sat down for dinner, like old times, and had a happy meal. Kusum was sure that something had happened, but whether it was in their favour was not yet clear.

Mehfuz did not like the idea of this marriage as well. He was highly status-conscious and also believed in religious sanctity. He did not like mingling too closely with people from other communities. His maternal uncles, Rasool and Maqbool Siddique, were the landed gentry of Raipur Najibgarh, which was almost 200 kilometres from Samnabad. However, they had small businesses around Samnabad and that is how they had come to know about the Mushtaqs and had decided to marry their sister Noori into the family. Wealth wise, there was no comparison between the two families. The Siddiques were well-known amongst the political circles in that area. They were staunch supporters of the ruling party, which professed egalitarian beliefs and ideologies and was a strong champion of the Muslim community. Money and political connections had made them quite arrogant. They were keen that Noori's sons, Watan and Mehfuz, marry into their family and were certain that their daughters, who were pretty and educated, would make good brides for the two brothers.

Anwar kept a discrete distance from his two brothers-in-law and had hardly visited them in over two decades of his marriage with Noori. However, this lack of interaction had been noticed by the family and had created a lot of resentment. Noori's parents were not alive; she had a married sister Amina whose husband worked with Rasool on the farms as a manager on a monthly salary. Amina's children, a daughter and a son, were mediocre in their studies and were also quite plain-looking. The brothers were keen that their sons marry Zahida and Zubaida, who apart from being good looking, were educated and well-cultured. Anwar, on the other hand, had proclaimed many times that he would not encourage any marriage alliance between the children of the two families as it was out of the question. But, the brothers were positive that when time comes, they would be able to sway Anwar's decision in their favour.

*****

The next morning, Roop Singh sent a message to both Anwar and Madhusudan and asked to see them for a quiet and clandestine meeting in his farmhouse in the evening. The farmhouse was 20 kilometres away and the road leading from their homes to the farmhouse was full of potholes and broken tar. Since there was no other alternative, both Madhusudan and Anwar decided to go together on a tempo, which was not in a good condition, but this was the common means of transportation in the rural interiors of the state. They covered the distance in silence, only exchanging polite pleasantries.

The decided time for the meeting was four in the evening so that the three could meet over a cup of tea, and have the entire evening for conversation after which they could return home in time for dinner.

All three adhered to the time and Roop Singh asked his staff to organise tea and snacks as they made themselves comfortable on the lawn at the back of the farmhouse. The lawn was quite uniquely planned. It was on a strip of undulated land and gave the impression of being situated on a hill. Right in front of it, about a hundred metres away, was a patch with teak and fir trees and a shallow but turbulent rivulet flowed through them. The rivulet never dried up and people claimed that its source was a sulphur spring up in the forest. Roop Singh knew that both Anwar and Madhu were admiring his farm and the garden; this thought made him feel very proud of himself. With a confident air, he opened the conversation and said, 'I have been thinking about what Madhu confided in me last evening. I would like to repeat what I have already shared with Madhu, that this is not a simple problem. It is rather complex with many ramifications and some pretty serious consequences for the children, the two families and for the entire community of our village. We have to be very calm and handle this with a lot of maturity. The sooner it is managed, the better it would be for all of us.'

'Yes, I agree with you Roop*ji*,' said Madhu and turned to Anwar to hear what he had to say.

Anwar avoided looking at Madhu, who understood that he and his family were still deeply hurt by what had happened that day. Anwar addressed Roop Singh and said, 'I really don't know what to say. For me, my wife and for Watan, this has become a closed chapter. We have accepted the verdict of the Sharmas and we are prepared to forget the entire thing and move on. A number of things, over which we don't have any control keep happening in life, and this was one such thing. It is behind us now. Yes, the relations between our families are strained but, relations break even between real brothers. We have accepted that too.'

'Anwar, you and your wife and your other children might have moved on but I am not sure if Watan and Malti have. I don't know whether they will truly be happy if they get married to someone else. Let's face the truth. Are we, as parents, prepared for this eventuality? On the other hand, do we have the courage and the conviction to support this marriage and also make our most honest and best efforts to win over our families and the community in favour of the decision of marrying them? This to my mind is the challenge,' said Roop Singh.

Madhu and Anwar looked baffled and perplexed. Turning to Roop Singh, they asked him for his views on how to handle this in the best possible way. The three men discussed the pros and cons of the situation and finally, thinking only about their children's happiness, they decided to get Watan and Malti married. They credited Roop Singh for solving their dilemma and said that they had complete faith in him. They agreed to follow his advice and counsel every step of the way.

The wives didn't appear to be as happy as the fathers when they heard about the impending marriage of their respective children. Kusum was more agitated than Noori. She foresaw the trouble that this alliance would bring to her family and didn't trust the capability of her husband in managing complex situations and relationships. Noori, on the other hand, saw this as a form of a minor victory with the Sharmas taking back their words. There was no overt reaction from either Watan or Malti. Mehfuz was visibly annoyed and told Anwar that instead of taking Roop Singh's advice he should have met Rasool and Maqbool instead as they would have told him what the actual reality was and how difficult or easy would such a situation be later. He also told Anwar that he had decided to leave for Najibgarh to meet his maternal uncles and take their counsel. According to him, this was the commencement of one of the worst troubles for the family the aftermath of which, at present, they were not capable of visualising. Anwar, warning Mehfuz not to leave for Najibgarh, said that this was their internal family matter and he didn't need any outside person's 'wise' counsel to worsen the situation. Mehfuz told him that he would be surprised to see how soon this matter escalates into a family and a community complication.

Anwar and Madhu both waited for a word from Roop Singh. Anwar was busy organising various meetings for the minister while Madhu's *pooja* work had entered into a busy phase as Ram Navami *poojas* were round the corner. However, the uncertainty and stress related with their decision was clearly visible on their faces. A week had passed and still there was no word from Roop Singh. Then, on the evening before Ram Navami celebrations, Roop Singh sent a message to both Anwar and Madhu and asked them to meet him at the panchayat hall where he had also invited four senior members of the panchayat.

Roop Singh narrated the whole situation after which the members of the panchayat started asking them questions about the affair, how did it start and for how long it had been going on. At the mention of the word 'affair', Anwar lost his temper. He said, 'Why don't you understand that there was no "affair" between Watan and Malti? Yes, Watan likes her and he had proposed to her and she had said that she would be prepared to marry him provided the elders take up the matter and decided. They have not been secretly having an affair or meeting in the farms or under trees after dark. The alliance has been initiated by them but now it will be an arranged marriage with the consent of the parents and the family. Our decision will be final and binding. So, I would urge you to stop referring to this relationship as an "affair" immediately.'

'Oh yes yes, we see the point. We needed to understand and clarify our own thinking. See, it is easier to deal with a case of a romantic affair when the boy and girl elope to get married. We have dealt with such cases and later, when the children come back, it is us only who encourage the families from both sides to accept the marriage. But, this is a different case; it is more serious and complicated,' said one of the village elder.

Anwar retorted with annoyance, 'As I said before, there is no affair and no question of them eloping. It will be a marriage where both the families will participate happily and the girl will be brought into our family with great dignity and respect.'

'You tell us, Chowdhury, how to handle this in the best possible way. I respect your opinion and experience,' said Roop Singh.

Chowdhury who was one of the most senior panchayat members shared his thoughts, 'The simple truth is that all religions spring from a sense of reverence for the universe, nature and all creation. Behind this reverence, there is love which is believed to be the source of the universe. There is nothing more, nothing less. The solution for all human problems rests in different manifestations of love, be it sharing or respect, faith or empathy, trust or transparent communication. There is no freedom without love. Both are two sides of the same coin and are interchangeable. Wisdom, respect and spirituality lie in simply recognising this truth, the truth about love and peace. The complications in life all emanate from feelings that oppose love and peace. All the dramatic complications of life are borne out of the interplay of conflicts. We all get involved, some more and some less, and in the end, all we really need are peace and love. Struggle for power and wealth is played out from time to time through greed, till someone facilitates the emergence of love and peace in the situation. We have a similar situation in front us. But, if we really think about, it is all about love and peace. We have to show a lot of maturity and understand that it is all about the happiness of two children.'

'These two families have lived like one family despite the difference in their religion and culture. It is all a matter of human love, compassion and respect. This will be a great example for our village and district. In the coming years, we'll be proud about it,' said Roop Singh, choked with emotion.

All the panchayat members praised Roop Singh and Chowdhury for the mature advice that they had given to Anwar and Madhu. Surprisingly, not a single member objected or created trouble for the families. Everyone was empathetic as they saw the two families as role models for the village. They were also impressed with Watan and Malti and the maturity which they had exhibited during this trying time.

Anwar and Madhu along with Roop Singh held several meetings with the panchayat heads to chart out the course for the future. It was decided that Malti would be adopted by a well-off but childless Muslim family. Roop Singh found such a family who readily agreed. Madhu made sure that they knew that he was not giving his daughter up for adoption because of money. He reiterated that Malti would look after them with love and *sewa bhavna* but this process was necessary for her conversion to Islam and then the *nikah* ceremony for marriage. Anwar and Madhu had both agreed on a registered marriage before the *nikah*. They agreed unanimously that the bride and groom should move to Delhi after the wedding, for at least a year; after that, they could come to visit the parents. It was also decided that Malti would start living with her adoptive parents, Sikander and Nusrat Ali Davar, after the formalities were completed and all her wedding ceremonies would be performed in her new *maika* only. Post the *nikah* ceremony, she would always stay at the Mushtaqs and would not visit the Sharmas.

After finalising all the details, the panchayat heads convened a meeting of almost all the village elders and communicated the news and their detailed plans for the marriage of Watan and Malti. Many Muslims, Hindu-Brahmins and members from other Hindu castes were present at the meeting. For some time, there was an uncomfortable lull but, then there were voices of consent and appreciation. Only a few asked questions related to how easy or difficult it would be to sever ties with their daughter for the Sharmas. Madhu had tears rolling down his eyes and many members suddenly got up and surrounded him. They patted his back saying that the entire village would be supporting both the families for this most wise and courageous decision. The adoption, registry of the marriage and the *nikah* dates were announced. There was an expression of relief on the faces of Anwar and Madhu. Roop Singh looked genuinely happy.

Kusum was not in the favour of a *nikah* because she felt that a religious conversion and adoption was not at all necessary. She believed that they would lose their daughter forever. Madhu explained in detail the reason behind the adoption, 'This is the only way to remain in the community and prevent being ostracised. Once she is adopted by the Muslim family, she wouldn't have anything to do with us after the marriage. She won't be visiting us and Watan would also keep away. We would communicate to the people from the district and our relatives that we have severed ties with our daughter, son-in-law and the Mushtaqs. This would not only secure my work as a priest but your *chauka* would also remain uncontaminated if this approach was adopted and publicised.'

While Kusum had her reservations, Noori was happy with the plan. She anyway thought that the traditions in the Sharma household were quite hypocritical and this plan would prevent all those influences filtering into her home. Keeping them at arm's length was the best thing that could have happened. Their expenditure in the wedding would also go down with no dinners and ceremonies. A registration and a quiet *nikah* would serve the purpose. She had already organised the gifts for the bride and her own clothes were also almost ready. Watan and Malti could leave for Delhi immediately after the ceremony was over. It was pointless for them to stay back and become the target of gossip and speculation. She had already thought about a name for Malti. Initially, she had chosen the name Sahiba for her daughter but Anwar's mother had insisted on Zubaida. Now, *Allah* had given her another chance. She had decided that she would change Malti's name to Sahiba right after the *nikah*.

*****

Anwar was quite unhappy with Mehfuz's attitude throughout the small and nondescript wedding. He sulked and was visibly sullen and irritable. He kept telling his mother that he was extremely disappointed that Anwar had not invited his maternal uncles. In fact, Anwar had not invited any member of the extended family as advised by Roop Singh. It was enough that the village elders were informed by the panchayat and everyone understood how delicate and sensitive the situation was. The greatest worry of Kusum and Madhu was the possibility of Madhu losing work of *pooja-path* which sustained the family, financially. Therefore, it was decided to keep the wedding as simple as possible, without any publicity and fanfare. The more people knew, the more there were chances of gossip and unnecessary distortion of the facts and the truth.

Rasool and Maqbool were livid with anger when they came to know that the wedding had indeed taken place. When Mehfuz had told them about the alliance, they were sure that the Hindus and the Muslims of the area would not let that happen. But, apparently they were wrong. They had their eyes set on Watan for one of their daughters and knew that Watan was far more eligible as a prospective groom when compared to Mehfuz. They had kept a close track of his academic and professional progress and were satisfied and proud of his achievements. They had, with surety, discussed his prospective marriage with one of their daughters, in their social circles. Mehfuz was, in a way, the second choice.

There was a heaviness in the air in the dining hall when Mehfuz entered to join Rasool and Maqbool for dinner. He sensed that he was not really welcome and both his uncles were being formal by greeting him in an emotionless manner with just a curt nod of the head. There were no questions about the wedding. The silence was broken by one of the children requesting Mehfuz to join them for kite flying after lunch, and Maqbool's son mentioning that Mehfuz must see the new aquarium.

Mehfuz stayed on with his uncles and tried to pacify them. He told them that he was as unhappy with this development as they were and did not want to go back to his parents. Over time, his uncles began to trust him again and engaged him in their construction business. He was even sent to the site where a complex of small flats was being constructed. The family also had plans to construct a small shopping mall which would have great market potential because of the rising disposable income in that area. Mehfuz, after a fortnight, called up Noori and informed her of taking up this job with his uncles, and also that he had given his consent to be engaged to Rasool's elder daughter, Saira. He told his mother that he didn't have plans to return to Samnabad for at least a year and that his marriage was being planned for the month of December, which was just 45 days away. He didn't ask Noori to tell his father to travel to Najibgarh for the wedding. There was no question of obtaining Anwar's permission because Mehfuz was sure that he wouldn't agree to his decision, and he also didn't think he needed it. He and his father had never gotten along. Noori was not at all surprised and was half-expecting this to happen.

Rasool and Maqbool were happy with the way Mehfuz was picking up work. He was also learning the ropes of the sordid side of the real estate business and had an interest in financial management. Maqbool, who managed the family's money matters, praised Mehfuz's management skills in a meeting. They had already started viewing Mehfuz as an asset to the family and were happy at their decision of calling him over to Najibgarh and involving him in the family business.

Saira and Mehfuz got married in a grand style. The wedding functions were ostentatious; there was a loud and almost obscene display of their newly-acquired wealth. Anwar, Noori and the children were not present in the wedding. Their ties with the families of Rasool and Maqbool were finally broken for good. Noori and Anwar had lost their younger son; they were shattered and devastated. The refusal of Anwar to marry Zubaida and Zahida to Rasool and Maqbool's sons was the final straw. People's egos were hurt and Anwar's decision was taken as an indicator of his lack of respect for the family and for Noori's brothers, and as an act of condescension for their lack of education, class and status. Anwar found good grooms for Zahida and Zubaida from a reputed Muslim family of Aligarh. Both the sons-in-law were educated and government servants. Anwar and Noori were very happy with the marriages of both their daughters.

Soon after her wedding, Sahiba had won the hearts of all the people she met and interacted with. Her cooking became a hit among Watan's friends circle and his work colleagues. Sahiba ran a good home and was proving to be a caring wife. She was equally popular in Samnabad at her in-laws' house. Not only did Anwar and Noori shower praises and affection on her, the servants and staff of the house also liked her immensely. For Zahida and Zubaida, she was an epitome of virtues and they couldn't bear to hear a word against her from anyone, particularly Noori.

Sahiba was in her third month of pregnancy when Watan sent her to Samnabad to visit his parents. She was in her fifth month when the doctor confirmed that she was carrying twins and that everything was normal and safe. It was difficult for Sahiba to see her father from her veranda and not be able to walk across to the house where she had spent her childhood. Kusum behaved rather peculiarly; she refused to acknowledge her presence even when Sahiba was in the courtyard. Kusum had become rather paranoid and believed that Madhu would lose all his work related to *pooja-path* if she is seen interacting with her daughter. She had confined herself to the two rooms of her house and had stopped stepping out into the courtyard. In fact, after Sahiba's wedding, she had not spoken with Anwar, Noori or the children even once. Bala and Krishna also stayed indoors and were not seen outside the house except when they went to school or to the market. Madhu did, on many occasions, exchange pleasantries with Anwar and inquired about Watan and Sahiba. But, he also felt that their big happy family had now lost its togetherness and camaraderie.

Anwar and Noori became proud grandparents of two beautiful children, a boy and a girl. They named them Kabir and Tamanna. Many friends, relatives and colleagues, a lot of them Hindus, came to wish them and to give their blessings to the newborns. But, Madhu and Kusum still stayed away. Bala and Krishna expressed their desire to see their niece and nephew but they were severely admonished by Kusum after which the topic of seeing the babies was never raised in the household. Sahiba was heartbroken and often felt a strong desire to run across and hold her father tight and give him a peck on the cheek. She was not close to Kusum so knowing that she was well was enough. Sahiba had realised that Kusum was the kind of person who would always find flaws with anything and anyone. She had learnt not to be happy and nothing could be done about it. Sahiba thought that Kusum drew unhappiness, trouble and misery to herself continuously and had learnt to revel in it.

Watan and his parents decided that it would be best if Sahiba stayed on in Samnabad for at least a year. It would be easier to bring up the kids. Finding a good domestic help in Delhi was not easy and had also become extremely expensive. Sahiba felt depressed at the thought of staying away from Watan but he promised to visit her during the weekends and make up for lost time. They were adjusting very well as a couple and now with the responsibility of two children, their bond appeared to get stronger with every passing day.

While Sahiba's serene presence in the house had created an atmosphere of calmness, the arrival of Mehfuz brought in a lot of negativity and tension. He had decided to bring his bride Saira to Samnabad on the advice of his uncles who told him that he should maintain relationships with the family so that he doesn't lose out on his share of inheritance. Anwar was extremely distant with him and his bride. Noori was happy to see him because in many ways, Mehfuz was like Noori.

One evening, on the dinner table, Mehfuz proudly informed the family that he had plans to meet a few politicians of the ruling party as well as the opposition because Rasool and Maqbool were planning to start construction in and around Samnabad very soon, and that they were about to sign a contract with a big builder. Anwar didn't get involved in these discussions at all and decided to keep out of all affairs concerning Mehfuz. He found his brothers-in-law completely untrustworthy. On another occasion, Mehfuz mentioned that he had heard that Roop Singh was getting a ticket to contest the *Vidhan Sabha* elections from Samnabad constituency. He asked Anwar to find out whether the ticket can be given to Rasool because he was planning to expand his business in the area and a little political clout would help his personal stature and social standing. Anwar didn't respond to the question and without finishing his meal, left the dining area and went to his room. A little while later, Noori came into the room and told him that he was very rude with Mehfuz and that he was also being very unhelpful. Anwar replied, angrily, 'Kindly tell your favourite child not to ever ask me to do anything for his maternal uncles. I have nothing to do with them or anyone from your maternal side as you very well know. Your son took this decision to marry their daughter, he took a personal decision to work with them. Then, he decides to come here, to my house, with his bride without seeking my permission and now he is asking me to help his uncle get a political party membership and a ticket? I work for the ministers but I am not in a political party and neither do I have a say in their politics. I am certainly not interested in doing anything for your brothers. I will not entertain such conversations. Please ask him and his bride to leave the house as soon as possible.'

Noori was petrified for she had not seen Anwar so angry before. She quietly moved out of the room. The elections were a good three years away and she was sure that her brothers would figure something out if they were so keen on doing what they were planning.

Krishna did well in his examinations and expressed a desire to study further. Kusum was not happy at the prospect of Krishna studying further because of the rising prices of virtually everything and the difficulties that the family faced in making both ends meet. Madhu, however, encouraged him and told him that he should try for government scholarships. 'If these were the old days,' he thought, 'I could have requested Anwar *bhai* to help him obtain the right forms and send his applications to the right departments.'

Well, nothing could be done about it now and he was sure that Krishna could figure out a way of doing things on his own. Krishna had made up his mind to clear his graduation and then try for admission in a good college to obtain a degree in business management. He had many friends in school whose brothers, fathers and even sisters worked in decent companies. These families grew financially comfortable and lived well. Krishna was very fond of his father and wanted to give him a comfortable and a stress-free life when he started working.

Sahiba was engrossed in bringing up her children. It was a full-time job to look after the twins. Barring the minor cough and cold, and a little stomach ache during teething, both Kabir and Tamanna were growing up well and were good-looking toddlers. Noori and Anwar doted on them. Tamanna would not leave Noori for a minute and Kabir was his mother's son. Sahiba was a contented woman. Watan would come once in 10 or 12 days and spend all the time at home. He would also help Sahiba take the children for their routine check-ups. He would take care of all the bills of the household. He took good care of his parents and was also attached to his sisters. However, he had also stopped speaking about Mehfuz and his interests and life.

Mehfuz was doing very well and was helping his uncles in running their business. He had almost completely taken over the real estate business. His uncles only offered their advice or took large financial decisions. Mehfuz was an ambitious and an avaricious man and saw to it that he took more than a fair share of the profits for himself. After all, he was doing all the legwork. He had kept a number of vendors and dealers under his control who regularly gave him his commission. To be discrete about his extra earnings, he gave all this money to Saira who had various cupboards, shelves and hidden places to stack the cash. She also kept, on the sly, investing in gold, silver and diamond jewellery that she never wore.

Rasool and Maqbool began to frequent Samnabad in connection to their business and also because of their growing interest in that region's politics. A year had passed and they were unable to dislodge the candidature of Roop Singh as the *Vidhan Sabha* candidate of the ruling party from Samnabad. The ruling party was very strong and had worked hard in the state as well as the district and block levels. The opposition was on a weak wicket but the new leadership in the opposition was trying, with all its might, to win the forthcoming elections.

Noticing Rasool throwing a lot of money around, Anwar's boss, the minister, called him to his office and said, 'Anwar *Sahib* we hear that this Rasool Siddique from Najibgarh is clamouring for the *Vidhan Sabha* seat from Samnabad. We know that he is your brother-in-law and quite annoyed because you got your son married to the pandit's daughter instead of his daughter. Personally, I think you did the right thing. They don't seem to be good people. But now, they have started blaming you and that pandit for messing around with religious traditions, norms and sanctity and projecting Roop Singh as the main culprit in all this. In fact, I have heard many Hindu people say that they have kept quiet this long only because of your proximity with the ministers, otherwise the Hindus in this area would not have let it happen. Hindus were more annoyed with the adoption and the conversion of their pandit's daughter to Islam before the *nikah*.'

Anwar listened to the minister in silence and then said, 'Sir, almost four years have passed. Nothing has happened. No negative comment or repercussion has taken place till today. This is all petty politics of the opposition and my brothers-in-law are colluding for greed of power and authority, and are also throwing their money into the party. Naturally the party will take their side and spread this kind of gossip in favour of them and against me. I have had nothing to do with them since I got married and have visited my in-laws only twice in my entire married life.'

'No no, I understand. I am not blaming you, just cautioning you. You and your family have to be a little careful. I would suggest that you keep your distance from Roop Singh for a while.'

'Yes, Sir, as you say,' said Anwar and returned to his seat.

The twins had grown considerably in the three years that Sahiba stayed with Anwar and Noori. On a few occasions, Sahiba had taken the children to meet Watan and a number of times he had come to spend some time with them.

Finally, Watan was promoted and moved into a larger flat. His salary also permitted him to keep two full-time maids. Sahiba managed the cooking herself while the maids helped in looking after Kabir and Tamanna. Watan was doing very well at work and his travelling had also increased a lot. He didn't want the maids to stay back at night, especially while he was away. Times were not good and even with all the care taken and police verification gone through, there was no certainty about their background and connections. Watan consulted his parents and decided to move Sahiba back to Samnabad till his travelling curtailed a bit. He also planned to speak with his seniors for a more stable role, given the unusual situation of his family and the age of the kids. He was sure that the bosses would work out something.

The elections were drawing close and Rasool had managed a ticket through the opposition party to contest the Samnabad elections. Mehfuz was put in charge of the election campaign as he was familiar with the area and knew most of the people in the village, the blocks and the district. The area had a sizeable Muslim population and a large Hindu community represented by almost all the castes. There were a few Christian families and almost no Sikhs, Buddhists or Jains. In the interior forest belt, there were two distinct tribal groups who were known as *adivasis*. They were peace-loving and docile people, mainly forest worshippers, who had recently commenced agricultural practices and grew millet and rice which they used for their own consumption along with vegetables, fish and frogs.

There were rallies being held all over the district and Noori and Sahiba could see the campaign cars running across the streets with banners and pamphlets. Mehfuz was staying with his uncles who had hired a large bungalow on the outskirts of Samnabad. There was news all over the district that Mehfuz was using Sahiba and Watan's wedding to build up immense animosity amongst the Hindu community.

'How could Roop Singh, being a Hindu Thakur, and Madhusudan Sharma, being a Brahmin, arrange the marriage of a Hindu girl into the Muslims? There was definitely a conspiracy here and the transaction of big money,' he could be heard shouting. People began to talk openly about this and many in the ministry also conveyed this to Anwar.

One evening, when Anwar was returning from office, he saw a few people standing at the crossing in front of his house and talking about Madhu and how he had married his daughter into a Muslim family. Anwar stopped and asked them what the matter was. The men, asked him to leave, otherwise he would be forced to leave his house and flee from the village. Anwar realised that it was a Hindu crowd and recognised a few in the crowd belonging to the opposition party. A few uncouth ruffians also abused him. Anwar hurriedly ran inside, bolting the door securely. He called out to Noori and Sahiba and told them what had taken place at the crossing and cautioned them to remain indoors for the large part of the day and not step out of the house in the evenings. They could wait for him if they needed anything from the grocery shop.

Sahiba became careful with Kabir and Tamanna and didn't let them stay in the courtyard anymore. Kusum and her children had become almost invisible and were not seen at all. Madhu was riding his scooter one evening when he met Anwar. They stood on one side of the road below a *neem* tree and told each other how worried they were about the recent developments and the rising Hindu-Muslim animosity. They decided that their families had to be extra careful because they were being targeted as the main cause behind the rising tensions.

Madhu told Anwar how disappointed he was with Mehfuz and his role in this negativity and the impending conflict, 'Mehfuz would go to any extent to ensure that Rasool wins the elections and defeats Roop Singh. They have the advantage of money and all the construction workers are on their side. It is going to be a very nasty fight. However, even if Roop Singh won, Rasool and his brother would keep fanning the Hindu-Muslim issue till it takes a ghastly turn.'

Anwar was also very worried at this sudden turn of events. Madhu, after a pause, began tentatively, 'I also have a doubt whether Roop Singh had facilitated this wedding and influenced the panchayat to win a special stand between both the Hindu and the Muslim groups by projecting the ultimate secular image and establishing his non-aligned religious credentials in the district.'

Anwar replied quietly, 'If this is indeed true, this entire thing seems to be backfiring now with the opposition raking the Hindu religious sentiments and Rasool spearheading the Hindu-Muslim conflict.'

Both the men stood in silence for a long time, helpless in the face of impending disaster.

*****

Sahiba sat in the veranda waiting for Watan to arrive from Delhi. He always kept his word and tried his best to spend all the weekends with the family. It was tiring for him but seeing the kids, Sahiba and his parents gave him immense happiness. Sahiba had also grown very fond of Noori and Anwar, and thought that she was lucky to have entered their family as a daughter-in-law. She thanked God for the wonderful twins that He had gifted her. She prayed that Kabir became exactly like his grandfather and father when he grew up and was sure that with training from Anwar and Watan, he would imbibe good values. He was already showing signs of a sharp mind.

Watan got down from the auto rickshaw, paid off the driver and called for his mother. Noori came out and hugged him and then Anwar came and held him by the shoulders and led him inside the house. Watan looked at Sahiba and gave her a smile and a subtle wink which made Sahiba blush. Then, all four of them walked into the house, chatting and looking very happy. Watan walked into the twins' room and planted kisses on their faces. They were fast asleep and he didn't want to wake them up, so he tip-toed back into the living room. Sahiba, as always, had cooked something special knowing that Watan would be arriving by dinner time.

It was a dark and damp evening. Sahiba went into the kitchen to check if everything was in order for dinner. The children were fast asleep after their evening meal and the maid was cleaning up their room. Noori, Anwar and Watan were sitting in the living room discussing the issue of Mehfuz and the forthcoming elections. The behaviour of Mehfuz was a big cause of concern and Anwar was in half a mind to convey to him that even his visiting them in the future would not be welcome. He told Noori to pack up all his belongings so that they could be shifted to Najibgarh shortly. Noori looked disturbed and helpless, but didn't say anything.

Sahiba heard the sound of firecrackers and asked Manju, the maid, to see what the matter was. Manju ran out to the gate and came back in a minute. She said that there was a wedding procession on the road and the firecrackers were a part of the celebration. Anwar noted that firecrackers were a big menace and were known to have caused many accidents. The family sat down for dinner and were appreciating Sahiba's amazing chicken korma when a huge crowd gathered in front of their gate. They were shouting and calling out to Anwar, asking him to come out. Anwar immediately got up and walked towards the gate.

Watan told Noori and Sahiba to move into the bedroom where the children were and wiping his hand, he went out to join his father. Noori dragged Sahiba into the nearby bedroom, whispering, 'Manju is with the children, let's stay here.' The first round of firing hit Anwar on the left thigh and he collapsed to the ground. Noori screamed and ran out. A bullet hit her on the shoulder and she also fell to the floor. Watan saw the crowd rush into the house as he ran towards the room where the two children were fast asleep. Sahiba was still in the bedroom but she could see that both Noori and Anwar were injured badly and were not moving. There was a crowd of over a hundred men in their compound and a few had entered the house. Sahiba did not move from the bedroom as she knew that apart from killing her, they would also rape her and that no member from the crowd would save her.

The crowd also jumped over the boundary wall between their house and the Sharmas'. They entered the house of Madhusudan and Sahiba heard a round of quick firing. She knew that some of her family members would definitely be dead. She saw Krishna jump the wall and disappear in the dark. Then, she saw a few men dragging the bodies of her parents and dumping them in the courtyard.

Sahiba stood in the dark bedroom and did not move an inch. Manju crawled into the room from the kitchen door and slipped under the bed. Sahiba saw a rifle lying on the veranda. When the entire crowd had moved into her father's house, she ran and grabbed the rifle and stood behind a pillar. She saw Rasool and Mehfuz enter the house from the front gate. She fired from behind the pillar. Rasool died on the spot. The crowd ran back from her father's house and surrounded her. Mehfuz shouted and asked her to stop firing. The crowd stood still as Mehfuz walked towards Sahiba with a rifle in his hands and grabbed her by the shoulders. She struggled to free herself and fired another two rounds. Two men were killed on the spot. Sahiba didn't know who they were.

The crowd finally dispersed with the arrival of the police. Sahiba was taken by the police that night and kept in the Samnabad police station. She found out that Noori and Anwar had died on the spot. Madhusudan and Kusum had innumerable bullets in their bodies and would not survive. Krishna had fled and no one knew where he was. Bala was miraculously alive and was found hiding in the house. There was not a scratch on her body but mentally she was completely destroyed. Watan had died protecting the two twins but the children were not in the house. Their decomposing bodies were found, three days later, in a garbage heap about 500 yards from Anwar's house.

That night thousands had died in the riots in Samnabad. Both Hindu and Muslim families were murdered and butchered, and hundreds of children were dead. Bodies were strewn all over the streets in Samnabad and innumerable courtyards were blood-stained with the bodies of young girls who were raped, murdered and desecrated. People who were left alive didn't speak and had seemed to have lost their minds. The village was a graveyard and the politicians, builders, police and the administration had enough work on their hands to care to fix things. Mehfuz and Maqbool won the elections and the ruling party faced a miserable defeat. The police locked up Anwar's house and handed over the keys to Sahiba in her prison cell. Bala stayed with Manju in her house. The boundary wall that separated the houses of Anwar and Madhusudan had been completely broken down by the stampede on the night of 20 July, the day the riots took place.

Sahiba was released from jail after completing her term of 15 years; she was released five years earlier because of her excellent behaviour and her contribution to counselling women who were facing life imprisonment for murder charges. She learnt *durree* weaving in jail and contributed to the running of the kitchen and cooked regularly for the inmates. She had not wanted to be released but then government orders had to be executed. She had not shed a single tear in the last 15 years. She never discussed the riot or her family or the events in her life even once with anyone in jail. People in jail only knew that she was a victim of the Samnabad riots. No one had the courage to ask her for more details. There was a fierceness in her look that forbade people to venture near her. She didn't let anyone come close and no one dared to question her or ask her about her personal life. She attended the morning Hindu prayers and also did her *namaz* five times a day. She had posters of Ram, Sita, Shiva and Ganesh and also photographs of Mecca and Madina in her cell. She accompanied a Sikh convict to the Gurudwara for prayers and didn't discuss her religious beliefs.

Sahiba saw Bala after 15 years when she was released from the jail. Bala had thinned down and looked older than her years. Bala couldn't recognise Sahiba as all her hair had greyed. Sahiba hugged her and told her that now that she was back, she would take care of her. Manju continued working for them and had become very attached to Bala. Sahiba opened her house, the house where Anwar, Noori, Watan, the kids and she once lived. She had it cleaned up and donated a lot of stuff and retained the bare minimum. She ran her own kitchen and decided not to construct the courtyard boundary wall separating the houses.

Since meeting Bala, Krishna was always in Sahiba's thoughts but Bala never spoke about him once. One evening, Sahiba casually said to Bala, 'I hope Krishna is well wherever he is.'

Bala replied, 'I don't think about him. You should not also.'

Seeing the look of confusion on Sahiba's face, she added, 'If we think about him, he remains living and we continue thinking about him. The more we think, the more we analyse and then become frustrated. But, if we accept that he is dead, we can move on.'

Sahiba understood what Bala was saying. After all, she had done the same in jail.

Roop Singh kept looking after them. He had grown old and had decent and pious sons. He was a well-meaning man but could never make it in politics. He took a lot of care of Zubaida and Zahida whenever they visited Samnabad from Aligarh. Sahiba was the anchor for her sisters-in-law. Bala, Zubaida, Zahida and Manju were like her children. She had to live for them and see them well and happy. Zubaida was convinced that women like Sahiba were born once in several centuries—

women of steel who rise above narrow concerns, women of wisdom and deep intuitive understanding.

Whenever Sahiba heard the elders discussing the riots that took place 15 years ago between the Hindus and the Muslims, she often wondered what the analysis and the fuss was all about. The motives behind the riots were not difficult to comprehend. The riots were not because of the hatred between the two communities for religious sentiments and differences. Religions don't fight with each other, men do. And men don't fight for differences in their religions—they fight for power and wealth, social position and authority. They only use the façade of religion. It always boils down to a fight between a few men and religion is used as a cover to exploit other people for the greed of a few. No one has the desire or the courage to hate God. The flames that rise out of riots are never flames of religious hatred or the hatred for God, the flames are of greed.

6

The Professional

Shailaja was the youngest daughter of Ravindra Sinha and Rupali Sinha. The Sinhas had hoped to have a son and were slightly disappointed when they came to know that their third child was also a daughter. However, that feeling soon subsided and they rejoiced at the arrival of another Lakshmi.

Mr Sinha had retired as a senior director of a multinational bank and was now settled in Mumbai. Rupali Sinha had worked in an advertising agency for almost 25 years and had a very hectic career. She had always been socially ambitious and now, even after her retirement, could often be seen at the parties of leading businessmen and popular film stars. The oldest sister Simran was in her late 30s. She was a chartered accountant and was doing excellent in her chosen field. She was single and had no wish to marry. The middle child was named Sama. She was an architect and had moved to the Gulf recently with her husband and her two-year-old boy. Her husband was also an architect. Sama was around 30 years old and there was a good nine-year difference between Sama and Shailaja.

Shailaja, throughout her childhood, felt an undercurrent of being the unwanted third daughter. This feeling was more a result of the attitude of her relatives than her own parents. Her father doted on her but Rupali was a strict mother who did not want to spoil Shailaja. She grew up to be a disciplined young woman who took a lot of interest in the household chores. Their relatives found it quite surprising that in today's day and age when girls are more interested in academics and building careers, Shailaja took an interest in learning how to run an efficient home. The reason behind their bewilderment could be that we generally take our homes for granted and feel that not much is needed to run them. However, only a homemaker would know the effort it takes to make it look easy.

Ravindra Sinha was a homebody. He and Shailaja often teamed up to achieve minor renovations in the house. One day, Shailaja found a curtain, torn and eaten up by rats, in the storeroom of her grandmother's house in old Delhi. That evening, father and daughter cut pieces of the curtain that had some beautiful Chinese motifs and made a collage with them. Then, they put it in an elegant frame. It now adorns one of the side-walls of their living room and is a stunning piece of art admired by one and all. There were many small paintings or artefacts created by the father-daughter duo adorning the bathrooms, adding an exquisite touch to the space. Rupali, Sama and Simran always appreciated Ravindra and Shailaja for these small but heart-warming gestures.

In a country like India not many are lucky to have the opportunity to enter the precincts of revered institutes of learning such as the IITs or the IIMs, the esteemed institutes of business administration. Students who go there are certainly the ones favoured and chosen by destiny to attain professional acclaim in life. Shailaja seemed to be one of those chosen ones. Surprisingly, she did very well in her graduate examinations. She topped her batch even surpassing the expectations of her teachers and her family. Her parents were glowing with happiness and her mother was convinced that now Shailaja would easily get admission in the most reputed MBA college, which she did.

Shailaja's institute's campus was impressive and majestic. She couldn't believe that she would be spending two years of her life there. Most of the 50 acres of the campus' land was covered with trees and there was greenery all around. Huge *neem* trees were a common sight and the newly-sprouted *neem* leaves filled the campus with an unbelievably fresh aroma. There were a number of pathways in the campus lined with these trees on both the sides. Other common trees on the campus were the purple and mauve jacaranda, the flaming orange and red *gulmohar* and the bright yellow *amaltas*. The combination of these purple, mauve, orange, red and yellow colours put to shame any other artificial attempts to enhance the beauty of the campus.

Boys and girls lazed around on the undulating and inviting green lawns. Innocent romance buzzed in the air and, at times, there would also be a spark of intellectual brilliance that would pick up momentum and blossom into enviable professional capabilities. There were a number of small ponds all over the campus which lent a feeling of abundance and richness to the terrain. Water indeed has the marvellous quality of introducing the feeling of abundance wherever it flows. Some ponds had manicured beds of flowers and patches of green grass surrounding them. Others were encircled with seasonal flowers. Both types of floral arrangements had their own charm.

Shailaja spent a lot of time in the cafeteria on campus. The aroma of the freshly-brewed coffee was too tempting and then there were *idlis*, *dosas*, *vadas* and *sambar* for breakfast that she just couldn't resist. The queues formed early in the morning because no one wanted to risk the possibility of breakfast getting over. One morning, while waiting in line for breakfast, Shailaja made friends with three other students—Kirti Trehan, Deepak Saxena and Dhruv Vasan.

Dhruv had a brilliant track record and already had about 10 years of work experience before joining the MBA programme. He was an engineer from one of the IITs and had done exceptionally well at work, climbing the hierarchical ladder fast and becoming the president of a business vertical in his early 30s. The organisation he was associated with had sent him on a two-year sabbatical for this course and was bearing all the expenses. He also had very versatile tastes—he was a music buff and was completely immersed in North Indian classical music. He came from a humble background; his father retired as a senior clerk in a government office and his elder sister was married to a government officer and lived in Chennai. His father had been disappointed when Dhruv refused a government job after finishing his engineering degree. Dhruv's early and impulsive marriage to Manvi, while he was still pursuing his engineering studies, ended up in a nasty divorce. Manvi refused to let him go without a heavy monthly maintenance. It had been two years since his divorce but his father didn't leave a single opportunity to remind him about his inability to take wise and sensible life decisions. His mother had always been inconsequential in domestic matters as well as in his father's life. She was always busy doing household work for which she was never appreciated. His father found flaws in her cooking, her washing and in all her efforts to clean the house. Dhruv stopped thinking about her plight years ago to avoid the emotional pain.

On the other hand, Kirti was from a wealthy family and had a different kind of air about her. Having been brought up in a worldly wise family, Kirti could get her way in any situation such as shifting to the best room in the hostel. She was always served coffee and food in the cafeteria the fastest and in the best plates, and in seemingly large quantities with additional servings of coconut chutney. She was even given an extra-large mug of coffee for the price of a smaller one. The rest of the students used to wonder how Kirti managed all of this. Did she tip the staff heavily or was it just her charisma? She was a chartered accountant and had decided to complete her business management course to improve her career prospects. She had put in five years of work in a large multinational and had resigned from the company before joining the course.

Deepak was temperamentally the most pleasant of the three and had completed his master's degree in commerce. He belonged to a family of very successful lawyers but had decided not to join his father's legal business. Instead, he pursued his passion—painting. He was the only child of extremely proud parents who were ecstatic about his artistic inclinations and were amazed at the passion and hard work he had put behind his seven art exhibitions all across the country. These exhibitions were critically acclaimed and he had also managed to sell a number of his works at exorbitant prices. He had a streak of genius but, at times, got a little complacent about his art and was often erratic about completing artworks on time and meeting targets which galleries set for him. There was, however, an endearing quality about Deepak. From his first day on campus, he appeared to be drawn to Shailaja. For Shailaja, he was a fascinating combination of a sharp intellect and artistic talent.

The four of them fortunately were allotted rooms in the same hostel and their rooms were almost adjacent to each other. The two men were on the second floor and the women were on the first floor. All the four rooms came with balconies overlooking the lawns on the back-end side of the campus. There was a lot of natural light in the rooms and they were spacious and well-maintained. Kirti had managed to get the most spacious room with the largest balcony and the washroom was practically attached to her room. She had slyly put a lock on the washroom door and had cajoled the security guard to prevent other students from using it. Shailaja thought that this was smart but unfair. However, Kirti was the kind of a person for whom smart was never unfair; it was all about using your intellect and influence to get ahead of others. Since Shailaja also benefited from this arrangement and got to use the relatively clean washroom, she never complained.

The classes began in full force. While a few faculty members were really brilliant and made students want to attend their lectures, the others were bookish and made their classes a bit boring. Most students attended their classes to fulfil attendance requirements instead of gaining knowledge; they could be found completing other assignments, writing emails or simply going through their social media accounts.

Deepak and Shailaja would sometimes skip these classes and sit beside one of the ponds, Shailaja sipping coffee and Deepak smoking. On one such day, Deepak happened to ask Shailaja, 'What role would you like to work in? Would you opt for marketing or something else? And what kind of company would you like to work in?'

'Why are you suddenly asking this?' Shailaja responded.

'No reason, just out of curiosity,' replied Deepak.

'Oh, I haven't really thought about it. Maybe finance or HR. I am not bad with numbers and HR interests me,' said Shailaja.

'And, where would you like to work?' asked Deepak.

'Nowhere, I would just work at home,' said Shailaja with a wink and a mischievous smile.

'Oh come on, we all work at home! Seriously, what kind of work? Which company or what kind of company?' asked Deepak a little impatiently.

'Deepak, you are not listening. I want to work at home, be a homemaker,' she said, firmly. 'You've clearly not thought about this,' Deepak said dismissing her, 'Think about it and we can discuss it later. But, I do wish you would stop being so childish.'

Shailaja got up angrily and said, 'Deepak I am very serious about working in the house. In fact, I do not want to work anywhere else in my life. Actually, I don't see the need to find any other work as there is plenty to do in the house for me.'

Deepak gaped at her and couldn't believe his ears.

'And, I have given this a lot of thought. I have thought about this for the last six years and have even discussed it extensively with my father.'

This hit Deepak very hard. He got up, straightened his shirt and pullover and said, his voice tinged with irritation, 'In that case, you should have gotten married, raised a family and worked in the house. There was no need for you to get this business management degree. You have just taken away a seat from some deserving candidate who would have utilised the degree to obtain a livelihood for himself or herself, and also taken responsibility for his or her family.'

Then, he walked away, leaving behind a fuming Shailaja. Deepak couldn't concentrate on his classes that day. By late afternoon, he felt exhausted just thinking about what Shailaja had said. He couldn't understand how Shailaja could be so casual and mention that she would work at home instead of utilising this degree and seeking a job.

'How could she spoil the chances of someone else studying here, getting a job and an income opportunity? We, in India, have to be more responsible. We should not play around with the chances life gives us and the destinies of other young people, especially when the employment scenario in this country is so bleak for hundreds of young people,' he thought. He decided to have a chat with Shailaja after dinner and make her see his point of view.

The cafeteria during dinner was noisy and it was impossible to have a conversation amidst the loud voices, the din of utensils and the sounds from the whizzing Usha fan.

The whiffs of the steaming *kadhi* and rice, colourful *aloo-beans ki sabzi*, freshly-made tomato chutney and cucumber *raita* were truly appetising. The aroma was making everyone's mouth water and the students made a beeline for the tables which had this wonderful spread. Deepak and Shailaja decided to wait for the crowd to subside. Finding the right opportunity, he asked her whether she'd have some time after dinner to speak with him for a while. Shailaja looked a little sceptical but then, after hesitating for a few seconds, she agreed. She knew the kind of conversation Deepak wanted to have with her. She wondered why the thought of her not working outside the house was troubling him so much.

They decided to take a walk on the path leading towards the library. This was a popular path in the campus and was known for its lovely broad trees and a beautiful pond on one side. It had the stately and exquisitely-carved brick-red and sand coloured library building on the right.

Deepak and Shailaja sat on a bench under a huge *neem* tree. Deepak felt a little uncomfortable as he always had the mental image of the Indian educated woman as someone who wanted her own space and voice in the society; someone who wanted the right to pursue her professional and creative calling. Then, what was this young, modern woman talking about? He could not imagine an MBA-qualified, bright spark of a human being happily spending the rest of her life dusting, cooking and washing utensils in the house. He was sure that it was a sure-shot recipe for depression. But still, he decided to listen to her carefully and try to get her out of this mindset. He understood that this might not happen in a day and decided to continue trying for as long as it took. After all, it was for her own good.

'OK, so tell me about your plan to work,' Deepak asked a little tentatively.

Shailaja looked at him with a soft smile lingering around her lips, 'As I told you the other day, oh only yesterday actually, I have no plans to work anywhere else except in my house.'

'But why? Don't you think you'll be wasting your education? You could do something larger and more meaningful with your life,' Deepak urged. He sounded desperate yet genuine.

Shailaja said, 'I would be doing something meaningful with my life. I would be present, looking after my children, my husband and my parents.'

'But, why do you have to be present in the home all the time? I mean, physically present. You can look after your family members even when you are out of your home for a few hours every day. I don't understand this logic. I really don't understand how you can run your home better with an MBA degree.'

Deepak saw Shailaja look a little disturbed and hesitant. She mumbled that it was getting late and they could have this conversation some other day.

'Oh come one, since we have got down to it, you might as well spend a little more time and explain your logic to me. This is really intriguing for me,' he said.

Seeing Deepak's confusion and desperation, Shailaja started to describe an incident that led to this decision.

*****

Shailaja was 13 years old when the first incident took place. She had travelled to Mumbai to attend a wedding in the family. There was a big gathering of relatives, friends and a number of cousins who were meeting each other after years. It was a very happy occasion and all the girls and women were decked up in their finest sarees and jewellery. In the gathering, there was a lady who was not a relative but the wife of Shailaja's uncle's friend. It was this uncle's daughter who was getting married. This lady would join them for breakfast, stay throughout the day and leave after dinner. Shailaja noticed that the woman just kept sitting in the veranda, conversing with whoever was around or reading a magazine or just looking out at the beautiful lawns. This happened for two consecutive days after which Shailaja asked her aunt about the woman. Her aunt told Shailaja that she was her husband's junior colleague's wife and was there out of a sheer sense of duty, to see if there was anything she could help them with. Shailaja observed that her aunt was very casual about it and took the lady's presence for granted. The conversation ended there.

On the wedding day, the lady came in the morning before breakfast as usual. She hung around, throughout the day, without doing anything. Her husband, on the other hand, was busy organising things for the reception and Shailaja didn't see him speak to her even once.

The bride along with all the young cousins, including Shailaja, planned to visit the salon for their makeup and hairstyling. This conversation was held in the back veranda where the woman could also hear them. After a while, she came up to Shailaja and asked her whether she could also accompany them to the salon. But before that, she had to take a detour to her house for some work which would take only 15 minutes. Shailaja and her cousins agreed to take her to the salon and Shailaja struck a conversation with her in the car. She told Shailaja that her name was Shalu Dogra and she was married to Dharm Yudh Dogra who served under her uncle in the government. She had a nine-year-old daughter and a 17-year-old son. While her son was in a boarding school in Dehradun, the daughter stayed with her in Mumbai. Shalu worked full-time in an advertising agency and had taken leave for the wedding since her husband had said that there would be a lot of work for her during his boss' daughter's wedding. Shailaja noticed that Shalu was a beautiful lady, practically a stunner, but she had extremely bored and vacant eyes.

Shalu directed the driver to take a detour to her flat. It was not very far from the salon but in those five minutes that they took to get to her place, the women in the car had discussed various options—should they wait for her in the car, should they drop the bride to the salon first and then drop Shalu, should they all go to the salon and then Shalu can go to her home and so on. Shalu requested to be dropped first and looking at

Shailaja, she said, 'I would be grateful if you could come with me to my flat. It'd be nice because there are a number of things that have to be carried back to the bride's house.'

They all agreed and Shalu and Shailaja got down in front of her apartment building. In the lift, Shalu told her that her daughter was not well and was resting at the flat. On further inquiry, she said that her daughter was down with a bout of regular typhoid and was being treated by a very well-known doctor in Mumbai. They reached the flat and Shalu rang the bell. Pinky, Shalu's daughter opened the door. Shailaja was shocked to realise that she was the one who was sick! Shailaja looked around expecting to see more people who would be looking after the child. Shalu, noticing Shailaja looking around, said, 'Pinky is a self-sufficient child and is quite responsible about taking her medicines and maintaining the temperature chart.'

She asked Pinky about her fever and the child promptly replied that she had recorded her temperature twice and written the reading down in the chart. It was 103 in the morning and half an hour ago, it was 102. Shalu asked her whether she had had her juice, bread and biscuits. The child nodded. She looked exhausted and pale. She told her mother that the maid had come to give her a sponge bath and had cleaned up the house. Shalu kept throwing a volley of questions at her daughter and didn't even comprehend how difficult it was for the girl to respond because of the sheer fatigue that she had from the high fever. Shalu then went into her bedroom and emerged after 10 minutes, carrying two bags. One contained a present for the bride and the other had her change of clothes for the evening and her make-up kit. A few half-hearted kisses were exchanged between the mother and daughter, and then they left the house. Shailaja turned back to see that the girl dragged a stool from the kitchen, climbed onto it and bolted the door from inside.

They were on their way back to the salon and Shalu looked absolutely normal. She asked Shailaja what she was planning to wear that evening. She also discussed the hairstyle which she wanted to get done in the salon and described how it would go with the *gharara* and *kameez* that she had specially got stitched for the wedding. Shailaja's thoughts were still with Pinky and she just couldn't erase the image of her tired face and the helpless and sad expression in her eyes.

'I could not forget the incident for months and thanked God for giving me a mother who was so loving and caring. After the wedding, when I returned home and narrated the incident to my father, he said that people have their own way of bringing up their children. He explained that all mothers love their children and all have their own approach towards nurturing their child. I remember he said that I shouldn't be judgemental,' she said with a long sigh.

Deepak was stunned and asked softly, 'What happened to Pinky? I hope she was fine?'

'I kept receiving information about Shalu and her family. But, last year, I found out that Pinky had developed drug addiction and the family has taken her to some rehabilitation centre in America.'

Deepak nodded his head and put his arms around Shailaja, 'I understand how you might be feeling. But, your father is right. There is both good and bad in every decision and situation, and we must know how to balance out things. It is important to know where to draw a line and work out the best solution possible. Nothing in a situation is only black or white.'

Shailaja merely nodded. After a moment of admiring the beautiful night sky, both of them walked back to their rooms. That night, Deepak slept well. Even though Shailaja's lack of ambition bothered him but in his heart, he appreciated Shailaja for being the sensitive human being that she was.

*****

It rained incessantly that winter. Winter rains are refreshing as they help in reducing the dryness that is created by the cold winter breeze. Shailaja and her friends used to spend their lazy Sunday afternoons inside the hostel with mugs of coffee and endless plates of *pakodas* from the cafeteria. Kirti's equation with the staff made it possible for them to obtain all their meals as well as cleaning services in the rooms. What an advantage to have in a hostel situation! Kirti was a master organiser and all her batch mates were sure that her competence in getting things done would assure her a quick rise on the corporate ladder, irrespective of where she worked. In addition to the hostel and cafeteria staff, she also seemed to hold sway over the faculty, the warden of the hostel and the directors of the institute.

Shailaja was doing pretty well in her classes. She secured As in most subjects and the faculty had grown very fond of her. Many times in class, she had been openly appreciated for the quality of her writing, her analysis and interpretation capability.

Time flew by and the first year of the course was nearing completion. Deepak and Shailaja had spent a lot of time together this last year. They could be seen together studying in the library and taking after-dinner walks. They got to know each other quite closely; Deepak liked her sensitivity and simplicity and she admired Deepak's courage and decency. In fact, their batch also found their pairing quite sweet and most of the class was convinced that they would end up getting engaged after the final examinations got over.

One evening, while Shailaja was with him on one of their many after-dinner walks, Deepak asked her, 'Are you still adamant about not working anywhere but home?'

Shailaja smiled and responded, 'Absolutely, nowhere else. I have made up my mind and this decision will never change.'

'Why this rigidity? Placements will begin soon. What will you say to the placement committee and the faculty and the directors of the institute? Will you even appear for interviews?'

'No, I will just tell them that I am not interested in a job and I will be setting up my own business. The plan is all worked out and is very clear to me, there's nothing to hide. All the knowledge that I have gained here will be applied, on a daily basis, in home organisation. What most people don't realise is that a home is a complete organisation and needs to be managed well, tactically and strategically. This is what we learnt, didn't we? And, contingency plans,' she broke into a throaty laugh.

'Shailaja, on the basis of just one incident you should not define and structure your future. You might regret it later,' he said seriously.

'There was not just one isolated incident; there were many more.'

And with that, she began to relate another incident that had shaken her up.

*****

Many years ago, a young couple lived next door. They were good people, completely devoted to each other. The husband worked in a reputed multinational and his wife stayed at home. She complained to Shailaja whenever she met her, be it on the road or in the lift or on an evening walk, that how bored she was with her life and how desperately she wanted to work. This kept happening for nearly six months and then one day, she informed her that she had got a job and was joining in a week's time. She had also hired a maid to look after her three-year-old daughter. Fortunately, her husband's office was just two blocks away so he would be coming home for lunch and would be able to spend some time with their daughter in the afternoon. He could also drop into the house, from time to time, to look after her. Things were all set. Shailaja felt happy for her but wondered whether it was wise to leave such a young child with an unknown maid.

Shailaja didn't meet the lady after she joined work as her working hours were long and arduous. She came home just before dinner, dog-tired, and had no time for a walk or socialising with neighbours. One morning, Shailaja bumped into her in the lift. The woman complained about the long hours at work and how burnt out she felt at the end of the day. Shailaja also noticed the dark circles under her eyes. Looking at the woman and hearing her rant, she was convinced that some people have the habit of making themselves unhappy. They just can't be happy and her neighbour was one such person.

A couple of days later, Shailaja returned from school late one evening. She paid off the auto rickshaw driver and as she was walking towards her building, she noticed a huge crowd had gathered in the lobby in front of both the lifts. When she approached the lobby, she heard the wailing of a woman and saw her sitting on the floor with her back towards Shailaja. Getting closer, Shailaja discovered that it was her neighbour with her unconscious three-year-old daughter in her lap. She asked around and found that the woman was waiting for the ambulance to move the child to the nearby hospital.

Shailaja, along with her parents, spent that evening and the whole night in the hospital with her neighbours. When her parents left to get dinner and purchase medicines for the child, Shailaja came to know about the details of the incident.

That evening, when the lady had returned from office, she had found her daughter asleep which was unusual because she normally slept in the afternoon and was very playful in the evenings. She went to her room and tried to wake her up. There was no response from her. She realised that the child was unconscious. The other maids in the building finally spilled the beans. They told her that her maid ate all the food that was meant for the child. She drank the milk, ate the fruits, the eggs and even the Cerelac. The child was hardly given anything to eat the whole day. This was going on for at least three months. The child was declared to be suffering from a dangerous level of malnutrition and was in the hospital for 10 days. The maid was thrown out, the woman resigned from her job and decided to stay home.

Shailaja completed her story and looked at Deepak. He didn't know what to say. They walked back silently to their hostel rooms, said goodnight to each other and made plans to meet for breakfast the next day.

In the morning, when Shailaja opened the door to pick up the flask of tea which Kirti's 'friends' left outside their door on a daily basis, she saw an envelope with her name on it and wondered what it was. She couldn't recognise the handwriting and thought that it could be an invitation to the many events that kept happening in the campus. She picked up the envelope and put it inside her handbag, deciding to read it while going for breakfast.

As promised, Deepak met her on the road outside and they walked together to the cafeteria. They exchanged their schedules for the day and planned to meet at five in the evening for tea and snacks in the canteen behind the library. The canteen served wonderful tea and snacks on Friday evenings.

Shailaja had to spend a few hours in the library for some reference work. She obtained the materials and the books, found a place near one of the larger windows overlooking the lawn and sat down to finish her work. She opened her bag to take out her pen, when she saw the envelope. She had completely forgotten all about it since the morning. She opened the white sheet of paper and saw Deepak's signature at the bottom of the note.

Deepak had written that he would like to know her better and would like to spend some time with her so that he could tell her more about himself. If she agrees, he would be happy, at some stage, to discuss if they could also explore the possibility of settling down together. He thought that he had found someone whom he was ready to accept as a life partner. If it would be alright with her, he would like to speak to her and later talk to his parents and when the time comes, visit her home. If everything worked out, they could perhaps get engaged before the term is finished and get married immediately after. He did not believe in prolonging things and at the same time it had to be a sane, balanced and an informed decision. In the end, he mentioned that he loved her and admired her a lot.

Shailaja smiled at the practical and formal tone of the letter. So unlike his paintings, she thought. Even though the letter had come as a shock to her, the contents of the letter were not. She had known for a long time that Deepak would propose to her eventually. She had expected it to happen and had a feeling about this since the first time they had met. The feeling became stronger during their evening walks. Even though she had not given it any serious thought, the feeling was lingering in her mind for quite a while. And now, since it was in black and white, she knew she couldn't avoid it and that she would have to say something to Deepak about his proposal. But, she didn't know what to say. So, she decided to avoid meeting him for a day or two to sort out her feelings and her thoughts. In fact, she decided to skip her classes and visit Aunty Ritu's place for three days. It was a Friday, so she would have the weekend to figure out her feelings. She rushed back to her room, quickly packed a few clothes, and left in an auto rickshaw for the short journey to her aunt's place.

Shailaja found Aunty Ritu in a good and effervescent mood. Ritu was a freelance journalist who covered political events and had made a mark for herself in the media circles. She was always full of stories and Shailaja loved spending time with her because it always helped her to get an update on current affairs and major political stories. Ritu was also an astrology buff. She dabbled in it herself and kept consulting a number of astrologers in the city. Shailaja thought that it wouldn't be a bad idea to consult an astrologer herself, especially after reading Deepak's letter. The advice of the astrologer might even help her sort out her thoughts about the future.

Ritu's friend and astrologer, *Acharya* Giridhar Sharma, came to meet them the same evening. He asked Shailaja for the usual information required for drawing out her horoscope and then sat down to make the predictions. *Acharyaji*, as he was reverently called by Ritu, told Shailaja that she would be getting married within the next 10 months. She would have a happy married life and would be blessed with two children. He also told her that her husband would earn his bread and butter through art and would not have a regular job. She would not work in an office either but would definitely be engaged in a professional career. He predicted that she would be in good health but had to be careful about accidents, especially accidents related with fire.

'Your Saturn period is beginning in another eight months and during the seventh year of this Saturn period, you should be careful and avoid being near fire or loose electric wires,' he said.

Surprisingly, Shailaja's mother had also told her that there were indications of accidents from fire in her horoscope. She, after consulting with a number of astrologers, had mentioned that keeping a black dog in the house as a pet would mitigate the ill-effects of Saturn. Shailaja was a bit surprised with the similarity in the readings of the two astrologers. However, it also helped her take *Acharyaji's* predictions seriously. With her mind at peace, Shailaja enjoyed the weekend listening to her aunt's political stories and indulging in some delicious Rajasthani home-cooked food.

Once back at campus, Shailaja told her decision to Deepak. He was happy to know that it was not a definite 'no' from

Shailaja. They realised that there was a high possibility of their friendship turning into a happy marriage. They decided to spend more time together. Dhruv and Kirti also picked up on the vibes but reserved their comments for a later time, when Deepak and Shailaja would share the development openly with them.

*****

The placement committee, the faculty members and the directors were shocked to learn about Shailaja's decision to skip all the placement interviews and work from home. Her batch mates were also confused wondering whether Shailaja had decided not to work at all or if she wanted to start something of her own. Deepak advised her to not explain herself to anyone and let people interpret what they liked. After all, she was not answerable to the world.

But, Dhruv couldn't accept Shailaja's decision. He created a furore in the institute and made it a policy issue. He rallied support of other students, went up to the dean and the directors and submitted a recommendation that students who were not serious about using a professional degree after obtaining it, must not be given admission in a professional institute. The seats being limited, the non-serious students usurp the opportunities from those who could utilise the education to build meaningful careers, benefit organisations and also shoulder the financial responsibilities of their families. At first, Shailaja was shocked to see that the demonstration was led by Dhruv, whom she had always considered a good friend. However, on deeper thinking, she realised that Dhruv, coming from a humble background, was full of complexes and had found the perfect opportunity to give it back to the people who he considered to be privileged, albeit in the most venomous way possible. Shailaja and Dhruv's relationship became strained and they could never be friends again.

The placement committee diverted its attention to other students and accepted Shailaja's decision to not appear in the placement interviews. Deepak appeared for a number of interviews, some for good companies and some for companies that were mediocre. He finally said yes to a major event management firm which operated out of Mumbai. Shailaja was happy because he was happy.

Deepak, Kirti, Dhruv and Shailaja did very well in their final examinations. However, Shailaja scored the best amongst the four and received a number of trophies and awards during the convocation ceremony. All the parents were there to see their children receiving their degrees on the stage. Deepak and Shailaja's parents met and liked each other. They instinctively decided to get their children engaged the same day. Deepak and Shailaja exchanged rings that evening but decided to not announce their engagement in the campus. Shailaja was still carrying the hurt caused by Dhruv's behaviour and wanted to avoid any other gossip concerning her.

*****

Deepak and Shailaja had been married for three years. They found their perfect companions in each other. They had mutually agreed to not have children before five years and were enjoying their extended honeymoon period. Deepak worked in the event management company for a year but gave it up to concentrate on painting. It was indeed Shailaja and her ideas that inspired him and gave him the courage to pursue his passion. Shailaja took over the task of organising his exhibitions that went off exceptionally well. Shailaja also ran a fantastically efficient home which was also done up most elegantly. It looked perfect, right out of an interior design magazine. Shailaja kept very busy but there were times when she found herself being occupied but not meaningfully engaged. However, there was nothing much to complain about. She and Deepak had everything going for them.

One day, out of the blue, Deepak suggested Shailaja to join him on a work-related trip along with their jet-black Pomeranian.

'I don't know why exactly I am going or what I am hoping to bring back—maybe some fascinating motifs or some striking colour combinations or designs which I could use in my paintings. But, the idea of a road trip with you does seem exciting. What do you say?' he asked eagerly.

Looking for a break, Shailaja agreed wholeheartedly. During dinner, Deepak suggested that they also take Munni, their 18-year-old live-in maid, with them. She would also enjoy a break and they would have someone to care for their beloved Pomeranian.

So, in the next couple of days, the four of them set out for their 'impromptu' trip along the carpet-weaving belt of India. The journey was indeed fascinating. They saw the entire process of weaving and dyeing, met a few master weavers and were amazed at their knowledge of wool variety, colours and designs. They encouraged Deepak to innovate and urged him to come back and spend some time with them. Overall, it was an interesting trip and a satisfied Deepak decided to drive back home. He requested Shailaja to pack up and be ready to move. All four of them started the return journey early morning the following day. They had enough food to last them till the evening and they planned to make two major halts on the way—one to have coffee before noon and the other for lunch. If the weather was okay, they could also stop for tea somewhere.

They did exactly as they planned and after an interesting lunch of chicken *tikka kebabs* and *parathas*, they pushed on. Deepak played some old Hindi film songs and they drove on an average speed towards the *ghats* that separated the major towns from each other. They drove through the beautiful teak forests and followed the rivulets as they happily flowed towards their destination. Then, suddenly, Deepak stopped the car at a small *dhabha* and said that he felt like having tea and taking a short walk. The maid, the dog and Shailaja also got down from the car and Shailaja told the maid to take the dog for a short walk as he must be stiff from sitting in the car for so long.

With disposable cups of tea in their hands, they walked down a narrow lane. The scene in front of them was breathtakingly beautiful. There were two ponds, quite large in size, full of pink and lilac lotuses and the undulating terrain was covered with lush-green grass. It was cloudy and had become a little dark so, Shailaja told the maid to come back quickly as it might start raining soon.

The dog, finding his freedom, went berserk and ran towards the ponds. A stray dog appeared from nowhere and the two dogs started chasing one another, playfully. This went on for about 10 minutes and then something happened that shocked everyone. Without warning, lightning struck near the ponds. Shailaja let out a scream as she thought that the dog and the maid had been electrocuted. But then, she saw them running towards them. The maid told them that a tree, some patch of grass and the stray dog had burnt to a crisp. The trees and the shrubs in the surrounding area caught fire. All of them were badly shaken up. Deepak asked them to hurry and get back into the car. As soon as they reached the car, they sped away without looking back.

Shailaja couldn't sleep for days after the incident. She became very quiet and Deepak noticed it but decided not to talk about it. He too was very shaken up by the incident as he had witnessed lightning strike for the first time in his life. He had read about it many times but had never really visualised how it actually happened.

A few days later, Shailaja visited an astrologer who welcomed her in the small consultation room. The room was full of charts and at a corner, there was a desktop. The astrologer was in his early fifties; he was a tall strapping man, well-built and exuded positive energy. He asked Shailaja what he could do for her. Shailaja said that there were certain issues that had been bothering her for quite some time. The astrologer drew up her horoscope and to check its veracity, asked a few questions.

'Please tell me if, about a week ago, you witnessed an accident in which a living creature died because of burning... most probably, in an open space like a field, near a water body surrounded with trees and shrubs. This living creature could have been a cow, a buffalo or a dog. The chances of a dog dying are high.'

Shailaja almost collapsed in her chair and then quietly nodded her head.

The astrologer continued, 'You have been saved. You are going through your Saturn period. You have a black dog, your pet, who actually saved your life. I can see that you will have a long life and you will be involved in occult sciences. You will do very well and save many lives.'

Then, Shailaja narrated the story of her life. After listening to her, the astrologer said, 'You had to go to the institute so you could meet Deepak. The incidents that happened with you which influenced your decision to work from home were in preparation to take up this work, the occult sciences. This is not some worldly work yet it spans many *kaals* or time zones: the past, the present and the future. All are contained in every moment. Many people can't perceive it but, we can understand it through astrology. You have to understand this science, then practise it and also evolve through meditation and *tantra* to acquire exceptional skills. I cannot teach you. You must go to Pandit Mishra as he is waiting for you. I have already told him that someone will be coming to meet him. In fact, I had this conversation with him about two months back.' He gave a confident smile.

Stunned, Shailaja went and met Pandit Mishra.

'There is existencc on many levels of awareness. We live below the level of cognitive awareness and also on many levels above cognitive awareness. You have to understand these levels. I will teach you the science but, you have to teach yourself to be aware. No one else can do that for you. You can only practise astrology if you become aware,' Pandit Mishra explained in a calm and soothing manner.

Shailaja felt herself drawn towards the science; she felt as if she had finally found her life's purpose. Pandit Mishra proved to be an excellent mentor. After five years of rigorous study, training and meditation, he permitted Shailaja to sit in his consultation sessions. Initially, Deepak was worried for Shailaja. He didn't understand the occult field at all. However, he couldn't stop her. He slowly realised that he was not meant to do that. Shailaja kept helping Deepak in his exhibitions while working hard on herself and on the mathematics of astrology. After 15 years of intense work, with the blessings of Pandit Mishra, she commenced her independent practice from a consultation chamber at her home.

Deepak and their children were very happy and proud of her journey.

'So, that is what you meant by working from home,' he would often tease her. Shailaja, on her part, would just smile.

7

Dark Clouds Without Silver Linings

Ramsevanpur was a small village on the border of Uttar Pradesh, touching Madhya Pradesh on the south-west. When we went into the village, we had no clue about the history of the community and its economic situation. We didn't have an easy entry into the village. As we were driving on the road, which directly led to the village, we were stopped by a small group of men who inquired about our credentials and the purpose of our visit. We told them that we were researchers with an NGO, engaged by the social work department of a university, and had an appointment with the pradhan of the village, Yusuf Siraj, and a senior panchayat member, Ram Yadav, regarding a research project. Most of them were not satisfied with our responses and there was a look of general disbelief on their faces. They doubted every word we uttered. While we were trying to explain our research, a couple of tall, well-built men jumped into our jeep and said, rather aggressively, that they would take us to the village.

Yusuf Siraj welcomed us but Ram Yadav looked annoyed and irritated. Siraj had organised tea and some snacks for us. Manoj Mishra from our team reminded Siraj about the telephonic conversation we had had with him about 10 days ago and requested him to organise our meetings with the families. We were told that our first meeting would start only after dinner, around eight in the evening, and all the other meetings would be organised in the next two days after contacting and taking permission from the seniors of the families. We agreed readily as there was no room for discussion and disagreement.

Our team consisted of Manoj Mishra, Satya Pandit, Vinay Verma and me, Vijaylakshmi Rao. I belong to Warangal but I have lived in the north all my life and received my entire education in Lucknow. I speak fluent Hindi and have had the opportunity to travel extensively in Uttar Pradesh. I had visited Ramsevanpur earlier as well but it had been a short visit and I hadn't got a change to speak with anyone then.

We had a couple of hours to find a lodge where we would stay for at least the next three days.

'It should be a clean place with dining facilities because looking for dinner late at night would be very inconvenient,' I said.

Siraj agreed with me and suggested a few places. Fortunately, we found one which seemed to tick all the right boxes. After checking-in and washing up, we were ready for the meeting 15 minutes before its scheduled time. It was unanimously decided that only two people from our team would go, preferably a man and a woman. Satya and Vinay decided to stay back and spend more time with Siraj. Manoj and I sat in the jeep and drove towards the house of Latif Ali. Ram Yadav also accompanied us but he looked grumpy and disapproving and didn't speak a word while we drove.

Latif Ali had five children—two daughters and three sons. His daughters were married and the youngest child, a son, was only four years old. He had got married when he was 22 years old and the bride was barely 11. The girl stayed with her parents for another year and it was only when she reached puberty that she was sent to her in-laws' house to live with her husband. She bore Latif's first child before she turned 13 years old. Latif told us that most families in Ramsevanpur used to be large, but now there were nuclear families because no other relatives, apart from one's parents, stayed together in the same house, anymore. However, no family had less than five or six children. Most families owned land and managed to grow enough grains to feed themselves.

'The real problems emerge when money is needed for medical treatment or education of children or procurement of household items as well as clothes for the family. There is no question of savings. Who has the money to save? In fact, most families reel under the burden of debts and heavy interests they owe to money lenders,' he said, nonchalantly.

Latif's wife Saira came in with cups of tea. She was in a torn *salwar* and *kurta* and looked rather pale.

'Could I spend some time with your wife, alone?' I asked, a little tentatively.

'Why?' he asked, his eyebrows raised.

We had to explain to him, again, that our research project aimed to do a comparative assessment of village life in India and in other countries. However, this was not true, not at all. In fact, we had come to Ramsevanpur to find out why so many women died here during and after childbirth. Our objective was mainly to discover why this occurred and what preventive steps could be taken.

These deaths were an alarming issue for us, but somehow the villagers did not want to speak about this topic; they were quite reticent about broaching this subject. We were, however, determined to get to the bottom of this problem. Latif said yes, rather reluctantly, but cautioned me not to ask personal and sensitive questions. I assured him that I won't and that I was not visiting their family to pry into their private and personal matters.

Saira took me to a banyan tree which was a little far from the house. She seemed eager to talk to me and began the conversation in a hushed tone, making it obvious that she would not like anyone else to hear what she was about to say.

Saira started, softly, 'I belong to a good and well-to-do family. My father lives in a village which is about three hours by bus from here. He married me off to this man because of family pressure. Latif is related to us. He is the son of my father's younger sister. Through this marriage, my aunt was able to extract a lot of money from my grandmother and my father.'

'Did you have the opportunity to attend school before your marriage?' I asked.

'Attending school was out of the question because in my family there was a strict *purdah* system. The girls were not even encouraged to visit the neighbour's homes. The village school was quite far from my house so going there was impossible. Also, the school had male teachers for some subjects and my father, the elders in the family and even the village elders would not allow girls to attend schools with male teachers. Moreover, my marriage was being planned since I was only seven or eight years old,' Saira had tears in her eyes.

She paused for a while and then added, 'I was married to Latif when I was 11 years old. After my marriage, I had to observe even stricter *purdah* rules and more stringent social norms.'

She explained how most girls in her family and in the village, as well as in other nearby villages, went through similar problems in their lives. All her friends were married off at a young age and quite a few were dead.

'But, why are they dying?' I was curious.

'Women in our village and the neighbouring villages die at a very young age because they suffer from various diseases and no one does anything about it.'

I asked her age and she looked unsure. 'My first child, my daughter, was born when I was almost 13 years old. We married her off when she turned 13. And, within five or at the most seven years, she has had four children,' she mumbled.

She calculated something on her fingers and said, 'I should be around 33 or 34 years old. That's quite old. Look, I have also started greying.' She showed me a strand of grey hair which she had deftly covered with her stole.

I could see that Saira wanted to share much more with me. However, she was extremely frightened of her husband and other family members. She asked me to meet her around six the next morning near the school in the village as she goes there every day to drop her son.

We walked back inside the house. Manoj and I thanked her, her husband and other family members for their hospitality and drove back to the lodge. I must have been unusually quiet because Manoj asked me whether something was disturbing me. I didn't want to go into unnecessary details, therefore, I quickly said that I was thinking about the difficult life that these village women led.

Next morning, Saira looked somewhat anxious and hurriedly took me to a small green patch of land behind a building. It was a secluded place and sitting on the grass, she asked me to sit and began to speak.

'Whenever I conceived a child, Latif would take me to a hospital in the tehsil town called Seona for a check-up, usually in my third month. I had come to know the lady doctor quite well as I had been consulting her for almost 13 years. The doctor would take an x-ray by using some modern machine and on the same day she would tell Latif about her diagnosis. At times, she would suggest an abortion and only rarely would she allow me to go through the entire pregnancy. I think she used to find out whether I was carrying a boy or a girl. If it was a girl, she would immediately abort and let me carry the child only if it was a boy. Then, after a month or two of the abortion, I would conceive again.'

I tried to hide the horrified look on my face, but Saira was not looking at me. She was staring at the horizon, absentmindedly fiddling with grass.

'You know, I have gone through 11 abortions, sometimes even two or three in a year. Latif wants six sons. He had told me initially that he doesn't care if this took 10 years or more. He has plans to send two of his sons overseas to earn well and the rest to join him in his farming work or in the welding shop.'

Saira added that in most families, the attitude towards women was similar and some women, unable to take the strain of childbirth, would die on the operation table in the hospital in Seona or if the delivery was at home, they would die in the hands of a local nurse or midwife. Some women also died during the abortions. I couldn't believe my ears, 11 abortions and only five children who were alive! In total, Saira had had 16 pregnancies in the last 13–14 years of marriage.

As I walked back alone towards our lodge, I wondered whether this was true for other women in Ramsevanpur as well, like Saira had mentioned.

Manoj and I visited Bipin Bain's family that afternoon. Bipin belonged to the Bain tribe which had been living in and around Ramsevanpur for decades now; they cultivated land and hunted animals like deer, wild rabbits, cats and dogs for food. They usually hunted using a bow and arrow and the children were trained to use it from a very young age.

Men in the tribe were prone to drinking heavily, and as a result, their women were much more hard-working than the men. Each family had a number of children, most of them boys and the entire tribe had very few girls. They preferred having boys and the girl child was aborted by women because of pressure from their husbands and other male family members. The reason given was that the tribe needed boys to hunt animals.

The men were polygamous because of the lesser number of women in the tribe. Many times, one woman was 'shared' by three or four men. There were hardly any wedding rituals except that when a girl moved in with a man, they exchanged flower garlands and there was eating and merrymaking before dinner.

Women could also move from one man to another. However, they had to remember whose child they bore. If it was a girl child, it was readily aborted and only boys were allowed to grow in the mother's womb. When the woman was pregnant with a male foetus, she was looked after and was given nourishing food. The male child was fed by many women who were nursing at the same time as it was believed that mother's milk in large quantities and from different women would strengthen the baby boy.

Bipin's first wife bore him six children—three sons and three daughters who were aborted. After the last abortion, his wife fell sick and Bipin spent a lot of money on her medical treatment but her health didn't improve. One evening, she walked down to the medical store to buy medicines and while returning home, she was struck by a speeding truck and died on the spot. She was only 32 years old. She was the only daughter of her parents who had spent an enormous amount of money on her marriage.

When I was leaving Bipin's house, one elderly lady came and greeted me from an adjacent house. Looking at me with a cynical smile, she asked, 'Has this rogue told you his version of the story? That bloody liar. He had his first wife knocked down by that truck. It was nothing but a cold-blooded murder. No one dares to speak about this because of his political clout. He was tired of spending money on her medical treatment. And then, when she was no use sexually, he had her killed.'

With angry, burning eyes, she looked at me and slowly moved back inside the house.

I was in utter disbelief and shock. We had to meet another family that afternoon. But, I suggested that Vinay and Satya go this time so that Manoj and I were not over-exposed in the village. I was very disturbed after listening about Bipin's dark secret. I wondered whether this was also happening with other families and women. After hearing the woman talk about the alleged murder, I realised that the problem was much larger and more sinister than what we had visualised. There were too many dimensions to this problem. What could we do about this? Should we get involved at all? There could be some serious repercussions concerning our safety and security in the village. At that moment, I felt like leaving the village and giving up this project. This work seemed pointless, too complex for us to deal with.

I woke up in the morning with a heavy head as I was unable to sleep because of what I had heard the day before. Also, the mosquitoes didn't help the matter much. I had rubbed almost an entire tube of Odomos all over my body but it didn't seem to work at all.

As I opened the door to go into the veranda where we generally had our morning tea, I heard a lot of screaming and shouting. I noticed that a crowd had gathered on the driveway inside the lodge premises. Wondering what it was all about, I began to climb down the staircase. Gopal, the caretaker, stopped me halfway and asked me to go back to my room. When I pressed him to tell me the reason for the commotion, he told me the whole tale.

Apparently, Satya and Vinay had met the family of Ram Yadav the previous afternoon. Satya had asked Ram's wife as well as his brother's wife a few awkward questions. It seems that the latter had been looking for such an opportunity only. She sermonised on the negative effects of child marriage and giving birth to so many children. She also spoke about the health hazard of going in for repeated sonograms and the many illegal abortions that were forced upon these women. She also raised her voice against the atrocities that the men of Ramsevanpur were inflicting on women and the girls. Ram's father overhead the conversation and immediately spoke to his son. He was very angry with him for having permitted the women to speak to us.

Now, he was standing in the veranda and yelling at the top of his voice, 'We do not want you meeting our families anymore and having such irresponsible and instigating conversations. You must leave the village immediately.'

Saying this, Ram stormed back towards his house. The crowd, parroting Ram, was demanding that we vacate the lodge and leave the village as soon as possible.

Manoj contacted the head of our NGO who had great political connections. After an hour, Ram Yadav came to the lodge again but, his tone had changed drastically. This time, he requested us to stay back and complete our work. He added that we would receive all the support required from him, Yusuf Siraj and the families in the village. However, he pleaded that we refrain from asking too many sensitive questions, especially to the women who were mainly uneducated and housebound. According to him, they were not aware of what should or should not be said.

We told him that we would be careful. We stayed back in Ramsevanpur for another day and met three more families. However, the women just wouldn't say anything anymore. They kept repeating how wonderful their families were, how their children were being educated and how loving husbands they all had. Their stories had changed completely. Vinay, Manoj, Satya and I exchanged knowing glances and we left it at that. We had realised that there is no point staying back at the village as we would not get any other answer. Thus, we returned back to our base the same day. After a week, Satya submitted a report to our senior which didn't say much except that the government and the local administrative authorities should pay more attention to the health and well-being of women and the girl children of these villages. After that, all of us got busy with different projects and travelled to other places.

Since my return from Ramsevanpur, I felt disillusioned with what I was doing. My understanding and perspective of rural India had been severely jolted. I realised the interplay of vested interests and how crime, exploitation and the political system were all connected in a very complex nexus within the local administration. I saw the casualness with which human life and well-being was treated. For most of the families, there was no love lost between a husband and wife and she was a mere vehicle or a means for providing the family the boys that it aspired for. The women's lives were very cheap indeed.

I was very restless and after a month of returning, I told Manoj all the thoughts that had been disturbing me for over a month. Manoj warned me to keep away from Ramsevanpur as there were too many social complications in that area.

'You, singlehandedly, won't be able to do anything. The prevailing social attitudes towards family and women have taken very deep roots and can't be changed overnight. These social archetypes take centuries to fester and cast a long shadow on many generations,' he said, sounding concerned.

I was not happy with Manoj's advice but I could understand where he was coming from. I heeded his counsel and put the village and its women out of my mind. But, however hard I tried to keep myself busy and focus on other projects, my thoughts would always come back to the women and their plight. So, I finally decided to travel to the village again during my holidays and spend some time with the women. I especially looked forward to meeting Bipin's wife, the woman who had nothing much to say, and definitely Saira, who had shared a lot about her life.

I managed to get a room in the same lodge and with the help of Sarju, one of the staff members there, sent a message to Saira to meet me in the evening. After an hour Sarju returned and blurted out something I was absolutely not prepared to hear. He said, 'Madam, I went to Latif Ali's house and was informed by their nephew that Saira *baji* is no longer alive. She passed away after a fatal accident approximately four weeks ago. She was hit by a truck when she was returning from the market. There was no one else in the house because Latif *sahib* is getting married today to Saira *baji*'s younger sister.'

I didn't know what to make of this. Was it true? How could I establish the veracity of the information communicated by

Sarju? My head began to reel and my thoughts were racing in the most negative direction. I wanted my mind to stop thinking but it was impossible to control the chain of thoughts. Saira's face was swimming in front of my mind's eyes and I could hear her whisper about her abortions and all the other things she had shared with me that afternoon. How did this happen and why had this happened? There was definitely more to this and I could detect something really amiss.

I went back to my room, called Manoj and told him everything. He implored me to return as he was worried that I would end up in a serious and complicated situation.

'I know what you are saying is sensible and rational but you know me, I have to stay on in Ramsevanpur and figure out what's happening. I can't come back just yet,' I said before hanging up.

I found out that Latif would be returning with his new bride and other family members the next day. I decided to meet him and convey my greetings and best wishes.

Next day, as soon as Latif saw me at his house, he turned pale and jittery. He greeted me with a weak, unwelcoming smile. He hesitated slightly before introducing me to his bride Fatima. I thought that she had an uncanny resemblance to someone I had met earlier. After a few minutes I recollected the case of Jyoti Sharma, a young girl who was working with an NGO a few years earlier and had gone missing from a village in the same state. The case made big news and Jyoti's photograph was splashed in a number of newspapers. I found Fatima uncannily resembling Jyoti. However, I suppressed the thought as it could be a figment of my imagination as I didn't have the facts with me. Fatima looked down most of the time and didn't say a word in the 15 minutes that I spent in Latif's house. There was no mention of Saira even by Latif's mother who never looked me in the eye. The entire family appeared to be avoiding me and therefore the conversation about Saira didn't take place at all. Bipin also came to convey his best wishes to the couple and seeing me, walked up to me and greeted me warmly. He said, 'I thought you had completed your project in your previous visit to the village. What brings you back?'

'I still have to write out certain parts of the report in detail, especially the parts where we speak of various communities, how they stay together and have a strong social bond. I have come back to obtain some more information on this as it would make the report even more credible and readable,' I said.

He assured me that I could sit with him again and he would be happy to share any other information which would assist me in completing the report. We decided to meet after breakfast the next day.

Bipin and I sat in his veranda for our conversation. His wife Ramoli gave us tea and *pakodas* made out of different vegetables. The *pakodas* were quite nice and I enjoyed drinking the tea with them. Bipin even explained how their tribe uses the oil of a flower called *betula* which resembles an overgrown hibiscus and is very pungent.

Sipping tea, I told Bipin that I had to write out a few things in descriptive form and would appreciate meeting other families.

'Actually the women who met us a day before we left, spoke in generalities and I didn't obtain enough information on family traditions, the role of women in the family and the issues they and their families face in their day-to-day lives. I want to talk to them again.'

Bipin merely repeated everything that he had shared with us in our previous meeting. Then I asked him about Saira and he froze. For quite a while, he didn't say a word. I asked him again and he replied, his tone curt, 'There are certain things that are better left out of meetings and discussions. We have no business to interfere in the affairs of other people. As for Saira, I don't have any information about the way she died. I believe that she had an accident but many people have different versions to tell. It is dangerous to meddle with this as there are many people involved. Do you know that Latif has the support of some very powerful politicians? Women are not safe even in their families. Let's just leave it at that.'

He got up in a huff and left without saying Namaste. I thought he looked a little anxious after saying what he had said. It seemed as if the words had just spilled out of his mouth and now, he regretted it.

I was able to meet quite a few people during my one week's stay in Ramsevanpur. A number of them said the same thing which Bipin had said but some went into more details and were more vocal. It became obvious that it was not a simple accident; Saira was the victim of a pre-planned and cold-blooded murder. It was not surprising as quite a few women had died in similar circumstances.

I met Ram Yadav on my way to the lodge one evening. He stopped my jeep and said, 'Don't mess around with our affairs. Who has given you the authority to interfere in our family matters? Who are you to ask the people of this village how Saira died or why Sunil Kantua's wife passed away? You have no business here. Pack your bags and leave our village now.'

He was shaking with anger and after gesturing rudely, he sped away. My legs began to tremble with fear and disgust and I called Manoj as soon as I entered my room.

'Six women including Saira have died in more or less similar circumstances in the last two years in Ramsevanpur. All these women had got pregnant more than 10 times each and they had had innumerable abortions. I can see a trend—male children are nurtured and female foetuses are aborted after the third or fourth month,' I said. I didn't realise I was shaking. I gulped down some water and then spoke again, 'Apart from these "accidental" deaths, a number of women have died on the operation table during the process of abortion and no one is actually bothered. Women can go ahead and die in huge numbers after they have birthed boys for the family. It is considered their primary duty in addition to looking after their husbands and their family. In any case, they age fast and their utility is over after the age of 35 or at the most, 40.'

I had got my information in bits and pieces from many people I had conversations with, which included both men and women. I was emotionally devastated and shared my feelings with Manoj, who listened silently.

'I can't comprehend this cavalier attitude towards women. It seems as if these women don't really matter, not for their husbands or even their grown-up children. Take Latif's family for instance, Saira passed away only a month ago and there is a marriage and much rejoicing in the family. Her husband is glowing with happiness and pride and her children appear to be having fun too. Then, what laws or humanitarian values am I talking about? Maybe Ram Yadav is right—who am I to interfere in their lives and disrupt their traditions, beliefs, attitudes and actions?' I knew I was babbling but I couldn't stop.

Manoj urged me to come back. Feeling depressed and tired, and not in the mood to speak with anyone, I hung up. I decided to skip dinner, pack up and leave by the early morning train. I was certain that I would be able to secure a fairly comfortable seat if I reached the station well in time.

It was already half past nine at night and the lodge staff was busy winding up things in the dining hall. I could hear them moving the furniture back onto the veranda from the patch of lawn in front of the main residential block. Suddenly, there was a knock on my door. I peeked from the peep hole and, to my utter surprise, saw Fatima, Ramoli and another lady standing outside my room. I wondered why the women had come to meet me so late at night. I was anxious and with bated breath, opened the door. The women tip-toed into my room and sat on the bed and the chair kept in a corner.

Fatima broke the silence and said, '*Didi*, please take us away from here. We are prepared to leave Ramsevanpur and go with you. We know that we will be safe and protected with you. We are prepared to work for our living. We are sure that you will find something respectable and meaningful for us to do.'

Fatima spoke in a different diction. She sat close to me and I had the chance to compare her face with the image of Jyoti Sharma. The resemblance was very strong. I was more convinced that the girl in front of me was Jyoti. I didn't want to question her though in Ramoli's presence and complicate the situation further. I was shocked anyway with what they were telling me and didn't know what to say. I wanted to help them but after knowing the reality behind the accidents, I was scared too.

'Do you even realise what you are saying? You are essentially asking me to take you away from here, get jobs for you, organise a place for you to stay and basically look after you. I don't have that kind of resources. And, let's imagine if I do manage to arrange all that, do you think your families will leave you so easily? Do you think they will not realise it was me and leave me and my family alone? They will blame me for instigating you to leave your homes. You are all married and with children. Is it so easy for you to walk away from your children and your families? Your parents will also not accept you if this happens. They will not leave me easily and may harm my family too.'

All three women sat down on the floor and began to cry. It was heartbreaking to see them so emotionally distraught. Fatima spoke, amidst sobs, 'Lakshmi *didi*, I am very unhappy. I have been married for barely four days and I can't describe to you what this man Latif has been doing with me. I am going through torture and at this rate, I will take my own life because I know that it will be very difficult to come out of his grip and his group of louts and pimps. You know, he has made plans for me to sleep around with his moneyed friends? The other day, I overheard him talking about how much he will be charging for me per night. He told me that he would also be sending me to some officials of the forest department.'

The two other women had similar stories to tell, heart-wrenching and very disturbing. I wanted to reassure them and provide support but, I didn't know how to move forward. It broke my heart when I asked them to leave.

I was confused and disillusioned. I again called Manoj and had a long conversation with him. He made me understand how this could also be a way to rope me into some kind of a scandal by Latif and Ram Yadav and his other friends. Maybe by evening, these women would come back in a larger group and ask for help to leave their homes. What will I do then? Manoj also reminded me about Saira and what had happened to her. He asked me to think about the dire outcomes if I meddled in any way with the women and their decision to leave their families. He advised me to leave the village immediately and get back home. I finally saw Manoj's point and decided to follow my earlier plan.

I reached the station on time, bought my ticket and found a porter to carry my luggage to the platform. I was preoccupied with my own thoughts and didn't notice the huge crowd assembling at the end of platform number four on which my train was to arrive. The crowd kept increasing and suddenly the cries of women filled the air. I asked a man standing near me what the problem was and why a crowd had suddenly gathered on the platform.

He replied, in a rather matter-of-fact way, 'Three girls were sold last night to three elderly men from the neighbouring villages in the hope that these girls would bear them their male heirs. This happens more amongst the tribal community because they survive on hunting and girls can't go into the dark forests to hunt. Therefore, no family wants more than one or two girls to do the household chores and bear children.'

I also found out that the three girls who had been sold were between the ages of 12 and 14, and the men were well over 40 years old. The girls were wailing helplessly and didn't want to leave their mothers and siblings. They are made to do a lot of household work in their husband's homes as the families normally were large. There was also a high incidence of AIDS and other venereal diseases.

This man seemed to be in a mood to talk and told me everything that he knew about these villages. Then, looking at me with a questioning look in his eyes, he said, 'Tell me, you don't seem to belong to this area. You look like an educated woman. What are you doing here? And why are you alone? It is dangerous to be completely on your own in this part of the world. Even a man is not safe in these villages.'

My train was delayed by an hour and after hearing the announcement, I went across to a tea vendor and bought two cups of tea. I offered the man a cup and told him the reason for my visit. Before I could even mention Latif, he started talking about him and Ram Yadav, and the various crimes that they were involved in. Then, he lowered his voice and said, 'A few years ago, a woman like you, from a university, had visited Ramsevanpur, and then she apparently lost her way in the forest. Till today, she hasn't been found. She was engaged in some project and had met me to seek help in filling up a questionnaire. It had questions about the village, the community and its traditions. I remember her name still; she was Jyoti Sharma from Kanpur. Her parents were in a state of shock with the news that she went missing and the lodge where she stayed, which is the only decent place to live in the village, was shut for almost a year.'

Then, he started fiddling in his pocket, 'You know, I had the good fortune of getting photographed when she interviewed me.' He took out his wallet and showed me the photograph of him with a woman. He said that he had met the woman about three years ago. The woman in the photograph was Fatima.

Yes, Jyoti Sharma was Fatima. Her case was hushed up because important politicians were involved. She was with Latif and his gang for months and was raped several times. Her family also helped in closing the case and refused to identify her. They were concerned about their two unmarried daughters and the reputation of their family. I was plagued with questions: Should I go back and speak with Fatima? If I did that then I was certain that I wouldn't be spared by Latif, his gang and the entire nexus that operated in the villages.

I heard the sound of the train approaching the platform and hurriedly boarded it, praying for it to start moving soon so I could be away from the wailing and the crying of the women.

Once back, I shared my findings about Jyoti with Manoj. He told me that he was convinced that the district administration had a few corrupt officers who were fully aware of the nexus that operated in these villages connected with such crimes. He advised me to drop Ramsevanpur and its neighbouring villages completely from my mind and never visit them again.

'Jyoti Sharma's case has been forgotten; so you should not rake it up. And, as far as the other women are concerned, you, on your own, can't take up the responsibility to fight for them,' he said.

I listened to him, silently. My head agreed with him, but my heart, not so much.

Days and months passed by and our team was travelling all over the country for our other projects. I applied for leave and decided to spend some time with my parents. They were also relieved to know that I was no longer involved in the work in Ramsevanpur. My father had retired from the government and had substantial experience of rural India. He told me to give up my romantic notions about villages because according to him, poverty attracts immense politics, exploitation and crime. It also makes people indulge in all kinds of illegal activities and behaviours. After my leave ended, I became fruitfully occupied in projects for school education and opted to work in the states in southern India as I had very little exposure to that part of the country.

I was lucky to obtain an interesting assignment in Karnataka. This project was with the Toda tribes of the Nilgiris who worshipped the forests, built homes that resembled mud igloos with unique embellishments and wooden doors. The Toda women did exquisite cross-stitch embroidery using only red, black and white threads. Their designs were symmetrical and angular but very attractive. My project was about Toda cultural traditions and norms, and also their socialisation processes and methods. The project lasted for two years and during this interval, I met an interesting gentleman from Germany named Karl. He was 40 years old and had worked in the development sector all his life. Karl and I became friends and the more we met, the more we discovered our shared interests and beliefs. He was a caring and sensitive human being who was truly dedicated to his work. He had spent a lot of time with Indian tribes and had studied their social and structural evolution. He had immensely contributed to the education of tribal children and had received awards from governments in Germany and other European countries. We had many common interests like travelling and music and our belief in close-knit families. I visited Germany with him and met his family in Berlin and he travelled to Lucknow and met my parents and brother. Initially, my parents were a bit sceptical and had doubts about my capability to adjust to an alien culture but then they relented after seeing how well Karl and I got along.

We got married and, after five years, moved to the US to work for the Social Work and Community Development department of Harvard University. Karl got busy on a project on education and I started working on an interesting assignment on integrated rural development. Soon, I delivered a beautiful baby boy who looked a lot like Karl. We named him Hans, but my parents called him Shashank. Karl found the name to be quite a tongue-twister with a complicated spelling. We explained the meaning to him but he couldn't get how the half-moon crescent on Shiva's head made for a great name.

'Perhaps it has something to do with acculturation and internalisation of social myths and beliefs,' he said, thoughtfully.

Once Hans was old enough to travel, we decided to take a holiday to visit Karl's parents in Berlin and then mine in Lucknow. We spent about a week in Berlin. The family found Hans adorable and he became fast friends with his grandparents. I began to admire Karl's mother because, despite keeping such a busy schedule in her school of languages in Berlin, she found the time to run an impeccable home, most elegantly done up. Her cooking was delicious but she was keen to learn to make simple *dal* and vegetables cooked in our style since Karl had developed a taste for our food and his father also enjoyed my cooking. I had taken a saree for my mother-in-law and she looked rather nice wearing it.

We landed in Lucknow two days before *Deepavali*. My parents' house was freshly painted and the garden looked beautifully manicured. My mother had changed the interiors also and everything looked just perfect. All of us sat around sharing family gossip. We missed Pankaj, my brother, who could not manage enough leave and therefore was still in Delhi and planned to celebrate *Deepavali* there with his friends. My parents were desperately looking for a girl for him. Karl just couldn't understand this and wondered how parents could take the ultimate responsibility of their child's happiness in marriage and find a life partner who would ensure the success of the marriage. He found it all too complicated to understand. I asked him to leave it and not waste time thinking about something which was so far removed from his own culture.

There were only two days to *Deepavali* and my parents were making frequent rounds of the market to purchase sweets, clothes, utensils and other things that were needed for the *pooja*. Karl loved the decoration of the house with candles and *diyas* for *Deepavali* celebrations. Both Karl and Hans were very excited to go to the markets as they had never seen such celebrations before. We had a wonderful *pooja* and then ate the delicious food cooked by my mother. There were my father's friends dropping in throughout the festival time and it was only on the third day that there was some respite in the evening.

We decided to take my parents out for dinner because they had worked really hard organising everything for the festivities. We took them to a well-known five star hotel in the neighbourhood. Karl and my parents were engaged in an animated discussion on Germany and Hans was half-asleep in my lap.

I watched the television which was a little far removed from where we sat. The evening news was on and my eyes caught a piece of news from a village in Uttar Pradesh—12 people had been murdered in a family. I missed the details as my attention was diverted to the dinner which was being served on our table. I only heard one word 'Sevapur' which reminded me of Ramsevanpur. But, I forgot all about it during dinner; my attention was directed towards feeding Hans. At night, I lay down and tried to sleep. My mind kept going back to the word Sevapur and I thought that if it was an important piece of news, it would definitely be covered by the morning newspapers.

The news of the gruesome murders was indeed the talk of the town as 12 male members of two families had been murdered in Ramsevanpur. I quickly scanned the news piece and saw that the names of all those involved in the murders were mentioned. The crime was committed by Fatima and Zubeida who were related to Latif Ali and by Sushma, Kiran and Leela who were from the family of Ram Yadav. These five women had hacked 12 men and boys belonging to the two families to death. Latif and Ram Yadav were also killed. The murders were committed at night by using *kulhadis.* After feasting on *Deepavali*, all the men were sleeping in a row in the living room and the women were huddled up in the two bedrooms. The pattern of planning and executing the crime was similar in both the homes. The five women who had committed the crime confessed to the police and described in detail how and why they had done it.

The murders were committed between one and two at night, at lightning speed. They had gotten the *kulhadis* sharpened two days earlier. The women had met and discussed the method which they would adopt for committing the crime and had vowed not to chicken out and go back on their plan. They had also decided to stay at home and plead guilty to the police and disclose everything to them. They were able to execute the plan perfectly and were not nervous or anxious at all.

The photographs of all the women were splashed in newspapers and TV channels during the entire week. Fatima was recognised by a lot of people as Jyoti Sharma but ironically, her parents in Kanpur refused to accept the fact and said that the police had confirmed the death of their daughter years ago. Fatima also never claimed to be Jyoti Sharma and that story died down soon. Many said that the political bigwigs were involved in the hush-up. Moreover, Mr Sharma had two younger daughters of marriageable age and they didn't want to spoil their marital prospects by associating themselves with a murderer.

There were only seven members left in the two families and they were all women and girls. The entire male population of the two families had been wiped out overnight. The five women involved in the crime told their gory tales of rape, prostitution and trafficking, abortions and female foeticide and murder, which was always planned and projected as an accident. They recounted the number of women who were killed in planned accidents by their families and friends. The stories were of torture and the women had lived through sheer hell. All five women said that they were driven to eliminate the men and boys because there was no chance that they would transform and mend their ways. They believed that the younger boys, sons and nephews would follow in the same teaching and training and would destroy the lives of other innocent girls.

Their confessions sent a tremor not only through Ramsevanpur but also through the entire state and the country.

Both the houses were locked because the women, related to the killed men, refused to live there after witnessing the scenes of death and massacre, blood and tattered flesh. They were taken away by their relatives to neighbouring villages.

The verdicts of the district courts as well as the high court were received positively by all five women. They were all given life imprisonment and were to be sent to different jails in the country. Even though they were convicted of brutal and planned murder, the judges refrained from capital punishment because they said that they had planned the murders in self-defence and to prevent the torture and abuse of the next generation of women.

In her last interview to the media, Fatima said that she is looking forward to her life in jail because her safety and security at least would be ensured. She could also go back to her reading and writing and would now be able to get back to work, even if it was just chopping vegetables and cleaning the floors. She will be paid for it and that is what dignity is all about.

However, one can never say anything about the conditions prevailing in jails. Dark clouds don't have silver linings. I only hope that they would finally find the peace that they were looking for.

8

Twilight Hues

The blue hues of the Nilgiris are breathtakingly beautiful. Viewing it from afar is a surreal experience as all the myriad shades of blue—of the sky and the mountains—appear to merge into one another. As I approached the range, I could feel a crisp freshness in the air and smell the aroma of the pine cones. The drive was up the mountains and I was eager to meet Pushpanjali, my dear friend from school days. She stayed in Kotagiri, a beautiful small town in the foothills of the Nilgiris. She had lived there for almost a decade. Her sons, Anant and Anuj, were pursuing their respective careers in Mumbai. Nikhil, her late husband, had taken the decision to settle down in the hills after two decades of a hectic work life in the Gulf. He passed away after a prolonged illness just about two months ago. Since then, I had been speaking to Pushpa almost daily but it was only last week that she asked me to come for a visit and spend some time with her in Kotagiri. She sounded lost and depressed and I couldn't help packing my bags and rushing down south to be with her.

Pushpa, in her early sixties, still looked as I remembered her—tall and slender with a beautiful face and long hair. Kotagiri seemed to have suited her for she looked well. Her skin glowed and her body appeared fit and toned. I suspected that the uphill walks and the fresh air had done her good. We were of the same age and had spent 13 years together in school, in the same class and the same section. We knew each other closely and had kept in touch even after she got married and moved away.

After settling in my room, which overlooked the forest and a pond, I walked to the dining room where Pushpa waited for me with a cup of coffee. She handed me the cup with a smile, but I could notice the melancholy look in her eyes. It was clearly visible that she needed company and someone to talk to. I was glad that I could spend some time with her. Pushpa had always been a quiet person who could not be indecent or aggressive with anyone. She had been reticent during our school days too and didn't open up easily. However, since she and I shared a comfortable relationship, she had always been able to talk about herself with me. Sensing that she still needed a little push, I started making small talk.

'You've been able to organise a lot, Pushpa,' I said, looking appreciatively around the room.

'Yeah, but not here at all,' said Pushpa pointing to her heart. Apparently, that was all the push she needed. All her pent-up emotions came rushing out and she told me how depressed and anxious she felt and how there were days when she just didn't know how to come out of the darkness that seemed to engulf her.

'I just don't know what to do with myself? Cooking food, cleaning up the house and all the other household chores hardly take up a few hours and, then, the day just seems to drag on forever. You know, I have also been suffering from insomnia and I can't sleep for long stretches at night. I keep tossing and turning,' she said, clutching the coffee cup tightly in her hands. She took a long sip and then added, softly, 'Now, I understand that Nikhil was the centre of my existence and there was so much to do in the house because of him. I wanted to make him happy in so many ways. My happiness was really tied to his,' Pushpa said.

I have been a widow for the last 16 years and that is why I could completely understand what she was going through. In fact, it was only the other day when someone had told me, with a rather cynical and a wry smile on their face, 'You know, there are more widows in the world than widowers', as if to tell me that I am not an exception and therefore there was nothing special about my situation. However, there is a lot of difference between the life of a widow and the lives of married women or women who are not married at all. This chasm will never be fully understood by those who have, fortunately, not experienced widowhood. That is the reason widows naturally gravitate towards other widows because of the similar existential truths that they face and share, which others, who have not faced widowhood, can't relate to. Maybe, that is why, Pushpa, after all these years, had specifically sought me out?

I had realised long back that widowhood transfers a woman to the twilight zone; it is like living between light and darkness. It is a life that is full of memories but also of desires that continually surface and subside. It feels like you are involuntary clinging to the past so there is always this pressure to wrench the soul out of it and bring it into the present, so that you can look towards the future. Then, there are some women whose only coping mechanism is to blank out the future completely. In the initial period, when you are undergoing the tragic sadness, the future, in any case, seems blurred or completely smudged with its outlines and contours barely visible. I understood that Pushpa was going through this phase, her loss was quite recent and to her, the future seemed bleak.

It takes time for the truth of widowhood to sink into the mind of a woman. Widowhood is not only a change to be managed, but a transformational experience at the level of personal identity. A woman's identity is sticky as it is and any metamorphosis is not easy to come by. Capturing the sense of an identity and describing it is no mean feat. Most of us don't think about our identities and may not even be aware of it. A sudden question about identity may leave a person confused and the response could be anything like a description of the person or her name, profession, age, etc. However, none of these can be described as one's identity; in fact, they are nothing but simple demographics and personal qualities. People generally require help, and a few intelligent questions, to connect with their identity. When widowhood strikes, the issue of identity suddenly emerges like an avalanche that begins to wipe out established cognitive and emotional maps and social moorings.

In India, especially in the middle and upper middle classes, the linkages with identity are very solidly anchored in the larger than life landscape of the husband and his family. With the change of the surname, which takes barely 15 minutes during the marriage ceremony, the woman unknowingly shifts her identity and even takes pride in what has happened to her. Nobody really bothers to check whether she understands the long-term implications of this 'shift of identity' or not. Most women experience a loss of individual identity as it substantially merges into that of her husband and his family. Our culture also eulogises surrender and self-effacing tendencies in women after marriage. The more they forget who they are, their unique selves and their special talents and adopt the sanctioned ways expected from a dutiful wife, the more they are praised by society.

Today, younger women are putting up a fight to protect their individual identity. However, this is just a little shift; this paradigm will not change easily as the larger context of social and family life is deeply entrenched in norms and traditions that have taken centuries to evolve.

Widowhood gives a jolt to a women's identity and connections since the man, whom the woman largely identifies with, is no longer around. The same was happening with Pushpa. The husband's passing away is as it is painful for woman who, in turn, is thrust on to the centre stage. She is begun to be perceived differently by the husband's family, her maternal family, by her own children and the society at large.

Psychologically, she is pushed into the category of being a single parent, in most cases, as well as being seen as someone's widow. Her late husband's shadow surrounds her and the word 'widow' continually reminds her that she is not alone even though she is now single. Her identity still represents someone who was with her but is no longer there, someone who has not left her completely. Widowhood, therefore, is a long shadow, a mirage and a receding paradox which can never be quenched.

The complexity of living between light and darkness, the stark reality and the past shadows, is not easy. It requires a set of completely different competencies which a woman is not exposed to before the event occurs. No family or institute imparts this kind of training or education. The woman is not prepared to face the transformation. The world says that a widow has to quickly pick-up coping competencies, not to live happily and start managing the burden of life. Life becomes an endless maze of responsibilities and, all said and done, the widow must walk alone.

Widowhood is all about confronting a void and living in vacant spaces. There is no one and nothing to fill it up with. It was not so much about the physical void but the vacant spaces created in the heart. The void was because of the lack of purpose and meaning in life. The husband was the meaning and the purpose of a wife's existence. I realised that it was completely true for Pushpa and it was my reality too. That is why I could connect with her and understand what she was going through.

There is nothing much left to do after losing one's husband. We are in the world yet out of it. This sounds quite schizoid but the texture of life becomes that way. People say that time heals everything, but time doesn't heal this—I can still feel the void after 16 long years. I think it is the same for all women; age, education, working or not working, rich or poor hardly matters. The only thing that matters is love. If there was no love between the married couple, then there was a void even while the husband was alive. There is no sense in being in a marriage without love. However, there are hundreds, if not thousands and lakhs of women, who have senseless marriages in this country.

'What do I do, Anna?' Pushpa's questions broke my trance and brought me back to reality. Pushpa was looking at me with a hundred questions in her eyes, 'Should I shift to a larger city like Mumbai, Bengaluru or Delhi? Should I find a job to keep myself occupied?'

'A change of place or getting a job would only suppress the discomfort that you feel; it would not sort it. This confusion is in your mind; you need to sort it out first,' I replied.

We explored many options, from exercise and yoga, to occasional travel, keeping pets, making a daily schedule of work and relaxation, increasing social engagements, and so on. Then, we realised that it was all about becoming peaceful.

'Pushpa, you need to accept this new reality and the change that has come with it, then, only your life would become meaningful. Nikhil has always been the larger purpose you seemed to have been living for, but now, you have to discover a goal or a purpose that transcends this "person-centricity".' I left it at that asking her to sleep on this thought, hoping that the mind and the soul would do the remaining work and come out with some meaningful solutions.

*****

Next morning, over breakfast, we got to talking about children.

'Children are best left alone to their own world and interests. The fact that in ill-health, they will take care of us is enough solace and reassurance. Otherwise, any other dependence on children must be avoided. The relationship between parents and children is always better with physical and social distance,' Pushpa said while buttering her toast.

'I wholeheartedly agree with what you are saying. I believe that children's respect for their parents is always more once they realise that parents have their own lives to lead and that they too can be independent and be busy with their various interests,' I said.

Pushpa had decided to be on her own, but visited Mumbai frequently to meet the kids. This parental relationship was working out well for all of them—her, the sons and the daughters-in-law.

'Pushpa, being alone provides space—physical and psychological. I am so accustomed to it now that I hate it when anyone intrudes upon my space. You know, I thank God for the freedom that he has given me. How many women have our kind of freedom? We are not answerable to anyone. I didn't have this kind of freedom when Raj was alive,' I said, in a nonchalant manner. However, Pushpa looked horrified.

'What are you saying, Anna? You said it in front of me but please don't say this to anyone else. You'll be misunderstood. How can you be happy and speak about your freedom from Raj? People will think that you were unhappy in your marriage,' said Pushpa sounding extremely agitated.

I realised that I had touched a painful nerve and would need to choose my next words carefully so as to not to hurt her.

'Pushpa, you have yet to accept what I have accepted in the last many years of my being alone—you are free. Why do you feel guilty in discovering your freedom? You had no control over what happened to Nikhil and you were not responsible for his illness and passing away. For all you know, he could be at peace and maybe might have even found his happiness wherever he is.'

She looked at me, tears pooling in her eyes. I reached for her hand, squeezing it gently, 'Time has moved on and so should you. Your life has changed, it is not the same anymore.

A sense of freedom would make a huge difference in your life. You will find new things happening in your life, and also peace and happiness.'

Looking at the shocked expression on her face, I added, 'Why does widowhood mean perpetual unhappiness and bondage? Pushpa, it is necessary and natural for anyone to want to come out of the shadows of the past.'

I looked around the room. Nikhil was a wonderful painter and Pushpa had put up his paintings everywhere. His photographs adorned the mantlepiece in the living room, her dressing table, the side board and even the front passage which led to the living and the dining area. Nikhil was all over the house even now. I had removed all the photographs of my husband from the house. There was only one left, in the study. Instead, I had kept artefacts that fascinated me and made my home beautiful. Suddenly, my home had become an extension of me and made me feel comfortable. On the other hand, Pushpa had decided to keep everything just the way it was when Nikhil was alive.

'Pushpa, just take a look around the house; there is Nikhil in every corner. You have to make this house, your home. My home doesn't have Raj's presence at all. That doesn't mean I never loved him or have forgotten him. I still carry his photograph in my wallet,' I said softly. Pushpa looked at me, puzzled and confused. But, she didn't say anything. She just got up to fulfil her daily ritual of lighting the lamp in the pooja room and placing some flowers in front of Nikhil's photograph in the living room. Then, she sat in the living room and prayed for about 15 to 20 minutes. I couldn't understand the logic of this ritual but refrained from making any comments. From our last few conversations I had realised that I had no right to judge her. Her life was different from mine and she had to manage it herself.

The next couple of days flew by quickly. I refrained from indulging in any philosophical or social discussions and intentionally kept the conversation light-hearted. On the fourth day, I went back to Delhi. I had had a good break in Kotagiri and missed the mountain air, the coffee estates and the forest expanse. I promised Pushpa to be back very soon. We kept in touch for a few months but then, to my utter surprise, I found her losing interest in maintaining contact. She would clamp up suddenly and just wouldn't speak. My calls also became infrequent because I didn't find her reciprocating and welcoming my conversations. It did worry me but I decided to give her some space. She had told me that she was attending Mandarin classes, something she had always wanted to do. Maybe her classes and the examinations were keeping her busy.

One night, a few weeks later, I was working on my laptop late in the night when I heard my mobile ring. It was almost midnight. I became a little worried as I approached my bedroom where my phone was being charged. Immediately, my thoughts went to my son who lived overseas. He hardly called at this time as he knew that I would be fast asleep. I looked at the screen and saw it was Pushpa. I was surprised at her calling me at this late hour and a bit apprehensive because of our recent lack of communication. I picked up the phone and was pleasantly surprised on hearing the excitement in her voice. We exchanged pleasantries for a few minutes and then, she broke the news.

'Anna, I have decided to marry my Mandarin coach. I know he is 13 years younger than me but it feels right, you know? After the wedding, which would take place within 15 days in Ooty, we would leave for Shanghai; that's where he lives.'

She went on and on like an excited schoolgirl. I didn't say a word till the end of our call. She was the one who spoke and I merely listened, without comprehending much. It was quite a shock for me. I did manage to understand that he was divorced and did not have any children. And, Pushpa's sons thought that her decision was crazy and both of them had refused to attend the wedding. She also mentioned that she wanted me to be there for the wedding and look after her house when she leaves. She was planning to return after six months and she would then decide what to do with her house and the rest of the property.

I immediately knew that I had to go to Kotagiri because this was a very serious matter. During our phone call, I had asked Pushpa to give me the phone numbers of her sons. She hadn't questioned me at all and passed on their numbers to me. I called Anuj first and spoke to him. He sounded hurt and worried. I told him that I was planning to go to Kotagiri the next day, and asked him to join me as well. He was evasive and didn't commit. Then, I called Anant, her other son, but he was travelling and I couldn't speak with him. I didn't think it would be wise to speak with their wives about this delicate matter.

Since it was the onset of winters, Kotagiri felt bleak and grey. Or maybe I was merely projecting my emotions onto the weather. Without wasting any time, I told Pushpa about the stupidity and the sheer madness of her decision.

'It is one thing to become friends with a man and an entirely different thing to get married at this age. And, how could you think about migrating to another country, leaving behind your family?' I asked.

She looked at me with a vacant and slightly shocked expression.

'Do you even understand the enormity of this move? Have you any idea about what life in China is all about? By the way, how well do you know this man? Your loneliness and vulnerability shouldn't drive you to this nature of madness. This will only bring you more trouble and pain, much more than what you are feeling today. Just stop and think what you are about to do. Or better yet, just listen to me and get out of this decision today itself,' I said the last part, assertively and categorically, leaving no room for discussion. Pushpa broke down and cried. She agreed to what I had said.

'I know what you are saying is correct. In fact, I also realised it but didn't have the courage to deal with it myself.'

I took the Chinese gentleman's number from her, called him up and told him that their wedding plans were not at all acceptable. To my utter surprise, he agreed without any argument or dissent and the matter was called off... just like that!

Anuj came down to Kotagiri the next day. It was a big relief for him. The mother and son sat in the veranda together, talking and laughing. After a long time, Pushpa looked relaxed and happy. In fact, I saw her genuinely smiling for the first time after Nikhil's death.

I sat in the living room, looking at the mother and son, pondering over the events of the last couple of days. I understood that emotional insecurity experienced during widowhood makes women vulnerable to exploitation. Also, men appear to be attracted to widows more than they are attracted to spinsters; probably, they find their softness and helplessness attractive. Widows also become easy victims to overtures by men who make false commitments and promises. Married men also seem to be looking for escapades with widows because of boredom within their marriages. Most of the times, widows, who have children to look after, don't even insist on marriages as they don't want to risk becoming distant from their children on account of a second marriage. This makes it even easier for married men. However, if the woman is not smart and strong, she could be hurt and exploited.

Often, widows who work are also financially exploited since men seem to be attracted to their wealth and power. This world is surely not a simple place. Widowhood places a woman in an open jungle where she has to constantly fight for her survival. This requires courage, strength and a lot of strategic sense. I decided to share these thoughts with Pushpa during my time in Kotagiri.

A couple of days later, Anuj went back to Mumbai. Pushpa and I locked up the house in Kotagiri and flew together to Delhi. After a lot of thought and discussions between the three of us, it was decided that Pushpa would join me in Delhi. Her wounds were new and, therefore, had the tendency to bleed. My injury, on the other hand, had become old yet it still hurt in the darkness of the night. Even though, I was still learning to manage the contradictions of life, I had accepted its unfairness. Pushpa had been waiting and just watching life pass from the shadows with timidity. She had to learn a lot and I was sure that she would.

*****

After coming back to Delhi, I resumed my work with widows in rural areas through an organisation involved in voluntary service. It kept me grounded and also grateful for the small blessings in life. Pushpa accompanied me twice to the office and couldn't fathom what I did in these villages. I said that I managed the accounts and documented the conversations that took place in meetings, in great detail.

'Ultimately, this is the information that is used to write the reports that are sent to international funding organisations that provide the funds to carry out welfare projects for the widows in these rural areas,' I explained.

Pushpa had more questions, 'How does this work help you manage life better as you are not even earning enough money to be comfortable.'

'I have enough money to keep my body and soul together. I am just happy not being financially dependent on my son,' I said with a smile.

During our discussion, I explained to Pushpa how extremely difficult it is to face and manage widowhood in the remote villages of rural India. Women have large families and the responsibility for feeding four to five children is no small task. Many widows don't have anything, not even a single-room house or any money for daily expenditure or any kind of savings. Women who have to shoulder responsibilities of such magnitude and have to indulge in a battle, on a daily basis, to overcome hunger, disease and abject poverty, don't have the time, the will or the pressing need to discuss their emotional and mental traumas. They are focused only on the day-to-day struggle for survival. They have seen death and destruction from close quarters and their sensitivities become blunt. They concentrate on the material aspects of life and not on their inner being. Keeping the body intact and in working shape is their battle for survival.

I told her the story of one of the widows I had met named Revati, 'Widowhood had left Revati completely bereft of money, so much so that she didn't have a penny to spend on the medical treatment of her ailing 13-year-old son. He was a tall teenager and Revati, without any other alternative, carried him on her back to the primary health centre near her village. Halfway to the centre, he died in her arms. With the help of a few farmers, she buried him in the empty patch of land which belonged to one of the?. Revati was grateful and in stunned silence, walked back to her village. She broke the news to her other children quietly. Then, she took her clothes and went for her bath as she had to go look for work to feed the others.'

After a pause to let the gravity of the situation sink in, I added, 'Revati is a hard-working woman. After the death of her elder son, she was devastated but she got back up as she knew that she had to be courageous for her kids. She realised that she was the sole breadwinner and had to look after her three other children. Showing extraordinary grit and determination, she got training in sewing, stitching and knitting and now she earns over ₹20,000 on a monthly basis.'

Both of us sat together, silently contemplating our respective lives. Even though Pushpa didn't say anything, I could sense a change in her demeanour.

*****

It was one of those rare afternoons, in the midst of December winters, when the sun had finally decided to make an appearance. Pushpa, Revati and I were sitting in my small lawn, soaking up the sunlight.

Pushpa was wrapped up in a heavy shawl and a scarf was tied around her neck and shoulders. Her shoulders hurt as she had typed out a long report in the office that morning. Dr Victor Mason, the director of the organisation where I worked, had met Pushpa on her previous visit and liked her. He had offered her a part-time job with a flexible schedule—she would have to spend two weeks in Delhi every month. Pushpa, after a little hesitation, had accepted the position. We had even worked out a paying guest arrangement for her. She would stay with me and pay me accordingly. This was less for the money but more for her confidence and self-respect. It had been two months since she had joined work and was doing quite well. She had adjusted with the office team and her sons were also happy with this arrangement.

'In more orthodox and tradition-bound communities and families, the woman is perceived to have caused the early death of her husband because she is ill-fated and they believe that her horoscope had this scripted for her. I find this really regressive. Being ill-fated is a dimension that a person doesn't have any control over and therefore a woman can't do anything about it. The blame for the demise of the husband is put on the woman. This is a huge blame and indeed a terrible guilt to live with. In many communities, widows are forbidden to bless newly-married couples lest their negative energies contaminate the happiness of the newlyweds. People can't imagine the hurt that this inflicts upon the person,' said Revati who was busy knitting a cardigan.

Since Pushpa started working, she and Revati had become good friends. They could usually be found chatting about diverse topics animatedly. I was happy to see Pushpa being less reticent than what she had been in the past. It seemed that Revati had read my thoughts and sensed what I was thinking.

'Madame, it's OK. I am very lonely and don't have anyone to talk to. I feel blessed that I have you and Pushpa Didi to vent out to. Both of you have brought light into my life. You know, I am just living for my children. Once they grow up and settle down, I'll be a happy woman. I find great satisfaction in my work. I pray to God to give me the opportunity to continue working always. I have also decided to work for widowed women after a few years. Like you two have helped me, I would like to help other widows, not that they would require my help. I believe God gives us, widows, strength automatically. We have already seen the worst in life that there is nothing more bad left to see. All the problems that come thereon feel very small. I can now easily navigate my ship because I've come out of the worst storm possible.'

With a soft smile playing around her full lips, Revati continued to knit.

9

Dadi Ma

'Ah, this is my Calcutta... no, no Kolkata,' smiled Dadi Ma, correcting herself, hastily. She was standing by the window of her fifth floor flat, all alone, looking at the rapidly-changing city.

'In these last 41 years, a lot has changed along with the name. The crowd and traffic have increased considerably. Now, there are more high-rise buildings which have somewhat ruined the beauty of the skyline. There are also many more flyovers but they have made city travel much more convenient. Sadly, the musical and the poetic soul of the city also appears to have been diluted. The city had a different spirit of joy and abandon four decades ago. Park Street and New Market were a delight in the evenings and so were the Calcutta Clubs and the Saturday Clubs,' thought Dadi Ma, with a twinge of sadness.

Dadi Ma stayed at Ballygunge Circular Road, one of the posh residential areas of South Kolkata. She had a two-bedroom flat with a storeroom, a kitchen and a balcony. She also couldn't leave the windows open to let in fresh air because of the mosquitoes and the drizzle which came into the rooms with the breeze. But, she never complained, the view made up for it.

Dadi Ma stayed alone with a part-time maid named Deepali who came for a few hours in the morning as well as evening to clean up the house and cook her meals. Deepali had two daughters; both of them were in their early teens. Her husband worked in a grocery store in a nearby market. They had been staying in Kolkata for over a decade and she had worked for Dadi Ma for pretty much the same number of years.

After Deepali would leave in mid-mornings, Dadi Ma, who had always been social by nature, would start getting restless and bored. The other flats on Dadi Ma's floor were occupied by young working couples who left early in the mornings and returned late in the evenings. It suffices to say that there was no one to keep her company. So, she started keeping her main door open to see the comings and goings of her neighbours. However, this gesture of hers was not appreciated by others and they complained to the president of the residents' association of the society, blaming her for prying on their personal and private spaces. Dadi Ma was asked to keep the door of her flat closed and, to everyone's surprise, she agreed. But, after a few days, the door was again found open and Dadi Ma was seen sitting outside, fanning herself; this cycle continued in a seemingly endless loop.

At the age of 73, Dadi Ma was still fit and energetic. She was particular about her clothes, her handbags, sandals and other accessories. Her personal grooming was lauded by everyone along with her taste in clothes and jewellery. However, the compliments ended there. Most of the people who knew her described her as a big gossip. It was a well-known fact that she had no other hobby other than talking about people, that too, behind their backs. She also had the tendency of being overly critical in her comments about people whom she didn't like—one of the reasons people maintained their distance from her.

But, all these comments about her character never stopped her from boasting about her large circle of friends. In reality, these 'friends' were actually acquaintances she had met during *satsangs* or at association meetings or while going up and down the elevator. In fact, she also counted all the people she saw through her main door, which was open for a good 10–12 hours a day even after repeated warnings from the association, as her 'friends'.

Her relatives were convinced that her becoming a widow in her early teens had led to a nasty streak in her character and had made her somewhat mentally unhinged. Some even went as far as to say that she couldn't see anyone happy and enjoying their life. Baldev, her nephew who visited her rarely, thought that her mercurial temperament was because of the difficulties she had faced in her life.

Dadi Ma was married off at a young age. She became a mother at 13 and a widow at 17. Her husband's family was well-off and, therefore, the land and the money that she was given saw her and her only son, Bakul, through their early years. After college, Bakul, on the recommendation of his grandfather, got a job in a junior cadre in the government where he served for almost 40 years and retired with a pension.

On the insistence of his wife, Bela, he had purchased some land in Cochin and built a small but comfortable house where he and his family moved after his retirement. Bakul managed to look after his family but never financially supported Dadi Ma. His wife resented him even gifting a saree to his mother. She thought that his mother had enough money to look after herself. Dadi Ma felt hurt about this. Bakul and his family visited Dadi Ma once in two years and they would stay with her for a week or 10 days. His wife didn't like cooking for her mother-in-law and thought that it was quite a task. It was a duty that she had to fulfil and would never do it if her husband didn't insist and create a fuss.

This year, Bakul and his family had decided to visit Kolkata during Christmas time and Dadi Ma was not too happy about this. She felt that they had timed their visit to see the Christmas festivities instead of spending time with her. Bakul noticed her mother's grumpiness and annoyance.

He discussed it with his family and planned to stay out of the house most of the time.

One day, Deepali, while mopping the floor, asked her, 'Dadi Ma, where is your son and his family? They are never at home. I don't think they have come to meet you. They want all the convenience of a home but actually just want to stay outdoors and enjoy themselves. I don't like your daughter-in-law at all. She was asking me whether you give me new sarees and jewellery for Durga pujo. I told her, "Of course! She cares for me and gives me everything I ask for". I think this lady is very clever. She is eyeing your money and belongings. God knows, she might be waiting for you to die so that she gets everything that you own. These ladies are not to be trusted at all.'

Deepali's words made Dadi Ma thoughtful. She wondered maybe there was some truth in what Deepali had said. Maybe Bela was actually waiting for her to die so she could usurp all her belongings. She must be a materialistic woman and that was why she chose to stay in Cochin, so far away from everyone. It must be because she does not want all the relatives to see what she truly is.

With all these thoughts whirring in her mind, Dadi Ma slowly got up and kept all her shoes, sandals and handbags inside a cupboard. She also took off her gold chain and gold bangles and kept them in the steel almirah's locker. Then, she double checked to see whether she had locked the cupboard and the almirah safely. She passed the mirror and looked at her reflection, appreciatively. At this rate, she might live for another 15 years at least, which would make her 88 and Bakul would be 75. It always baffled her that there was just a difference of 13 years between mother and son. She didn't feel like his mother anyway, more like an elder sister. Bela was five years younger than Bakul. Dadi Ma was hurt by her daughter-in-law's attitude this time around. She hardly stayed at home or spoke with her.

There is so much to talk and share between a mother-in-law and a daughter-in-law but they never developed that kind of camaraderie. During such times, she really missed having a daughter.

*****

Bakul and his family were still sleeping when Deepali was almost finished with her work. She grumbled and told Dadi Ma that she didn't have the time to return and clean the bedroom still occupied by them as she had work in other houses as well. 'By the way, what is this Dadi Ma? Mother-in-law is up from six in the morning and the daughter-in-law is fast asleep till now? This doesn't happen in families which have traditions and discipline. She is really taking advantage of your goodness, Dadi Ma. If I were in your place, I would have asked her to pack her bags and leave. Sometimes, I do feel sorry for you. By God's grace, till now you are fit and fine but what will happen when you grow weak? Will they even look after you when you are sick and bedridden? I don't think so. You should also not expect anything from them. Mark my words—you will be all alone; they, for sure, will not be there for you. Kindly remember my words and plan everything accordingly. It is better not to have children than to have these kind of children who don't care at all,' Deepali rambled on and on. Simmering with anger and frustration, she went in to the kitchen to wash the utensils. She was horrified to see the large number of plates, bowls and glasses piled up in the sink. She called Dadi Ma to the kitchen. 'Come and see what happens in your house. While you were sleeping, your son and his family were having a feast! I am sure they didn't even wake you up and ask you to join them, did they? They didn't keep anything for you in the refrigerator also. This is the height of being mean and petty! What kind of children do you have, Dadi Ma? I would hate to have such ungrateful children! I would wish they would rather die—'

'Don't say such inauspicious things!' Dadi Ma cut her off as she had experienced the pain of losing someone close. She knew she couldn't go through it again. She took a deep breath to calm herself down and spoke slowly, 'I have a belief that whatever we say goes out to the universe and it becomes true. It is mentioned in our old scriptures too. So, always say good things. You should also practise it. And as for my family, they have come on a holiday. Let them enjoy! You tell me how can they take an old woman like me to the market late in the evening? They know that I have dinner by 7 pm that is why they did not keep anything for me. And anyway, outside food doesn't suit my delicate tummy anymore. You have started talking too much, just concentrate on your work and go,' admonishing Deepali, Dadi Ma went into the living room.

It was almost noon and Dadi Ma was getting jittery about lunch. She didn't know whether Bakul and his family would have lunch at home or not. Deepali would finish her work in an hour and leave. She never did any extra bit of work and Dadi Ma didn't want to ask her to wait; she was already in a foul mood. She finally decided that Bela would have to cook if the family decided to eat at home. There was fish and chicken in the fridge and plenty of vegetables. Dadi Ma thought that it would be a nice change from Deepali's insipid cooking which she somehow tolerated.

When it was almost one and no one came out, Dadi Ma peeped into the bedroom. Bakul and Bela were sitting and were discussing something in hushed tones. Jai, their 27-year-old son, was fast asleep and Shanti, their daughter who was 25, was in the washroom. Bakul saw his mother and asked her to come in. Dadi Ma hesitated for a second and then entered the room to find two large bundles of cash on the bed. She wondered what was going on. Bakul said, 'Ma, Bela has saved this cash over the years. We are thinking of investing it in some gold jewellery. We were planning to go to New Market tomorrow for our purchases.' Dadi Ma nodded and hurriedly left the room without any comment.

Dadi Ma went to the balcony and sat on the cane chair. She loved sitting here, gazing at the trees across the road. She thought that maybe Deepali was right in her assessment. Bakul and his family didn't care about her at all. In all the years that Bakul had been working, he had never gifted her even a single saree. He didn't even know how his mother managed her life and had never ever inquired whether she needed anything. On the contrary, he always demanded things like furniture, clothes or cash. In fact, there was also a time when Dadi Ma would send a portion of her accrued fixed deposit interest to him to meet his monthly expenditure. Still, there was never a gentle word from him or his family.

Dadi Ma was lost in her thoughts when she heard Bela say that she planned to cook lunch for everyone. After a while, the smell of delicious curries wafted through the air. Dadi Ma felt quite happy at the prospect of having good home-cooked food after years. Bela had cooked chicken curry for Bakul and the children, and for Dadi Ma and herself, she had prepared fish curry with some lentils and vegetables. Soon, thcy were joined by Bakul who had a packet and a jewellery box in his hands. He knelt down next to his mother and gave her a beautifully embroidered saree and a heavy gold chain with a gleaming diamond pendant.

'Ma, I have waited so long for this because I wanted to give you something good. Since now, I am finally a little comfortable with money, all of us decided to give you something special for your generosity and kindness,' he said handing her the presents. Dadi Ma discreetly wiped her tears and thanked him. She praised his choice, and added that she would wear the saree and the chain on New Year's Eve. She also decided that she would proudly tell Deepali how wrong she was in her judgement of her son and his family.

The lunch was very well made. Dadi Ma complimented Bela on her cooking and Bela thanked her, her happiness and pride clearly visible. The children sat with their grandmother that afternoon and for the first time in years, they seemed like a happy family. Dadi Ma realised that Shanti and Jai were good children, undemanding and supportive. On their part, both the kids admired Dadi Ma for bringing up their father on her own. They thought that their grandmother had demonstrated immense courage in doing so.

That afternoon, Shanti asked Dadi Ma to share some tales about her father and happily listened about his childhood antics. Dadi Ma also told stories of her own childhood. Thus, the afternoon was spent happily after which everyone retired to their respective rooms for a siesta.

*****

That afternoon, while leaving, Deepali had told Dadi Ma that she would come a little early in the evening as her elder daughter was not well and her husband would be taking her to a doctor. Since she could not leave her younger daughter alone in the evening, she would have to leave early to be with her. Shanti was present when this conversation had taken place and she was convinced that Deepali took advantage of her grandmother's age as well as the fact that she lived alone and was dependent on her. She wanted to say something but held her tongue.

In the evening, Deepali prepared hot cardamom tea and served it along with pastries and Christmas cakes that Bakul had picked up from the nearby market. There was a festive atmosphere in the house.

While sipping on his tea, Bakul explained his shopping plans to his mother, 'We plan to finish all our shopping tomorrow only, so that we would be free for the next two days. Then, we all can visit the uncles, aunts and cousins in Kolkata.'

Dadi Ma agreed readily and told Bakul that she would inform the extended family about their impending visit.

It was already six in the evening and it had become a little dark and cold. The whole family sat in the living room sipping tea and making plans for their shopping trip.

'Bakul, you have dinner outside in case you get late. Also, take the spare key tomorrow so that you can come inside without any hassle,' Dadi Ma was saying when the doorbell rang. Bakul walked to the door and opened it. The security guards from the lobby of the society were standing outside. They said that there were people downstairs who had come to meet Deepali. Bakul asked the guards to let them come up so Deepali could meet them outside the flat. The guards looked a little sceptical but said that they would ask the men to come up.

When the doorbell rang for the second time, Deepali opened the door and found four men from her neighbourhood. One person beckoned Bakul to see him separately and walked towards the lift. Even though Bakul found this gesture odd, he followed the man who told him, without preamble, that Deepali's husband and daughter had met with an accident while going to the doctor. Her husband had died on the spot while her daughter was in critical condition at the hospital. He said that they didn't know how to break the news to Deepali. Bakul looked at him in stunned silence. Finally, he called out to Bela and told her to take Deepali inside and gently tell her about the accident. 'It'd perhaps be a better idea to inform her of her husband's death later,' he added softly.

Bela broke the news of the accident to Deepali in a gentle manner. On hearing about the accident and hospital, Deepali almost fainted and insisted on leaving for the hospital. Jai, Shanti and Bakul accompanied her. At the hospital, Shanti told Deepali about her husband's demise. Deepali froze and looked straight ahead with a glazed expression in her eyes. Deepali's daughter was still not out of danger and the doctors were doing their best to stabilise her. Bakul, Jai and Shanti decided to stay with Deepali while Bela looked after Dadi Ma who kept inquiring about Deepali and her daughter.

After about an hour, Deepali was suddenly out of her trance. She remembered her younger daughter and wanted to go and see her. Bakul said that he would stay back at the hospital and asked Jai and Shanti to accompany Deepali. The colony where Deepali stayed was called Kasba and it was on the outskirts of Kolkata. It was a network of the narrowest-possible lanes that one could imagine, infested with gutter filth and garbage. There was hardly any space to walk but Jai and Shanti silently followed Deepali who expertly manoeuvred her way towards her shanty. When they reached it, Shanti saw that it was so small that it could be barely called a hut. The younger daughter was watching a small black and white television. On seeing Deepali, she ran towards her. But when, she noticed Jai and Shanti, she stopped and looked at them. Then in fluent Bengali, she asked her mother about the guests who were visiting them in the shanty. Deepali ignored her question and instead asked her whether she had eaten anything. She said that her father, before leaving for the hospital, had given her some rice and vegetables. Shanti noticed that Deepali addressed her Shyamoli. She was an attractive girl, tall for her 13 years, sturdy and strong. She asked them to sit and then told her mother that her father had left the house about three hours ago and would be coming back any time. Shanti and Jai watched the expression on Deepali's face. They could see helplessness in her eyes, which were almost pleading to the two of them to take charge and break the sad news to the young teenager. Shanti sat next to Shyamoli and taking her hand in hers, broke the news to her. The girl didn't react at all. After about 10 minutes, she inquired about Mitali, her sister, and was told that she was critical and in the hospital. Shanti observed as Shyamoli silently took charge of the whole situation. She consoled her bawling mother and even helped her pack for the hospital. Looking at the young girl, running around stuffing clothes and other things in a plastic bag, made Shanti realise that grief, sometimes, matures a person much before their time.

*****

Mitali had stabilised by the next morning but the doctors wanted to keep her under observation for a couple of days. She had sustained head injuries and had fractured her left arm. She was given blood transfusions and the doctors were worried about her fluctuating blood pressure. The body of Deepali's husband, along with other papers, was handed over by the hospital to the family. After some discussion, it was decided that the cremation and other rituals would be completed by the morning. Deepali refused to go to the cremation. Instead, she bathed and requested Shanti to take her to Dadi Ma's flat.

'Shyamoli could stay in the shanty with the other family members. She will be taken care of,' she said, sobbing.

Shanti agreed and hailed an auto. The ride was bumpy as Kasba colony had many potholes and unlit lanes. Throughout the journey Deepali didn't say a word. Her mind was a jumble of thoughts. She was worried about the money which had to be paid to the grocery shop by the weekend; she had heard her husband tell the shopkeeper that he would get his salary soon and pay him. She had to go and tell her husband's shop owner boss what had happened and ask for her husband's pending dues. Then, there was Mitali who was still in the hospital; her bills were also increasing by the minute. There were so many things to be handled now. She wondered whether she would have to find jobs for both the girls now so that they could start earning and help in running the house. Since she was still young, in her early thirties—she had married young and her first child was born when she was barely 15—she was also worried about men chasing her once they heard that her husband was no more. She had to protect her daughters and herself from the lecherous men who were all over Kolkata.

She was lost in her thoughts and didn't realise that they had reached Dadi Ma's flat. She saw Dadi Ma sitting solemnly in the living room. Deepali fell at her feet and for the first time, broke down. Dadi Ma asked Shanti to get a glass of water for Deepali. She consoled her and told her to be brave, 'Everything is going to be alright. You have to be courageous for your daughters. You have to look after them and protect them and therefore, you have to first look after yourself.' Shanti returned with a glass of water as well as some food. Dadi Ma forced Deepali to eat a little and then took her to her bedroom.

While Shanti prepared a bed for Deepali, Dadi Ma explained about the after-death rituals to both the women, 'There is a custom in some parts of India that says that on the day the body of her husband is cremated, the wife has to leave her home and spend the night at a relative's house. There are many reasons for this—since it is a frightening and depressing time, the woman is better off being in the company of others that night. Sleeping well is necessary because she has to shoulder many responsibilities next day onwards. If the wife stays at home, people would keep asking her questions and make comments which would further disturb her and prevent her from sleeping.'

Then, Dadi Ma gave Deepali a thin blanket and asked her to rest. However, neither Dadi Ma nor Deepali could sleep that night. Early in the morning, Dadi Ma heard Deepali sobbing which made her sit on the bed and stroke her head gently. Deepali sat up, and clinging on to Dadi Ma's legs, she said, 'I remember Dadi Ma, the other day I told you that it is not good to have children who don't love you and care for you. It is better not to have such children. You told me not to utter such inauspicious words because they go out in the universe and make bad things happen. How do you know all this? You were so right. I have been cursing people throughout my life. If

I had known this thing about the universe, I wouldn't have said such things. Look, the universe has punished me in just three days. You are so wise and all-knowing. Dadi Ma, please bless me and my daughters. I have decided to leave all the other jobs and just be with you so that I can serve you and take care of you. In this way, the universe will forgive all my wrongdoings.' Deepali began to cry again. Dadi Ma, without saying anything, continued stroking her hair and in about ten minutes, she fell asleep.

*****

After two days, Bakul and his family had made plans to leave for Cochin. Mitali was discharged from the hospital and was taken home by Deepali who was living between her home and Dadi Ma's house, trying to manage work in both the places. Bakul and Dadi Ma, with Bela's participation, discussed and sorted out a number of important issues. Bakul and Bela also volunteered to take both of Deepali's daughters to Cochin and admit them in a school, on the condition that they, like Shanti, would also help in household work in their free time. They assured Deepali that all their expenses would be borne by Bakul and whenever possible, Dadi Ma would also help. It was also decided that from now on, Deepali would stay with Dadi Ma on a full-time basis, and would not work elsewhere. Deepali fell at the feet of both Bakul and Bela and with tears in her eyes, said, 'Please forgive me for talking ill about you. You are not what I thought you were!'

Then, she related how Dadi Ma had berated her when she spoke against them. Bakul consoled her and said that everyone makes mistakes in life and we should learn from them and move on. Deepali didn't stop talking about Bakul and Bela's goodness with whoever she met.

Deepali was also convinced that Dadi Ma had supernatural powers because she had said something which had actually come true. She told everyone that Dadi Ma was blessed with supernatural powers and that she could foresee the future. Many people began visiting Dadi Ma to ask her about their future and some would even bring along their horoscopes. Since Dadi Ma was born into a Brahmin family and had imbibed a little knowledge about Vedic astrology, she tried to help the people who flocked to her door as much as she could. As her interest grew in astrology, she started reading the few books on the subject that she already had. Thanks to Deepali's loose tongue, Dadi Ma's problem of boredom was also solved. She loved talking to people and this information about her 'supernatural powers' gave her the opportunity to meet new people and spend time with them. The appreciation and respect that she received from people seemed like an added bonus and boosted her self-confidence.

These interactions with people, though infrequent, went on for a few weeks till one day a large group of people came to meet her with gifts. Some even offered her money because her prediction for a young couple had turned out to be true. This young couple had been childless for a number of years and Dadi Ma, after looking at the woman's horoscope, had told them that she would conceive soon... and it happened! Initially, she hesitated to accept the gifts and the money but on Deepali's insistence, she acquiesced.

After this incident, the floodgates seemed to have opened. Dadi Ma's name and fame in astrology spread far and wide. She started reading more books on astrology and also began taking guidance and tuition from a few established astrologers in Kolkata. Soon, she didn't have any free time left. There was also a substantial increase in her earnings. Even politicians, ministers and corporate leaders began to visit her. Bakul, Bela and her grandchildren were amazed at her abilities and were very proud of her. Dadi Ma also taught Deepali how to read and write, and soon, she became Dadi Ma's manager of sorts, maintaining her appointments, scheduling meetings, etc. This went on for almost seven years. Dadi Ma established herself as an astrologer, coach and counsellor.

*****

Dadi Ma celebrated her 80th birthday in her own sprawling bungalow in a posh residential area in South Kolkata, which was rated even better than Ballygunge Circular Road. 'I could live here till my 88th birthday,' she thought, smiling. Deepali also became a well-known figure amongst Dadi Ma's important clients, who were mostly top politicians and ministers. One day Deepali said to Dadi Ma, 'Ma, I now believe that whatever one says to the universe comes true. I said that you have supernatural powers and look so many times you have shown your powers. I have realised that we should only say good things to the universe and good things will happen. Bad things must never be thought of but more importantly, they should never be uttered. Today, I have understood the meaning of Dadi Ma—it means grandmother and you are truly a "grand" mother.'

10

The Colour of the Mind

'The mind is everything. What you think, you become.'

—Buddha

There couldn't have been a better location for the institute. It was situated on the edge of a forest with a sparkling stream flowing behind it. The forest expanse was truly invigorating and, on most days, one could find students taking a leisurely stroll amidst the many trees, rejuvenating themselves. Teak trees grew in plenty as did neem and banyan. Interspersed amongst these trees were the radiant amaltas or the golden rain trees which blossomed in the scorching heat of the summer and looked beautiful in their yellow and light orange glory. At night, the velvety dark sky was a treat for the eyes because the contrast between the diamond-like sheen of the stars and the inky black sky was not visible anywhere else except in that area.

For the students, the time spent at the institute was an experience of a lifetime as they would not get an opportunity to live in such a glorious place after they graduated. The institute had a legacy of over a hundred years. It offered a number of courses including a full-time two-year-long residential graduate programme of business administration, which was affiliated to the university. The institute was known for its excellent faculty and the diversity of the student community. There were around 200 students and they belonged to different religious groups, states, socio-economic backgrounds and age groups. Some students had worked earlier and some had joined the MBA programme immediately after their graduation. There was, more or less, an equal representation of men and women in the programme.

One of the strengths of the institute was its range of co-curricular activities. There was something to do for every student—music, photography, sports including swimming and polo, sculpture and painting, sewing, stitching and embroidery, among others. Surprisingly and contrary to popular stereotypes, more men than women pursued sewing and stitching as a hobby. Gandharva was one such student who took to sewing, stitching and embroidery as a duck takes to water. He often told his friends that he had discovered his true potential and would pursue fashion designing after completing his MBA. Often, he could be found in the sewing centre, missing important classes like logistics or supply chain management as he found those subjects rather boring.

His best friend Deepika always chided him saying he was not putting in the required time and effort to do well in these difficult subjects. But, Gandharva never paid heed to her advice. As expected, in the second semester's internal examination, he barely cleared the supply chain management paper.

Deepika reminded him again about the rules of the institute and the policy of the university, 'I hope you remember that a student has to pass in every subject in order to clear the overall MBA examination.'

'Oh relax, will you! First, I haven't failed. Second, even if I did, I would have one more chance to appear for the examination,' he said, carefully cutting a piece of fabric.

'I know but, what if you can't clear the paper in the second chance as well? Then, you would fail the overall examination and would not even receive your MBA degree.'

Deepika knew that Gandharva was very weak in the subject and urged him to study as the final examinations were not too far. Gandharva nodded, barely listening, but, the next day, she again found him in the sewing centre instead of preparing to do better in the subject.

Gandharva was not bothered about his results. He was very clear that his aim was not to top the institute but to just get through the examinations, so he could finally pursue his passion—fashion designing. However, there were times, especially at nights, when his father's face would suddenly come in front of his eyes. His father was a technical supervisor in a factory and had taken a large loan to fund his studies. He was paying a substantial chunk of his meagre salary towards the repayment of that loan. It was at these times when he felt truly vulnerable, when he knew that he couldn't afford to fail the overall MBA examination.

Time, as is its nature, passed very quickly and Gandharva realised, with a jolt, that there were only five weeks left for the final examination. He was not prepared at all, especially for supply chain management. However hard he tried, he just couldn't concentrate or put in any effort for this subject. One evening, he sat with the books and realised that since he had missed a number of classes, he could not understand any of the concepts mentioned in the chapters. It was a technical subject and even Deepika couldn't be of much help. Gandharva started to hyperventilate and decided to approach Rasik, the faculty favourite, who, without studying too much or being a bookworm, managed to do well in all the examinations. This fact had always troubled the other students, including Gandharva, who attributed this ability to many different reasons, some entirely implausible. However, the simple reason was that Rasik never missed classes and thoroughly prepared the assignments and other homework that the faculty assigned to the students. Thus, pinning all his hopes on him, Gandharva knocked on Rasik's door. After hearing his plight, Rasik, in a very forthright way, told Gandharva that he didn't see any possibility of his passing the supply chain management paper because he lacked the basic understanding of the concepts and models. Gandharva panicked and frantically started looking for Deepika who, at that moment, was in the library making notes for her sociology examination, which was due in a month. When Gandharva finally found her, he rambled on about his predicament. Deepika listened to him patiently and suggested that he should select a few chapters and read them thoroughly to understand the basic concepts and models. She added that she would help him prepare a list of prospective questions which could be asked in the examinations.

Still, Gandharva was very worried and was sure that he would fail the supply chain management paper and would not get his MBA degree. His father's dejected face swam in front of his eyes whenever he closed them. Neither he could sleep nor could he concentrate. He took last year's question papers from Rasik and studied the trend of questions. The more he went through them, the more he realised that the paper was not easy and required a thorough knowledge to score even passing marks.

All Gandharva knew was that he had to pass the MBA examination; he just couldn't afford to fail. If he didn't get his degree, his father would never forgive him and might even throw him out of his house. And, his mother, who sincerely believes that her son is the one who would help them all escape their life of drudgery, would be completely heartbroken. His mother had already suffered enough—her parents had died when she was only 10 years old and her grandmother, who thought of her as a burden, brought her up by giving her just two meals a day. Her mother had often told him, with moist eyes, how after a torturous childhood she was looking for a happy wedded life but her husband, Gandharva's father, had not been very kind to her either. Regular beatings and constant swearing had been a part of her life. Thinking about her mother gave him the boost that he needed. He resolved to find a way to manage this crisis and started thinking of ways to at least secure passing marks in the supply chain management paper.

The examinations began as scheduled. Gandharva looked quite relaxed and whenever he was asked by his peers about his performance in the various papers, he told them that he had done well. Deepika was quite relieved to see Gandharva happy and confident about his performance. Time, as usual, flew by and the examinations were finally over. The junior batch, as per tradition, had organised a farewell dinner for the soon-to-be graduates and sent out invitations to all of them. The principal, the dean and all the faculty members were also invited to the do.

Professor Tamanna Singh, who taught supply chain management, was also one of the invitees. She was a senior professor and had an excellent reputation as an academic. She was also a formidable disciplinarian and played a crucial role in the placement committee. Since she lived quite far from the institute, she had decided to stay back at the campus and complete an editorial assignment before attending the farewell.

While Prof. Singh was in her room, writing the editorial column which she planned to complete in the next two days, she heard a faint knock on the door. She wondered who could have come to meet her at that time. Nevertheless, she asked the person to come inside. Gandharva walked in hesitantly and greeted her. She was surprised seeing him and asked him for the reason of his unannounced visit. Gandharva stood silently, staring at his shoes. When he didn't say anything for another minute, which seemed like a lifetime because the silence was heavy and uncomfortable, Prof. Singh asked him to sit down and offered him a glass of water. She asked, softly, 'What is the matter, Gandharva? Why aren't you saying something? Is everything alright?'

'Well, ma'am, I don't know how to begin. It is a little embarrassing,' he almost whispered the last part.

Prof. Singh strained to hear what Gandharva was saying. She leaned towards him and asked him to speak up freely.

'Actually... the thing is...' he began haltingly.

'Go on,' the professor said kindly.

'Ma'am, I have not been able to sleep at all for the last three nights. Whenever I close my eyes, I see your face and therefore I thought that I should come and speak to you because I can't hide it from you anymore,' Gandharva spoke in a rush, almost choking on the last few words.

Prof. Singh became worried and thought that this could be something to do with an emotional involvement with someone in the institute, or had this boy gone a bit too far with someone? She had seen him a number of times with Deepika. Could that be the problem?

'I don't understand what you are trying to say. Please explain properly. Don't be frightened,' said the professor.

'Ma'am, I can't hide this from you anymore. I cheated in my supply chain management paper. I haven't been able to sleep since then. I keep seeing your face every night. Please punish me however you deem fit ma'am,' Gandharva broke down and sobbed bitterly.

The professor was shocked. She closed her eyes, trying to make sense of what she had just heard. After a minute, she asked, 'Were you caught cheating by the invigilators?'

Gandharva shook his head, staring down at the glass in his hands.

'Then, why are you telling me? What is the point of confessing to me today?' the professor seemed confused.

'No, ma'am, no one caught me doing it and no one knows about it but, I had to tell you. I couldn't hide it from you. I respect you too much,' said Gandharva.

'But, not so much as to not cheat?' she asked pointedly. 'Anyway, do you understand the repercussions of this?' she asked.

'Yes, I understand that I will be rusticated from the institute,' said Gandharva.

Then, she asked him to tell her how he managed to cheat without anyone noticing. Gandharva described the entire process that he had adopted in detail. He told her that he had scribbled notes on the thighs of the trousers he had worn to the examination hall that day.

'How did no one see the writing?' asked the professor.

'I was wearing a long kurta which hid that part of the trousers. I had also written the concepts on the back of the kurta,' he admitted, a little sheepish.

The professor couldn't think straight. On one hand, she was impressed with Gandharva's idea—hiding the answers in plain sight but, she was also disturbed with this sudden turn of events. She asked Gandharva to leave her alone so she could get her thoughts in order.

Even though her sense of discipline was rather strong, she couldn't ignore the courage shown by Gandharva in confessing to her. She wondered what the boy must have gone through to muster up such courage and confess to her about what he had done, knowing fully well about the seriousness of the outcome. She was confused and felt emotionally burdened. She knew she had to tell the principal but, the grief-stricken face of Gandharva kept coming back to her. Time had come for her to go to the hall where the farewell dinner had been organised. She walked inside and saw Gandharva with Deepika; both of them looked rather forlorn.

She also noticed Dr B. K. Sharma, the dean of the institute, who was a good friend of hers. She decided to confide in him about the situation at hand and chalk out a plan of action. She finally admitted to herself that the principal would also have to come into the picture because this issue would certainly lead to rustication.

'But, what would happen to Gandharva's life after he is rusticated? Will he ever get a job? Will the institute not think about this?' thought Prof. Singh sadly. She knew that institutes were largely driven by policy and strict norms, especially when such behavioural deviations occur. She also understood why these anomalies needed to be viewed through the governance lens.

'Perhaps rightly so, there should be a line that should never be crossed.'

Prof. Singh decided to sleep over the issue before discussing it with Dr Sharma the next day. In her long academic career, she had faced such a problem for the first time. The thoughts of Gandharva and his future kept her awake most of the night. She had a fitful sleep and when she woke up in the morning, the thought that Gandharva had shown exceptional courage in confessing to her kept hammering into her mind.

'No one knew about his cheating and the invigilators were also unaware, he could have hidden it from me too,' she thought, her resolve strengthening.

She met Dr Sharma and told him about the cheating incident. Like her, Dr Sharma was also amazed at the meticulous planning that Gandharva had done for cheating in the examination. However, Dr Sharma and the professor were of divided opinion about the fate of the boy. While Dr Sharma felt that the boy, if not corrected now, could repeat this later on in life and get into grave trouble. Prof. Singh was of the view that he had demonstrated exemplary courage by confessing and if he was punished now, he would be completely shattered and destroyed for life. The only point that they agreed upon was the fact that if the principal was informed, she would immediately issue a rustication letter.

They both debated for a long time about how this could be tackled. Dr Sharma explained that they would be going against a number of policies of the institute, 'You know Tamanna, this is pretty risky. We must understand that we are senior members of the system and we will be doing something that goes against the culture of the institute. We are talking about deliberately hiding facts.'

Pondering over his comments for a while, Tamanna said, 'Sir, apart from administration and governance responsibilities, I think we have a larger responsibility towards the entire life of a student—his character building and how he can preserve the exceptional qualities of head and heart that he possesses. It is not easy to have this kind of courage. He knows that after this disclosure, his career, in fact his entire life can go for a toss. Yet, he came forward and spoke the truth which is not easy at all. How many of us can claim this kind of courage? Our mind automatically seeks safety and protection. Those are the usual colours. However, admirable minds have exceptional courage as the colour of the mind.'

Finally, Dean Sharma agreed with Tamanna. After this conversation, they decided to not discuss the matter with anyone else at the institute. Gandharva failed the exam and was asked to appear in a supplementary examination which was held a month after his batch had graduated. Dr Sharma was one of the invigilators for the supplementary exam. This time, Gandharva, with help from Deepika and Rasik as well as extra classes from Prof. Singh, had prepared for the whole month and managed to pass the exam without cheating.

*****

On a sunny winter morning, seven years after the cheating incident, Prof. Singh, now the dean of the institute, opened a letter addressed to her. It read:

'Dear Professor Singh,

It has been several years since we last met. I had visited your esteemed institute to hire management trainees for our organisation. This is to thank you for training and preparing the students in an exceptional manner to professionally handle their work and careers in organisations such as ours.

I would like to specifically mention one student named Mr Gandharva who is doing great work at our organisation. He is an effective leader with the right values and attitude. He is admired for both his character and competence. We would again like to visit your institute for selecting students as management trainees this year...'

Prof. Singh stopped reading; she had tears in her eyes. The letter seemed to be a testament that proved to her that she had been right in standing up for her beliefs all those years ago. She hurried up and showed the letter to Dr B. K. Sharma as well. He read through the letter with a sombre expression on his face, and then he said softly, 'All these years, I had thought that I hadn't done the right thing by withholding this information from the institute's governing body. However, I am glad I listened to you. Courage is indeed a beautiful colour of the mind which is rarely displayed so well.'

Both the teachers, after seven long years, sat together in silence, their faces turned towards the sun, their eyes closed in gratitude and a guilt-free smile on their lips.

About the Author

Priya Somaiya, Executive Director, USHA Social Services (USS), is one of India's leading organisation development (OD) and human resource (HR) consultants.

In the course of a career spanning more than three decades, Dr Somaiya has assayed several roles, including that of an OD and HR consultant, a mentor, an executive coach to senior leadership (CXO level), a change interventionist and a thought leader in the social development space. She has played a pivotal role in co-creating and advancing the community development vision and mission of a leading corporate firm in India. She has enabled leading business organisations—Hindustan Unilever, Sanofi India, ACC, Tata Group, ONGC and *Hindustan Times*—to handle intricate organisational complexities through various initiatives such as succession planning, senior leadership team development, potential and talent assessment and coaching and mentoring.

In her current role in USS and USHA Consulting Services (UCS), she provides strategic leadership to community development and consulting practice areas within Usha International Limited. She spearheads community development initiatives in areas of entrepreneurship for rural women (spread across SAARC nations) and rural integrated development through non-formal education, the arrest of distress migration and poverty alleviation. Under her leadership, Silai schools have grown to become a national movement aimed at women's empowerment.

Dr Somaiya holds a PhD in Organisational Psychology from Allahabad University, India.